A Psychoanalytic Reflection on Narcissistic Parenthood and its Ramifications

A Psychoanalytic Reflection on Narcissistic Parenthood and its Ramifications: The Forgotten Echo proposes a new perspective on narcissism, focusing on its destructive impact within relationships.

Hila Yahalom discusses the patterns and ramifications of traumatizing upbringing by narcissistic parents, exploring the resulting development of a defensive-behavioral pattern and personality structures in the child which constitutes a mirror image of narcissism. Yahalom assesses a wide range of psychoanalytic theories in presenting a broad outlook on narcissism, its roots, and the manner by which pathological narcissism may manifest in interpersonal relationships as 'narcissistic abuse'. This book considers the narcissist's perverted occupation of the psychic space of others, with both participants usually blind to the phenomenon – a blindness that is reenacted in therapy, affecting its course. This book contains clinical vignettes from the author's work as well as examples from the life stories of Heinz Kohut (Mr. Z), Franz Kafka, and Maria Callas.

A Psychoanalytic Reflection on Narcissistic Parenthood and its Ramifications: The Forgotten Echo will be of great interest to psychoanalysts and other clinicians working with narcissism, parenthood, and dysfunctional family relationships.

Hila Yahalom, MD, MBA, is a psychiatrist and psychotherapist. She is currently a candidate at the Israel Psychoanalytic Institute, and lectures on diverse psychiatric and psychoanalytic topics. She previously served as the director of a psychiatric ward at Sha'ar Menashe Mental Health Center in Israel.

A Psychoanalytic Reflection on Narcissistic Parenthood and its Ramifications

The Forgotten Echo

Hila Yahalom

Routledge
Taylor & Francis Group

LONDON AND NEW YORK

Designed cover image: "Maria Callas on Visible and Invisible Strings"
Image painted by Hila Yahalom

First published 2025
by Routledge
4 Park Square, Milton Park, Abingdon, Oxon, OX14 4RN

and by Routledge
605 Third Avenue, New York, NY 10158

Routledge is an imprint of the Taylor & Francis Group, an informa business

First (Hebrew) edition published by Carmel Publishing House 2022

British Library Cataloguing-in-Publication Data
A catalogue record for this book is available from the British Library

Library of Congress Cataloging-in-Publication Data
Names: Yahalom, Hila, author.
Title: A psychoanalytic reflection on narcissistic parenthood and its
ramifications: the forgotten echo/Hila Yahalom.
Description: Abingdon, Oxon; New York, NY: Routledge, 2024. |
Includes bibliographical references and index. |
Identifiers: LCCN 2024004004 (print) | LCCN 2024004005 (ebook) |
ISBN 9781032625386 (hardback) | ISBN 9781032625379 (paperback) |
ISBN 9781032625393 (ebook)
Subjects: LCSH: Narcissism. | Parents—Psychological aspects. |
Families—Psychological aspects.
Classification: LCC BF575.N35 Y343 2024 (print) |
LCC BF575.N35 (ebook) | DDC 155.4—dc23/eng/20240318
LC record available at https://lccn.loc.gov/2024004004
LC ebook record available at https://lccn.loc.gov/2024004005

ISBN: 9781032625386 (hbk)
ISBN: 9781032625379 (pbk)
ISBN: 9781032625393 (ebk)

DOI: 10.4324/9781032625393

Typeset in Times New Roman
by codeMantra

To the family I came from and to the family
I established, with great love

Contents

Acknowledgments

My heartfelt thanks to the many who were involved and who supported and encouraged me in the process of writing this book. I am deeply grateful to Dr. Salman Akhtar and Dr. Michael Eigen for their generous and warn endorsement of the book, to Susannah Frearson and Priya Sharma at Routledge and to Professor Merav Roth for their helpful guidance along the process of publishing this English translation of the book.

To Ahuva Schul, who accompanied my journey to this book from its very first step, whose magnanimous generosity and faith in me encouraged me to dare. My thanks for all that she is for me.

To Tami Dror-Schieber, who read the first version of this book when it was still intended to be an article, contributed from her extensive knowledge, helped me deepen and expand the perspective and writing, and supported me throughout the challenging and exciting moments of the process.

To Tami Nir-Gottlieb, who read the first version, encouraged and advised generously, instilled in me the courage to publish, and supported me in challenging moments throughout the process.

To Luba Klukin, the brilliant Hebrew-language editor I was fortunate to work with on the first, Hebrew version of this book, for making the editing process a shared, fruitful, and friendly journey. Her contribution to this book was priceless, and I am grateful that she had put her heart and soul into it, improving this book greatly.

To my dear husband Gili and to our children Omer, Ori, and Tamar, my pride and joy, each of whom supported in his own unique way and allowed me to invest myself in the writing journey.

To all my teachers and mentors, for everything I have received from them, which accompanies my work.

To all those who shared their stories and insights on social networks and books, bringing their personal tales, some of them anonymous, some are not. All across the globe, underneath different skies, in different cultures, and in different tongues, a similar story of occult human suffering re-emerges. Joining the echoes of all those voices together crystalizes into a deafening cry.

Last but not least, I thank my patients, who trusted me and entrusted me with their heartache, shared their innermost world with me, and gave me the right to accompany their journey and learn from it. Without them, this book would not have taken shape. I hope that through their stories some understanding can be achieved, some of the veils removed, and some solace brought to others who, day after day, year after year are trapped in the abyss of agony and nameless pain.

Note from Publisher

Every effort has been made to contact the copyright holders of material in this book. Any omissions brought to the attention of the publishers will be corrected in future editions.

Chapter 1

Introduction

The myth of Narcissus is well known as the story of the handsome youth who fell in love with his own reflection died of that empty love and turned into the familiar flower. Despite being titled 'Echo and Narcissus', Echo's story failed to gain similar recognition, and her existence is all but forgotten.

> She saw him in his present misery,
> Whom, spight of all her wrongs, she griev'd to see.
> She answer'd sadly to the lover's moan,
> Sigh'd back his sighs, and groan'd to ev'ry groan:
> "Ah youth! belov'd in vain," Narcissus cries;
> "Ah youth! belov'd in vain," the nymph replies.
> "Farewel," says he; the parting sound scarce fell
> From his faint lips, but she reply'd, "farewel."
> (Ovid, 8 AD 3:613–3:620)

'Echo and Narcissus' was written by the Roman poet Publius Ovidius Naso (Ovid),[1] as part of the mythological epic 'Metamorphoses' (Ovid, 8 AD). According to the myth, Echo the nymph fell in love with Narcissus, who was unable to love. Echo could not form her own words. The Goddess Juno cursed her, punishing Echo for distracting her with her prattle whilst Juno's spouse, Jove, was fornicating. The curse prevented Echo from expressing herself and she could only repeat the last words of others, echoing them. Thus, Echo could but repeat the last words of Narcissus as she watched him fall in love with his own reflection, wither and die.

Narcissism is discussed in the analytic literature in abundance. But just as Echo's lot was to be 'erased' from the story, the tale of those devastated by the destruction the narcissist's vulnerability leaves in its wake is unacknowledged.

In this book, I seek to bestow 'Echo' with a voice and argue that a close relationship with an individual afflicted with a severe narcissistic disorder[2] is almost inevitably abusive. That abuse is subtle and covert, with both parties to the relationship usually unaware of it. The essence of this abuse is the narcissist's occupation of the victim's psychic space. The narcissist is dependent upon the other, needing

DOI: 10.4324/9781032625393-1

him in order to nourish and vitalize himself,[3] thus assuaging feelings of emptiness accompanied by the fear of a psychotic breakdown.

The narcissist hurts in subtle ways, but a very specific pattern emerges, like stenciled cutouts, of a relationship based upon the abuser's need for symbiosis and control. The damage inflicted upon the victim's psych and personality structure is characterized by a pattern just as repetitive and stenciled-like. The victim feels controlled like a marionette. His separate existence and subjective essence are erased. Like Echo in the myth, the victim is filled with shame which enhances his dependence upon the abuser and the need for his approval, and is being drained of content and of an authentic, vivacious self.

> The nymph, when nothing could Narcissus move,
> Still dash'd with blushes for her slighted love,
> Liv'd in the shady covert of the woods,
> In solitary caves and dark abodes;
> Where pining wander'd the rejected fair,
> 'Till harrass'd out, and worn away with care,
> The sounding skeleton, of blood bereft,
> Besides her bones and voice had nothing left.
> Her bones are petrify'd, her voice is found
> In vaults, where still it doubles ev'ry sound.
>   (Ovid, 8 AD, 3:490–3:499)

The traumatizing pattern became known as 'Narcissistic Abuse', a term that has become common, especially in popular parlance. The word abuse is harsh, perhaps deterring, but it is of importance to call a spade a spade. The deeds leave no visible bruises, but they certainly leave their mark on the soul and inflict intense pain. Physicians have imaging technology enabling them to determine whether a recurring trauma took place. They might notice old fractures and deformed bones. Those who care for the psych are bereft of such means. Fractures of the mind might manifest themselves as depression, anxiety, 'deformations' or disorders of the personality, and other symptoms, none of which are distinctively related to a specific etiological factor. Relating symptoms to their cause is made more difficult still, by the fact that at the core of this injury is the perpetrator's denial that something is wrong, alongside the silencing and the blaming of the victim. The perpetrator's actions cause the victim to doubt his own reality and blind him to it, hence the uppermost importance of identifying the abuse and validating the experience of those victims.

The word 'narcissist' has become derogatory, and many depict the narcissist as the epitome of evil who inflicts harm maliciously. Such perception provides with a simple explanation, alongside a defensive illusion, that the world contains absolute good and evil, easily distinguishable from one another. Such perception might also provide the victims with a protective shield, enabling them to recognize the evil in others and acknowledge they are being harmed. That is an essential step toward healing, but also a defense mechanism which, while allowing for a relieving expulsion of unwanted psychic elements from the 'self' to the 'narcissist', hinders a deeper, more comprehensive understanding – that Narcissus is the outcome of rape. In Ovid's version of the myth, Narcissus's mother, Liriope, was violated by the river god, Cephisus. I maintain it is not a choice, and that it is important to re-member those traumatizers act like automatons, because they themselves were, and still are, deeply hurt children.

The book maintains that the rigid and offensive pattern of behavior reflects a primitive object relations pattern characteristic of individuals with severe narcissis-tic pathology. Every close relationship with an individual afflicted with a pathologi-cal narcissistic personality might be abusive, but the deepest, most comprehensive, most devastating injury occurs within the parent-child[4] relationship, and worst if both parents are afflicted. The book focuses on the ramifications of the abuse taking place between narcissistic parents and their children, but the dynamics characteris-tic of those relationships are the basis for understanding the narcissist's offensive-ness in all relationships, including couples' relationship and workplace bullying. The processes and principles described along the book are applicable to all narcis-sistic relationships, even though the book examines them through the perspective of the parent-child relationship.

Like Echo, the child of the narcissistic parent is born with a potential for a voice and a vitality of his own, but soon his voice is lost and little more is left than an echo of the parent's wishes and personality. Thus, a relational-developmental trauma occurs (Stolorow & Atwood, 1992). This damage is inflicted upon the soul at its core, preventing the child from acquiring his own experience of self and of separation, therefore arresting his psychic development. A child thus damaged remains narcissistically injured himself and will be prone to engaging in relation-ships that reenact this abusive pattern all through his life. He might become an adult that knows not but to echo his fellow man's narcissism as a way to offer him-self as a love object, pleasing and satisfying the narcissistic needs of others as the terms of relationship, just as it was with his parents. Alternatively, these children might become abusive narcissists themselves or fall somewhere on a spectrum be-tween these two extremes.

Narcissistic abuse, like gravity, cannot be seen, but it is just as tangible and constantly affects the orbit of the child's life. The parent is engulfed by blindness, usually unaware that his behavior is disturbed and abusive. The child fails to notice it as well, as he knows no other reality and has developed within his psych a defen-sive split which blinds him to the existence of the abuse. The blindness causes dis-sociation between the traumatic agent and the mental suffering of the traumatized, thus enhancing the suffering and the feeling of 'losing one's mind', which is innate to such relationships.

The same blindness is reenacted in therapy, and perhaps that is the reason why the professional literature left a certain void or a missing link when it comes to the subject of narcissism and narcissistic abuse. The existence of such a void is best evidenced by the fact that it has been filled in recent years with an abundance of material, primarily from the United States – YouTube videos, posts, forums, and books galore. Most of the content was created by people declaring themselves to be victims of such abuse. Amongst these content creators, few are mental health professionals. An almost universal, recurring pattern was that their understanding of having been abused came as a late epiphany, after enduring years of mental suffering they could not explain, and that the recovery process could commence only once they could acknowledge that. An entire community revolving around the topic has evolved, with a jargon of its own, disconnected from the professional community. The term 'Narcissistic Abuse' mentioned above is a part of that jargon. The disconnection between the professional community and the de-facto need has opened opportunities for individuals lacking any professional education, who out of pure intentions, or not, offer themselves as therapists based on their personal experience.

There is no reason to assume that the psychoanalytic theory lacks anything in understanding the relationship between the narcissist and his objects. On the contrary, only through delving into the psychoanalytic literature can one find a deep, thorough, and exhaustive understanding of the processes at play. Nevertheless, in this particular field, something has been 'lost in translation' between the professional community and those in need of it, a 'confusion of tongues' or perhaps an act of examining different parts of the same elephant. As mentioned beforehand, the abuse in question is elusive, subtle, and covert, and because its very existence depends on the blindness of both participants to the 'elephant in the room', the patient will not easily present it in therapy. Healing, nonetheless, depends on acknowledging it and seeing it with eyes wide open.

What is the entire elephant then? The greatest theoreticians and best researchers have taught us to observe the narcissist's personality traits and understand what lies behind them, shedding light on different aspects with their insights. However, I sensed that something was missing in connecting these aspects, a sort of a missing link required to complete the puzzle and explain the full depth of the pathology and its elusiveness. I believe the missing link is the way in which the narcissistic pathology manifests itself in interpersonal relationships, comprising an essential yet under recognized part of the elephant. It is argued in the book that one of the harshest and most significant manifestations of this pathology is the narcissist's perverted treatment of his objects. This perversion, not necessarily sexual, is the manifestation of a defense mechanism against the psychic pain brought about by reality, including the reality of being separate from others, and is a constant, integral part of narcissistic pathology. It is a manifestation of the narcissist's need to crawl beneath its object's skin and control him from within. The more I was exposed to patients and stories that exhibited genuine trauma caused by a relationship with a narcissist, the more convinced I became that severe narcissistic pathology would always be accompanied by perverted behavior toward the narcissist's objects. Indeed, the missing link presented itself just as I was reading writings about perversions, opening the door to a broader perspective and a deeper understanding of narcissistic psychic dynamics.

The act of acknowledging isn't a simple one. Professionals are rightfully reluctant to diagnose those who are not their patient, meaning the narcissistic abuser.

Good, professional methods are geared toward the patient's intra-psychic representations rather than their experiences and relationships in reality, which are subjected to distortions and interpretation anyway. However, trauma-therapy requires a different approach. One cannot treat trauma without acknowledging its existence and understanding what has transpired. In the case at hand, the failure to acknowledge the trauma might be a reenactment of its essence. We have an obligation to help the patient find words for the incomprehensible, that which must not be experienced and that which has been dissociated. In this regard, Alice Miller's writings stood out due to her emphasis of the real past experiences of the patient as a child. Miller wrote:

> Metapsychology…is concerned with cathexis, with intrapsychic dynamics, object and self-representations, but not with facts…Its concern is the meaning attached to experiences and not the reality behind them. Nevertheless, we do analyze parents, too, and we hear about their feelings toward their children and about their narcissistic needs, and we have to ask ourselves what the consequences of all this are for the development of their children…Can we blind ourselves with the argument that an analyst is only concerned with intrapsychic processes? It is as if we did not dare to take a single step in order to acknowledge the child's reality, since Freud recognized the conjecture of sexual seduction as the patient's fantasy. Since the patient also has an interest in keeping this reality hidden from us, and still more from himself, it can happen that we share his ignorance for a long time. Nevertheless, the patient never stops telling us about part of his reality in the language of his symptoms.
>
> (Miller, 1979, pp. 73–74)

Miller defined the subject of her work as the effort to "come closer to the origins of the loss of the self" (ibid, p. xx) and she makes the connection between narcissistic parenthood and the formation of a false self in the child:

> Accommodation to parental needs often (but not always) leads to the "as-if personality" (Winnicott has described it as the "false self"). This person develops in such a way that he reveals only what is expected of him, and fuses so completely with what he reveals that-until he comes to analysis-one could scarcely have guessed how much more there is to him, behind this "mask view of himself"… Understandably, these patients complain of a sense of emptiness, futility, or homelessness…A process of emptying, impoverishment, and partial killing of his potential actually took place when all that was alive and spontaneous in him was cut off.
>
> (ibid, pp. 12–13)

Miller first attempted "looking for a way, within the framework of psychoanalysis" (ibid, p. xxi), but eventually, as of 1988, she chose, out of her criticism, to no longer regard herself as a psychoanalyst. Much has changed within the rich texture of psychoanalysis since then, but even had it stagnated, Miller's decision seems to me like throwing the baby out with the bathwater. I find the understanding is there, written in the psychoanalytic body of literature, and I believe psychoanalysis can pride itself on bringing about a change in the way children are treated and raised, including via Alice Miller and her analytic training. I also believe it unadvisable to hasten the removal of the patient's defenses in the way Miller seems to suggest. Whilst I concur with Miller that there must be room for the facts and the recognition of them, I believe there has to be room for investigating and interpreting the patient's tale. These acts are almost opposing. Premature historical interpretations will be experienced as a traumatic attack on the defenses, whilst regarding the past as the patient's 'inner experience', meaning a product of his distorted reality testing, might constitute a traumatic reenactment as well. Nonetheless I believe that if we tread cautiously alongside a patient who was narcissistically abused on our way to the core of his psych, we will discover with him the narcissistic elephant in its whole, and we will be able to recognize both intrapsychic dynamics as well as validate reality whenever it is required.

I hope this book will start filling the void that was caused and bring about awareness that would enable to observe faster that a patient experienced or is experiencing trauma from a narcissistic relationship. In addition, I would argue that the pattern of damage caused by narcissistic abuse deserves recognition as a clinical entity in itself, just as narcissism is a clinical entity in itself. I make the plea to give Echo words of her own, first by accepting the term narcissistic abuse, which seems to assert itself and second by applying the term Echoism.[5] I shall seek to infuse this term with a theoretical understanding and turn it into a comprehensive name for an adaptive-survival pattern of behavior, a pattern of object relations and of personality traits which evolve as a negative of the narcissist's pattern of object relations.

I would argue that echoism is a type of narcissistic disorder in itself, which has unique features distinguishing it from other types of narcissism, as well as common ones. I also believe it is important to have a separate noun which will enable researching the dynamics between the narcissist/abuser and his weaker object, the echoist, hoping the existence of such a noun and entity would contribute to theoretical investigation of the subject.

Notes

1 There are many versions to the Narcissus myth. Ovid's version, written around year 8 AD, is regarded by many as the classic version.
2 From here on the term 'narcissist' will be used instead of 'a person afflicted with a severe narcissistic disorder' or 'narcissistic personality disorder', despite its harsh and judgmental connotation. The term is used in a descriptive-diagnostic manner and is required for clarity's sake, as we are discussing persons afflicted with a narcissistic disorder which propels them to hurt, to whom the term 'narcissist' will be dedicated, and those hurt by them, who would often develop a narcissistic disorder themselves.
3 Throughout the book gender-specific pronouns are used rather than the neutral but plural 'they'. This is done in order to stress the individuals involved in the relationships described. Please note that these are arbitrary and interchangeable; narcissists and their connections can, of course, be either gender.

4 For clarity's sake, I shall continue to refer as 'children' to fully grown children of narcissistic parents as well.
5 After I chose the word Echoism, comprised of the called for combination of the name Echo and the ending -ism also used in narcissism, I found the word is being used online in popular parlance as part of the jargon of narcissistic abuse. My theoretical conceptualization of echoism is different. It regards it as a unique and specific type of a narcissistic disturbance, and not a state 'devoid of narcissism', as in the popular usage of the word.

Bibliography

Miller, A. (1979). *The Drama of the Gifted Child, the Search for the True Self.* Translated from the German by Ruth Ward. Basic Books, 1981.

Ovid, P. N. (8 AD), *Metamorphoses* (Translators: Sir Samuel Garth, John Dryden, Alexander Pope, Joseph Addison, William Congreve). Passerino, 2017.

Stolorow, R. D. & Atwood, G. E. (1992). *Contexts of Being: The Intersubjective Foundations of Psychological Life.* Routledge, 2002.

Chapter 2

Pathological Narcissism, Pathogenic Narcissism

The Narcissistic Disorder

The term narcissism "has been both abused and overused" (Kernberg, 1975, p. 16), creating confusion. The term is used to describe an assortment of different things, including a normal developmental stage, healthy or pathological self-investment, character traits, a personality disorder, and in popular parlance, it has become a slur. There are many psychoanalytic theories concerning narcissism, sometimes contradicting one another. This book does not presume to bring forth an exhaustive review of those theories. Nonetheless, it is necessary to clarify what is the abusive narcissism which will be discussed and what are the psychic processes active within the relationships of a person afflicted with a severe narcissistic disorder. In the book, narcissism shall be described from several perspectives and using several theories, hoping this sort of usage, even if somewhat scattered, will add up to a comprehensive image of the elephant in discussion.

The first to borrow the tale of Narcissus from the field of mythology to that of the psych was the English physician Havelock Ellis, whose research interest was sexuality. Ellis (1898) wrote that exaggerated self-love was 'Narcissus-like'. The term narcissism was coined by Paul Näcke, a Russian-born German physician. Näcke, who also translated Ellis's article to German, wrote an article about sexual perversions, which dealt primarily with excessive masturbation (1899). He was the first to add the German suffix 'us', parallel to the English suffix 'ism', thus creating a new word, the term narcissism.

In his article *On Narcissism* (1914), Freud mentioned he had acquired the term narcissism from Paul Näcke. Freud described a primary narcissism, a natural state in infancy, in which the child's libido is invested in himself and not directed toward objects. The object, at that state, is perceived as inseparable from the infant. In a person afflicted with a narcissistic disorder, there is a regression to narcissism which Freud named a secondary narcissism. In this state, the narcissist's emotional capabilities in the inter-personal domain are restricted to the extent that like the infant, he cannot be fully aware of the existence of others as separate beings, cannot tolerate the experience of being separate, and keeps investing his libido in himself rather than in others. Freud equated the libidinal cathexis to the distribution of the

DOI: 10.4324/9781032625393-2

cytoplasm[1] of the amoeba, a unicellular organism that has pseudopodia, extensions that resemble feet, emanating from it. There's a given amount of libido and its distribution varies the way the distribution of the cytoplasm between the 'body' of the amoeba and its extensions varies. Using this metaphor, one can regard narcissism as a trait that's on a range, on its one end, there's an excessive investment in the cell body, or excessive self-cathexis, and on its other end an excessive investment in the extensions, the Other, at the price of self-depletion. Over the years, there have been extensive theoretical changes and this metaphor became obsolete, but there appears to be a consensus that there is a range from normal, even healthy, narcissism to a myriad of pathologies of variable severity.

Even though Klein referenced narcissism directly only twice in her writings (Klein, 1946, 1952; Segal, 1983), her cogitation serves as an essential layer in understanding the psychic life of the narcissist. Klein, in effect, places narcissism within the context of object relations and clarified the psychic mechanisms active in the narcissistic disorder. The process of 'projective identification' which she has described is essential for the understanding of the psychic dynamics characteristic of this disorder. In one of her references of narcissism, she wrote: "autoerotism and narcissism are in the young infant contemporaneous with the first relation to objects – external and internalized" (Klein, 1952, p. 434). The other time in which she referred to narcissism was in the article 'Notes on Some Schizoid Mechanisms'. She wrote:

> The violent splitting of the self and excessive projection have the effect that the person towards whom this process is directed is felt as a persecutor. Since the destructive and hated part of the self which is split off and projected is felt as a danger to the loved object and therefore gives rise to guilt, this process of projection in some ways also implies a deflection of guilt from the self on to the other person... Another typical feature of schizoid object relations is their narcissistic nature which derives from the infantile introjective and projective processes... when the ego ideal is projected into another person, this object becomes predominantly loved and admired because it contains the good parts of the self. Similarly, the relation to other persons on the basis of projecting bad parts of the self into them is of a narcissistic nature because in this case as well the object strongly represents one part of the self. Both these types of a narcissistic relation to an object often show strong obsessional features. The impulse to control other people is, as we know, an essential element in obsessional neurosis. The need to control others can to some extent be explained by a deflected drive to control parts of the self. When these parts have been projected excessively into another person, they can only be controlled by controlling the other person.
>
> (Klein, 1946, p. 104)

Klein's successors made a crucial contribution to the conceptualization of narcissism. Segal (1983) wrote: "The narcissistic structure originates in the paranoid/

schizoid position under the dominance of envy and the defences against envy. It depends on the operation of splitting, denial and projective identification" (p. 275).

In writing about narcissistic personality pathology, I shall refer to a person whose relationships are prominently characterized by 'narcissistic object relations' as described by Rosenfeld (1964). Before clarifying what narcissistic object relations are, it is appropriate to discuss whether narcissistic relationships can occur between two persons. Seemingly, if narcissism means investment in the self at the expense of investing in others, the term contains an inner contradiction. However, Freud described such relationships amongst people who choose for a love-object a person representing their own self. According to Freud (1914, p. 89), a narcissistic object such as that may be a person representing to the lover 'what he himself is (i.e., himself)', that is, someone resembling him in one or more fundamental traits and who arouses in him identification, someone representing 'what he himself was', i.e., the child he was as is perceived in his inner representation currently, a person representing 'what he himself would like to be', i.e., his ego ideal, or 'someone who was once part of himself'. It would appear that in the love of a parent to a child, all four possibilities coexist.

The narcissistic object relations, according to Rosenfeld, are relations based on the defenses of splitting, projections, and incorporation, which nullify the ability to relate to others as separate subjects. All of these may lead to an abusive-perverted behavior toward the object.

This type of relations is particularly characteristic of narcissistic personality disorder (NPD), but may also present, with varying severity, in different characterological pathologies.

Rosenfeld wrote:

In narcissistic object relations omnipotence plays a prominent part. The object... may be omnipotently incorporated, which implies that it is treated as the infant's possession; or the mother or breast are used as containers into which are omnipotently projected the parts of the self which are felt to be undesirable as they cause pain or anxiety. Identification is an important factor in narcissistic object relations. It may take place by introjection or by projection. When the object is omnipotently incorporated, the self becomes so identified with the incorporated object that all separate identity or any boundary between self and object is denied... In narcissistic object relations defences against any recognition of separateness between self and object play a predominant part. Awareness of separation would lead to feelings of dependence on an object and therefore to anxiety. Dependence on an object implies love for and recognition of the value of the object, which leads to aggression, anxiety, and pain because of the inevitable frustrations... In addition dependence stimulates envy... The omnipotent narcissistic object relations therefore obviate both the aggressive feelings caused by frustration and any awareness of envy. When the infant omnipotently possesses the mother's breast, the breast cannot frustrate him or arouse his envy... any disturbing feeling or sensation can immediately be evacuated into the object without any concern for it, the object being generally devalued. In severe narcissistic disturbances we can invariably see the maintenance of a rigid defence against any awareness of psychic reality, since any anxiety which is aroused by conflicts between parts of the self or between self and reality is immediately evacuated. The anxiety which is thus defended against is mainly of a paranoid nature, since narcissistic object relations date from earliest infancy when anxiety is predominantly paranoid... The rigid preservation of the ideal self-image... is felt to be endangered by any insight and contact with psychic reality.

(1964, pp. 332–333)

Kernberg and Kohut's writings on narcissism are extensive. Both saw it as a condition which is based on a grandiose self, but this is where their views diverge (Kernberg, 1975).

Kohut (1971) regarded the grandiose self as a normal and essential developmental aspect, which will remain as a pathological structure in the adult, should narcissistic injuries occur, leading to a developmental arrest. Such injuries are the result of a premature, accumulative, and traumatic frustration of archaic selfobject needs, i.e., the object-parent, experienced as part of the self, fails to fulfill primary infantile needs. These selfobject needs include mirroring – the need of the child to be 'seen', admired, and approved of by the parent and even a need for the parent to share the child's grandiose fantasy, and a need for merger, or symbiosis, with an idealized parent imago, that is a need to have an idealized version of the parent and feel part of that idealized parent. An individual with a narcissistic pathology is left with archaic selfobject needs, without them having gone through processes that transmute and internalize them into the psychic structure (transmuting internalization). Thus, he is left with unfinished, weakened, psychic structures and is dependent on others for the execution of intra-psychic processes required for maintaining a sense of self-cohesion. He would keep seeking in others a mirror to reflect his grandiosity, and a need to merge with an idealized other will keep gnawing at him, though that need might be denied or split off. As opposed to Kohut's apprehension of the grandiose self as a normal phase, Kernberg regards it as a pathological structure, different from normal infantile narcissism. Kernberg (1975) stresses both the grandiose self's defensive function and its roots in significant innate aggressive drives. He views narcissism as a disorder in which, alongside a disturbance in self-regard, there are specific disturbances in object relationships. Kernberg described the way people afflicted with NPD will present excessive self-reference in their relationships with others, will manifest an intense need for love and admiration from others, apparently in contrast with the outwardly presented self-confidence, and will display a shallow emotional life, a compromised ability for empathy, and envy toward others. They tend to idealize some people from whom they anticipate 'narcissistic supply', i.e., an outward stoking and strengthening of their perception of self-regard, while discounting and depreciating others at the same time. Those 'others' might be their former objects of idealization, once the narcissist senses there's nothing more awarded by them.

> In general, their relationships with other people are clearly exploitative and sometimes parasitic. It is as if they feel they have the right to control and possess others... and behind a surface which very often is charming and engaging, one senses coldness and ruthlessness... On the surface these patients appear to present a remarkable absence of object relationships; on a deeper level, their interactions reflect very intense, primitive, internalized object relationships... and an incapacity to depend on internalized good objects.
>
> (Kernberg, 1975, p. 16)

Kernberg views narcissistic pathologies as a part of the borderline personality organizations. He stresses the outwardly high functioning, socially and with regards to impulse control, which is often found amongst persons with NPD, which differentiates them from the 'typical borderline patient'. Like Rosenfeld, Kernberg regards a disturbance in object relations as a fundamental factor in the narcissistic disorder. He regards the development of pathological narcissism alongside a range of dysfunctional object relations as the outcome of bad internalized object relations, in contrast with the development of healthy narcissism and a capability to love, which develops from good internalized object relations (Kernberg, 1975).

While a vast utilization of projective identification plays a central role in narcissistic object relations, I find that there is an important complementary mechanism, described by Bollas (1987), that of 'extractive introjection'. According to Bollas, extractive introjection will always be accompanied by the corresponding usage of projective identification. Even though Bollas does not relate extractive introjection specifically with narcissism, I believe it is a universal mechanism within the object relations of those afflicted with a severe narcissistic pathology. According to Bollas, while in projective identification one is rid of an unwanted element of himself by projecting it onto another, in extractive introjection, there is an almost opposite process:

> Extractive introjection occurs when one person steals... an element of another individual's psychic life. Such an intersubjective violence takes place when the violator (henceforth A) automatically assumes that the violated (henceforth B) has no internal experience of the psychic element that A represents. At the moment of this assumption, an act of theft takes place, and B may be temporarily anaesthetized and unable to 'gain back' the stolen part of the self. If such extraction is conducted by a parent upon a child it may take many years of an analysis before B will ever recover the stolen part of the self.
>
> (ibid, p. 104)

Bollas gives the example of a parent who lashes out disproportionally at a child who had spilled his drink. Just before the outburst the child feels remorse and is upset with himself, but now "These elements have in a sense been stolen by… the parent, who assumes [the child] is not upset… [the parent] arrogates to himself alone the elements of shock, criticism, and reparation" (ibid). The danger is that if such processes are continuous and consistent, the person subject to them will dissociate himself from those psychic elements. For instance, if one assumes a grandiose stance in which all that is good and just and all knowledge are his, while continuously depreciating and diminishing another, one might instill in that other the sensation that he lacks knowledge, lacks capabilities, and is overall bad, especially if that other person is weaker from or dependent on the first. In this manner, one robs the other of his psychic elements and appropriates them. "The victim of extractive introjection will feel denuded of parts of the self" (ibid, p. 107). Bollas sums up his article on the subject thus:

> When one person invades another's psychic territory he not only deposits an unwanted part of himself, as in projective identification, but in some respect he also takes something… the projector enjoys limited peace of mind, a psychic state that is extracted from the recipient, who is left in confusion.
>
> (ibid, p. 110)

The covert abuse I wish to discuss is characteristic of all types of pathological narcissism. In DSM-V (APA, 2013), an effort was made to improve and expand the disorder's definition compared with its predecessor, DSM-IV, but it remains a superficial and limited definition. One must clarify that in this book pathological narcissism refers to more than that limited definition and contains both the grandiose narcissist, who conceals his insecurity with an arrogant and aggressive behavior, and the vulnerable narcissist which Akhtar named covert or shy (Akhtar, 1989, 2000). The vulnerable narcissist, while possessing within himself a covert grandiosity, may be outwardly introverted, lacking in self-confidence and sensitive to rejection. While it is likely that the abusive patterns described in this book are more common amongst narcissists of the first kind, the same psychic mechanisms are activating the covert narcissist and thus he also might become abusive, especially when feeling safe and in power, for instance with his children.

The potential for causing significant harm to others exists when the narcissism arises to a mental disorder proper, when the patterns of object relations are comprehensive, rigid, and maladaptive. The abuser may appear normative, even impressive, since the disorder will be manifested mainly in his close relationships, whereas the rest of the world will be presented with the 'ego ideal' and the split-off functional side of him. In close relationships, he might act on a need to be the center of his objects' world and demand from them satisfaction for his emotional needs in a way usually required by a child. When the narcissistic pathology is severe, it is to be expected that nothing but symbiosis will be interpreted as love and that any reference to the reality of separateness will evoke terror and a sense of disintegration so severe, that the narcissist will do all in his power to refrain from experiencing it. He might exert pressure or emotional force, and in the severest of cases even physical force, in order to control the other and direct him into a scenario consistent with the way he wishes to see reality. The Other, used as an object, might feel objectified, invisible, silenced from protesting and expressing himself, humiliated and trampled for the lack of regard for his needs or respect for his autonomous separateness, and penetrated-raped for the lack of boundaries. The narcissist's relationships are tinged with the colors of his pathology: he uses splitting in order to avoid being in touch with parts of himself perceived as negative and through projections places those parts in others. Should the narcissist find criticism, perceived or real, in the words of another, or should the Other refuse to let the projections in, the narcissist's defenses will be undermined and he would commonly respond with an attack. Lack of confidence and a feeling of inferiority are swapped for grandiose defenses, which will manifest as condescension, righteousness, and entitlement. Envy will become a conviction that others envy him, causing him, often unconsciously, to sabotage someone else's success. Fear of abandonment turns into a possessive iron grip on the other.

The French psychiatrist and psychoanalyst Hirigoyen (1998) wrote:

Abusive narcissists are considered asymptomatic psychotics who find their equilibrium by discharging onto another person the pain they can't feel and the internal conflicts they refuse to acknowledge. They do wrong because they can't exist any other way. They themselves were hurt during childhood and, in turn, this is how they try to survive. This transference of pain at the expense of another permits them to attain self-confidence and self-esteem... A Narcissus... his life consists in searching for his reflection in the gaze of others. The other exists, not as an individual, but as a mirror. A Narcissus is an empty shell with no real existence; he is a "pseudo" person who creates illusions in order to mask his emptiness. His fate is an attempt to avoid death because he has never recognized himself as an individual and has been obliged to construct a game of mirrors to give himself the illusion of existing. Even if, like a kaleidoscope, the game repeats and multiplies itself, the foundation of his individuality rests on a void... the narcissist needs nourishment from another substance. When life does not exist, one attempts to appropriate it or, failing that, to destroy it so there will be no life anywhere. An insubstantial reflection lives inside abusers and a victim is only another reflection, not a real human being. Any situation that calls into question this mirror construct, masking a void, will unleash a chain reaction of destructive fury.

(pp. 124–127)

I find Hirigoyen's words both precise and too harsh. On the one hand, they describe the universal psychic mechanisms of the disorder with precision. On the other hand, they turn one into a homogenous inhumane 'narcissus'. Indeed, the patterns of abuse and the trauma are as identical as though all narcissists came out of the same assembly line, and their ramifications wound the soul, but it is also of importance to remember that these are people with all their complexity. Each of them has his own painful history and injuries that, even though one can name them with a generalizing professional noun, are still personal and private. Each one has his own unique mixture of advantages and disadvantages, alongside the common abusive behavioral patterns. I shall make the effort to present a comprehensive and balanced picture which includes the abuser's sad and injured inner world. My goal is neither to justify the abuse nor to lessen the abuser's responsibility, nor is it to encourage victims to put up with what is being done to them, but to get to the bottom of the phenomenon and seek the truth, since possession of it might bring about relief. It is easier to recover from an injury if one understands it was a result of someone else's anguish rather than a calculated malice. The nature of pathological narcissism is to bring about self-destruction in addition to the destruction of others.

Destructive Narcissism, Narcissistic Rage and Aggressiveness, and the Death Instinct

The unique nature of narcissistic aggressiveness, the narcissistic pathology's destructiveness, and the considerable mark of the death instinct on it contribute to the great abusive potential inherent in this pathology.

The narcissist is an ouroboros, the mythic serpent eating its own tail, creating an infinite circle. He ingests himself, and in attempting to revitalize himself, brings death upon himself. The circle which was created is closed to the outside world and contains no transformation or psychic evolution. It is an emotional state of an absence of separateness or of pre-separateness, which never evolves into separateness. The narcissist seeks to deny his need of others and wishes to be the source of life, while annihilating the other's vitality. He seeks to deny his neediness, his vulnerability, and even his mortality by means of an illusionary self-sufficiency. By wishing to have all the potential, he turns his existence into a locked-in, lifeless existence, lacking in self-awareness or an awareness of others. He is unable to give life and unable to receive life into himself. This is a distinct manifestation of the triumph of the death instinct over the life instinct (Freud, 1920), a desire to destroy and go back to a primary state, disorganizes, non-separated, which is also a state of 'nirvana', a symbiotic, painless state of peace of mind. Rosenfeld (1971) links the narcissistic withdrawal from relationships and the death instinct. He wrote that the death instinct "always becomes manifest as a destructive process directed against objects and the self" (p. 169) and that this process is most virulent in severe narcissistic conditions.

Rosenfeld also linked envy, which is so characteristic of severe narcissistic pathologies, to the death instinct and reminded us that Klein regarded primitive envy as "a direct derivative of the death instinct" (ibid, p. 172). Rosenfeld described a destructive narcissism and a libidinal narcissism, both of whom coexist in most patients, in varying proportions side by side. The destructive narcissism is directed against libidinal object relationships and against parts of the self which experiences the need for an object and a desire to depend on an object. Its inherent envy and death drive pair to destroy all that is good in the object, as well as the differences between the object and the subject. With libidinal narcissism, the good in the object is idealized, and the subject appropriates it as his own. Thus, narcissistic destructiveness is aimed inward as well, against the life instinct itself, against libidinal parts which seek a relationship with the object. Segal (1983) emphasized the destructiveness and self-destruction inherent to narcissism as well. She described how the death instinct and envy give rise to destructive object relations and internal structures. According to Segal, Klein (1957) described envy "as a spoiling hostility at the realization that the source of life and goodness lies outside" (Segal, 1983, p. 270). Elsewhere Segal wrote:

> One could formulate the conflict between the life and death instinct in purely psychological terms. Birth confronts us with the experience of needs. In relation to that experience there can be two reactions, and both, I think, are invariably present in all of us, though in varying proportions. One, to seek satisfaction for the needs: that is life promoting and leads to object seeking, love, and eventually object concern. The other is the drive to annihilate the need, to annihilate the perceiving experiencing self, as well as anything that is perceived.
>
> (Segal, 1993, p. 1)

Kohut (1972) described the aggression which arises from the infringement of the narcissistic balance. He maintained that this aggression is distinct and separate from other types of aggression. The causes at the root of this aggression are shame and narcissistic rage brought about by a narcissistic injury. These result in a compulsive need to undo the injury.

> The need for revenge, for righting a wrong, for undoing a hurt by whatever means, and a deeply anchored, unrelenting compulsion in the pursuit of all these aims which gives no rest to those who have suffered a narcissistic injury-these are features which are characteristic for the phenomenon of narcissistic rage in all its forms and which set it apart from other kinds of aggression.
>
> (p. 380)

Based on the selfobject needs described by Kohut, one can define two major types of narcissistic injury. Even though these types apply to the formation of the initial narcissistic injury which occurs during childhood, I shall refer to them here from the viewpoint of the narcissistically injured adult, the narcissist. The first type is an injury to mirroring needs, the need to find one's aggrandized-self reflected in the Other, who serves as a mirror. This kind of injury would include all that undermines the narcissist's conviction of his greatness, such as an insult, real or perceived, the withholding of a special treatment the narcissist expects, being confronted with a reality that contradicts the narcissist's belief that he is unique and superior and so forth. Kohut gives as an example the evil stepmother's reaction to the mirror's proclamation that Snow White is fairer. Just like her, the narcissist cannot bear the evidence which undermines his conviction in his greatness, i.e., destabilizing his narcissistic balance. Just like in the tale of Snow White, the narcissistic solution is to wipe out the evidence. In Snow White's case, it was an attempted murder, but one can also wipe out evidence by means of a somewhat more abstract destruction – by sabotaging someone else's success, devaluing them, or by denying reality. The other type of narcissistic injury is an injury to the need to merge with an idealized other. This injury may manifest by rejecting a narcissist, by some empathic failure, and even by events which are seemingly insignificant, such as holding an opinion different from the narcissist's or behaving in a way different from that which the narcissist expected, thus emphasizing the reality that one is separate from the narcissist and not under his control. In Kohut's words:

> The enemy, however, who calls forth the archaic rage of the narcissistically vulnerable is seen by him… as *a flaw in a narcissistically perceived reality.* He is a recalcitrant part of an expanded self over which he expects to exercise full control and whose mere independence or other-ness is an offense… the most intense experiences of shame and the most violent forms of narcissistic rage arise in those individuals for whom a sense of absolute control over an archaic environment is indispensable because the maintenance of self-esteem–and indeed of the self–depends on the unconditional availability of the approving-mirroring functions of an admiring self-object, or on the ever-present opportunity for a merger with an idealized one… It is this archaic mode of experience which explains the fact that those who are in the grip of narcissistic rage show total lack of empathy toward the offender. It explains the unmodifiable wish to blot out the offense which was perpetrated against the grandiose self and the unforgiving fury which arises when the control over the mirroring self-object is lost or when the omnipotent self-object is unavailable.
>
> (ibid, pp. 386–387)

For the receiving part, a narcissistic injury is unbearable, because it dismantles the grandiose self-regard or the experience of merging with an idealized selfobject, which serve as a flimsy foundation for the cohesion of the self. In other words, the narcissistic injury removes all defenses from underneath the narcissist's feet and sends him dropping into the abyss falling apart. This is the reason I regard the narcissistic anxiety mainly as an anxiety of a psychotic breakdown.[2] Kohut himself mentioned that while in narcissistic personality disturbances the fragmentation hence described is temporary and fleeting, in psychoses, which in his view also reflect a fragmentation of nuclear narcissistic structures, that fragmentation of the self is permanent or protracted (Kohut, 1972, footnote on p. 370). The narcissistic injury brings about regression. It arouses aches and mental states from the past which the victim experienced in childhood, with the concomitant affects of shame, fear, frustration, and helplessness. The adult might react to the injury with a temper tantrum, just like a two-year-old, but with all the intensity, fortitude, sophistication, and vindictiveness of an adult. This combination might make the narcissistic rage particularly painful and frightening, in essence a traumatogenic factor. In the extreme cases, it might also become lethal, and the news reports will discuss a normative person who out of nowhere, and without warning signs, committed murder.

Narcissistic rage may manifest in two different ways. The first is a raging wrath. The second is an alienated withdrawal of the narcissist from the object, accompanied by the withdrawal of all the affects and acts which portray warmth and human contact. The oxymoronic combination 'a thundering silence' is embodied fully when a narcissist ignores his object of anger.

"I know my father's facial expressions when I displease him so well", Noah told me. "His eyes become fiery, his face becomes red and it seems like smoke is about to come out of his ears. Then he shouts so loud the veins in his neck become engorged and it seems to me like the roof of the house is about to fly off. Sometimes he slams his feast against the table and I feel like it's me he wants to hit. He has a second kind of rage: his lips tighten and stretch, his skin pales and his gaze freezes. He is silent and might ignore me and not say a word to me for days on end. Sometimes I don't even know what I have done, but the message is clear – I'm not worthy of attention. I feel as if he wipes me out of existence, as if he would rather I'd vanish into thin air since I am not what he wishes me to be, or as if I made such an offence to merit a death sentence. As a little boy I was so afraid of the loud outbursts. He used to raise his voice at me, at my brothers, at Mom. I'd run to my room, get into my bed and imagine I'm somewhere else, dreaming of being grown up and leaving this house, but I think the silence was just as bad".

Noah aptly described the destructiveness of the two types of rage, which like in Robert Frost's poem 'Fire and Ice', suffice in their opposing and unique ways to bring about devastation. The narcissist is fire and ice, fluctuating between two extremes which are just as destructive. The one is a defensive ice of remoteness and isolation, where he is cold and alienated, petrifying those who emotionally need him. The other is fire, which in its greediness to appropriate the object and control it from within, consumes them both.

Notes

1 The semifluid substance of a cell.
2 And from a different theoretical perspective – one must again mention Rosenfeld's observation, which dated the narcissistic object relations from early infancy, when anxiety is predominantly paranoid.

Bibliography

American Psychiatric Association (2013). *Diagnostic and Statistical Manual of Mental Disorders, 5th Edition: DSM-5.* American Psychiatric Publishing.

Akhtar, S. (1989). Narcissistic Personality Disorder. Descriptive Features and Differential Diagnosis. *Psychiatric Clinics of North America, 12*: 505–529.

Akhtar, S. (2000). The Shy Narcissist. In: J. Sandler, R. Michela, & P. Fonagy (Eds.), *Changing Ideas in a Changing World: The Revolution in Psychoanalysis. Essays in Honour of Arnold Cooper* (pp. 111–119). Karnac.

Bollas, C. (1987). *The Shadow of the Object*. Routledge, 2018.

Ellis, H. (1898). Auto-Erotism: A Psychological Study. *Alienist and Neurologist, 19*: 260–299.

Freud, S. (1914). On Narcissism: An Introduction. In: J. Strachey (Ed.), *The Standard Edition of the Complete Psychological Works of Sigmund Freud* (vol. 14, pp. 67–102). The Hogarth Press, 1957.

Freud, S. (1920). Beyond the Pleasure Principle. In: J. Strachey (Ed.), *The Standard Edition of the Complete Psychological Works of Sigmund Freud* (vol. 18, pp. 1–64). The Hogarth Press, 1955.

Hirigoyen, M. F. (1998) *Stalking the Soul: Emotional Abuse and the Erosion of Identity.* Helen Marx Books, 2000.

Kernberg, O. (1975). *Borderline Conditions and Pathological Narcissism*. Rowman & Littlefield Publishers, 2004.

Klein, M. (1946). Notes on Some Schizoid Mechanisms. *International Journal of Psychoanalysis, 27*: 99–110.

Klein, M. (1952). The Origins of Transference. *The International Journal of Psychoanalysis, 33*: 433–438.

Klein, M. (1957). *Envy and Gratitude: A Study of Unconscious Forces*. Hogarth Press. Reprint: (1975). *The Writings of Melanie Klein*, Vol. 3: *Envy and Gratitude and Other Works, 1946–1963* (pp. 176–235). Hogarth Press and the Institute of Psycho-Analysis.

Kohut, H. (1971). *The Analysis of the Self.* The University of Chicago Press, 2009.

Kohut, H. (1972). Thoughts on Narcissism and Narcissistic Rage. *Psychoanalytic Study of the Child, 27*: 360–400.

Näcke, P. (1899). Die Sexuellen Perversitaten in der Irrenenstalt. *Psychiatriche en Neurologische Bladen, 3*: 122–149.

Rosenfeld, H. (1964). On the Psychopathology of Narcissism: A Clinical Approach. *The International Journal of Psychoanalysis, 45*: 332–337.

Rosenfeld, H. (1971). A Clinical Approach to the Psychoanalytic Theory of the Life and Death Instincts: An Investigation into the Aggressive Aspects of Narcissism. *The International Journal of Psychoanalysis, 52*: 169–178.

Segal, H. (1983). Some Clinical Implications of Melanie Klein's Work—Emergence from Narcissism. *International Journal of Psychoanalysis, 64*: 269–276.

Segal, H. (1993). On the Clinical Usefulness of the Concept of the Death Instinct. *The International Journal of Psychoanalysis, 74*: 55–61.

Chapter 3

The Narcissistic Parenthood

The Range of Narcissistic Parenthood

Freud (1914) described how parents' (normal) love for their children leads to the recognition "that it is a revival and reproduction of their own narcissism, which they have long since abandoned" (p. 91). The offspring is "His Majesty the Baby" (ibid) and he:

> shall not be subject to the necessities which they have recognized as paramount in life... the laws of nature and of society shall be abrogated in his favour... The child shall fulfil those wishful dreams of the parents which they never carried out... Parental love... is nothing but the parents' narcissism born again.
>
> (ibid)

Hence, parental love is narcissistic by nature. One cannot fulfill this enormous, demanding, and marvelous role of a parent in a manner that is devoted, "unresented" and "good enough" (Winnicott, 1953, p. 94) without such narcissistic investment. It is of importance to stress that, prior to discussing 'Narcissistic Parenthood', a term I shall designate to situations in which the parent's narcissistic investment is pathological. Parenthood is narcissistic when the intensity of the narcissistic processes is excessive or when they persist without the transmutations and adaptations needed in light of the child's growth.

The behavioral patterns of narcissistic parenthood are the derivatives of the parent's narcissistic object relations. They are characterized by controlling the child and denying separateness – an omnipotence which will manifest itself through projective identification and incorporation. They are also characterized by envy and the defense against it. They are in effect failings in parental functioning, and as Winnicott wrote: "failure of [the external object] indirectly leads to deadness or to a persecutory quality of internal object" (ibid).

Manzano, Espasa and Zilkha (1999) describe the narcissistic scenarios of parenthood. In this process the parent projects upon the child "a representation of the parent's self...cathected with narcissistic libido" (p. 467). This is a process of projective identification and incorporation[1] or rather a re-introjection by the parent

DOI: 10.4324/9781032625393-3

of that which was projected by him. The Process may "wholly or partially oblit-erate the boundaries between self and object" (ibid, p. 469). In other words, the child is experienced as an inseparable part of the parent's self. He is required to take the projections in, to be what the parent needs, and not what he truly is, and to allow himself to be food for the parent's soul, incorporated by the parent. In these cases, the narcissistic scenarios of the parent impose a conflictual overload on the child and nest in him "parasitically" (ibid, p. 473). The parent may project different aspects of his self-representation onto his child. These might include the parent's infantile self, i.e., he might see himself as a child in his offspring; the ego ideal, i.e., what the parent would have wanted to be; or he might project onto his child the representation of his own parent.[2] In this manner, the scenario the parent creates is an expression of a narcissistic relationship between self and self. It is a relationship occurring in the parent's inner world albeit enacted in the real world through the parent's projection of his own self-representation onto his child, thus staging him to portray the scenario. Manzano et al. argue that the ultimate goal of the process is invariably the attainment of narcissistic satisfaction, but there might be other goals as well, such as a defensive denial of loss or a disguised satisfaction of repressed oedipal drives. "To paraphrase Freud, the shadow of the parents may be said to have fallen on the child, either directly or by way of the shadow of the parental internal objects" (ibid, pp. 467–468). Manzano et al. stress the universal and normal nature of this mechanism, which may be beneficial and constructive for the child, as long as "the narcissistic relationship… is gradually superseded by an object relationship in which the child is acknowledged and loved predominantly as a distinct individual" (ibid, p. 469). If, however, the narcissistic element is exces-sive, the ramifications on the child's psychic development might be pathological. These processes might be pathogenic "if they interfere with this development and conflict with reality—in particular, with the reality of the existence of a growing child that is inconsistent with the parental projection on to him" (ibid).

Miller (1979) wrote:

> The difficulties inherent in experiencing and developing one's own emotions lead to bond permanence, which prevents individuation, in which both parties have an interest. The parents have found in their child's "false self" the confir-mation they were looking for, a substitute for their own missing structures; the child, who has been unable to build up his own structures, is first consciously and then unconsciously (through the introject) dependent on his parents.
>
> (pp. 13–14)

Eigen (1999) described how by its very nature, parental love is also toxic:

> Emotional nourishment and poisons can be so interwoven… that nourishment one needs to support life is toxic… a parent who loves may pour limitless nega-tive energy into the child. This is… an offshoot of the fact that the child is the spontaneous object of the parents' deepest feelings… All that is in the parent

floods the child. Thus love is mixed with... anxious control, worry, death dread, ambition, self-hate... Parents often view children as extensions of themselves, food for ego... Parent-child boundaries are variable and fluid. The child must digest messianic expectations fused with everyday life. To an extent, we learn to use what psychic nutrients we can and avoid what is toxic. Often, we more or less succeed, but not without casualties.

(pp. xiii–xv)

The American psychologist Susan Forward (1989) described abusive patterns of parenthood which she called toxic. Those patterns are effectively the manifestations of a narcissistic pathology. According to Forward's definition, toxic parents are parents whose negative behavioral pattern is consistent and dominant in their child's life, and who inflict trauma on the child by means of abuse and denigration. She likens the psychic harm such parenthood inflicts to that of a toxin, spreading through the child's being. The pattern which Forward describes is characterized by a harsh criticism of the child, by the lack of emotional availability of the parent, by a role reversal forcing the child to take care of the parent, and by conveying a message that being different or refusing to capitulate to the parent's wishes renders the child 'bad'. The child fears his parents in general, and fears being angry with them or criticizing them in particular. According to Forward, as the child matures, these parents keep treating him as a little child, controlling him through manipulations, emotional blackmail and the incitement of guilt, or through money. Forward likens the toxic family to a multiple car pile-up, one generation damaging the next (intergenerational transmission). She describes how in such a family there are spoken rules, such as a prohibition to talk back to the parent, and unspoken rules which for the child are nonetheless loud and clear and share the fundamental message that the child is forbidden from leading an independent life without needing the parent. Forward wrote that in such a family, the child's sense of identity and illusion of safety depend on his letting himself be enmeshed with the parent and experiencing himself as enmeshed, since the alternative is being shunned. The child pays for the temporary feelings of approval and safety with his selfhood and becomes dependent upon approval and validation from others. In a subsequent book, *Mothers Who Can't Love* (2013), Forward already refers to such mothers as 'narcissistic'. Forward begins her book with the story of a patient of hers, who wished to warm herself in the sunlight: "it sure looked like the sun and it was bright like the sun, but there was absolutely no warmth coming from it. And this wave of sadness came over me—the sun was just like my mother" (p. 1). According to Forward, these mothers struggle to love themselves, are lacking in self-confidence and therefore have a need for acknowledgment and a need to be the center of attention, as well as a need to sabotage their daughter's developing confidence and self-esteem, which serves to increase their own. Forward stresses that these mothers harm their daughters unintentionally:

Much of their behavior is driven by forces outside their conscious awareness, or emotions they are afraid of confronting: a crippling sense of insecurity, an unshakable feeling of deprivation, deep disappointment in their own lives. As they look for relief from their own fears and sadness, they use their daughters to shore up their feelings of power or agency or control. The hallmark of all these mothers is a lack of empathy, and their intense self-centeredness blinds them to the suffering they create.

(ibid, p. 20)

Narcissistic parenthood shapes the child's personality. "The outline of the child's personality is sharply etched by the acid of the parents' anxiety" (Mitchell & Black, 1995, p. 69). It is impossible to comprehend the process in its entirety by observing intra-psychic processes and representations alone. Winnicott stressed this in his article "Ego Distortion in terms of True and False Self" (1960):

To get to a statement of the relevant developmental process it is essential to take into account the mother's behaviour and attitude, because in this field dependence is real, and near absolute. *It is not possible to state what takes place by reference to the infant alone.*

(Winnicott, 1960/1965, pp. 144–145)

The Characteristics of Narcissistic Parenthood

I shall list eight main characteristics of narcissistic parenthood. These characteristics are artificially divided for didactic reasons but in effect many are overlapping or intertwined. The vignettes may also suit several characteristics of the relationship between a parent inflicted with narcissistic pathology and his child. For example, the parent's criticism might derive from envy, a need to control or both. The characteristics of narcissistic parenthood are a manifestation of the aforementioned mechanisms. The child internalizes them and might develop similar patterns by way of intergenerational transmission.

A Lack of Boundaries and Separation

A narcissistic parent tends to regard his child as an inseparable part of himself. Any deviation from a state of symbiosis is experienced by the parent as alienation and provokes annihilation anxiety and deterioration in the behavioral pattern. One often gets the sense that the parent is 'living through' his child and experiencing the child's life as his own. The parent behaves intrusively and demands to have his way with the child's mind and often with the child's body as well. I've heard countless stories of houses where locking doors was forbidden, houses where the parent had no qualms about barging into the bathroom, even that of an adolescent or a mature child, no hesitation about touching the child's body possessively and intrusively, as if it was his own, or going through the child's belongings and demanding unrestricted access to the child's inner world.

Kohut (1971) opined "The parents' pathology and narcissistic needs contribute decisively to the child's remaining excessively and protractedly enmeshed within the narcissistic web of the parents' personality" (p. 79). According to Kohut (1977), "narcissistically disturbed parents… deprive their children of the requisite narcissistic nutriment" and their personality is pathogenic (p. 276). These parents "are reluctant to give up the merger-enmeshment with the child whom they, phase-inappropriately, because of the defective condition of their own self, still need to retain as part of their own self" (ibid, pp. 274–275). These chronic narcissistic relationships cause a developmental arrest from which the child struggles to extricate himself (Kohut, 1971).

Such a child might have contradicting feelings. On the one hand, only when he fully exposes himself to the parent and lets him intervene in everything, does he get to feel closeness and a relief from anxiety; on the other hand, he is subject to severe intrusions. In all likelihood, he would come to interpret closeness and love as a symbiotic lack of separation and in the absence of such symbiosis would feel excluded from the mind and life of the Other. A relationship becomes something required in order to maintain an illusion of wholeness, as well as a threat to his independence and to his selfhood. The parent demands that the child would become an indistinguishable, enmeshed human-clump, and feels a need and an entitlement to be the most important person in his child's life and to keep his claim to this status even when the child is grown up, acting like the master of his child.

The lack of boundaries is bilateral, and the child might find himself inappropriately exposed to the parents' relationship. He might witness quarrels or sexual insinuations between the parents, who fail to perceive him as a separate subject and therefore act and speak as if the child is absent. At times, the atmosphere in the house is saturated with the primal scene's vapors, a scene to which the child is not only exposed, but in which he also takes part. He might serve as a substitute partner for the parent of the opposing sex. The mother would idealize her son and convey to him that she prefers him over his father, thus castrating the father and denying the son of him. Or the father might make a partner of his daughter, burdening her with his grievances with her mother, thereby ruining the mother as a model for identification and idealization for the daughter. Thus an oedipal drama is formed, in which the child 'triumphs' over the same-sex parent. Such a pyrrhic victory denies the child of the normal developmental course of identification with and internalization of the same-sex parent. The end result is a hollow simulation of a grown up, trapped within the oedipal conflict. The child is faced with the oedipal drama having failed to attain basic skills needed to contend with it, since prior developmental stages were not achieved. The formation of the triangular space (Britton, 1989, 2004) is affected, i.e. the recognition of the parents' relationship as one child is not a part of. That recognition forms a basis to acknowledging the reality of being separate from the other.

Abigail, a patient in her forties, was married to a man who failed to fulfill her expectations of him to become rich and renowned like her father, and whom she treated with outright contempt. She idealized her son and described how she used to preach him not to follow his father's footsteps. I felt she was trying to mold her son into the internalized image of her father, who has left home when she was a small child and whom she admired. In other words, having expectedly failed to heal her childhood wounds through her choice of a partner, she tried to do so through her son – projecting onto her son as a means to keeping a relationship with her object-father and to fulfilling oedipal drives. In order to achieve that goal she had to control her object-son. Throughout the years, she regularly went through her children's possessions and read their letters and diaries. She spoke disdainfully of her son's pleas that she refrained from wandering around the house in front of him in her undergarments, and spoke proudly of the "hungry looks" she received from his male friends. She often criticized her son's female friends and found a fault with each and every one of them, especially with those who seemed closer to him or interested in him romantically. When he would entertain one of them in the living room, she used to hang around, listening intently, mocking in our sessions the "stupidity" of the girl in question. As years went by, Abigail became increasingly worried about the fact that her son had yet to have a romantic relationship. When he turned eighteen her preoccupation with the topic became obsessive. She got caught in the thought that he might be avoiding a relationship because of a small manhood. One day she told me how, using one excuse or another, she barged into his room while he was dressing up in order to see for her own eyes and put her worries to rest. The room was not locked since she forbade it. When I asked how her son reacted she lashed at me: "What exactly are you saying? That I have no right? Who are you to tell me, what are you talking about? I'm his mother. I used to bath him, there's nothing he has that I hadn't already seen, one would think what I did to him!" Abigail could not fathom that her son had grown up. From her tone of voice and the furious-ominous look in her eyes, I could easily guess why her son could only protest feebly, knowing he would be subject to the full scope of her narcissistic rage, in a petrifying and silencing response that leaves no room to reply. To Abigail, separateness was excruciating and dangerous to the extent that she had to attack any mention of the reality of its existence.

Criticality and Judgment

Since the child is experienced as an inseparable part of the narcissistic parent, he is held to perfectionistic standards, to criticism and to rejection. The criticism is judgmental, i.e. inflexible and inordinate. The parent projects onto his child his ego ideal – the way in which he wishes to see himself – and criticizes him when he fails to meet the high standards he was held to. Oftentimes, the criticism derives from a projection of the parent's weaknesses and insecurities and is driven out of a failure to view the child as separate or serves as a means to avoid an emotional reckoning with these parts of the parent. The child is attacked by the parent's areas of self-hatred and internalizes a perception of himself as defective, not good enough, incapable.

The hatred toward parts of the parent's self or parts of the parent's introjected objects is now turned outwards, toward the child. The child is subject to both idealization and devaluation by the parent, alternatingly overvalued and degraded and sometimes both at the same time. A deluding and inconsistent experience of an incomprehensible and unexpected world is formed, as well as an experience of a split self. On top of that, the criticism is an expression of the parent's envy as well as a manifestation of an obsessive need to omnipotently control the object. Criticism will be aimed at the child's functioning and appearance as well as desires, needs, opinions, and beliefs, who must not oppose those of the parent. In order to receive (an illusion of) acceptance and love from the parent, the child will have to meet the bar set for him by the parent. He is condemned to live in an ongoing anxiety to fail and might perceive himself as a failure even despite a reality of successes, for the sole reason of failing to meet his parents' high expectations, which are internalized and become his own. The child has to adjust himself in order to fit into a pre-tailored suit, and he stifles his desires, his talents, and his true opinions, namely, his true self. Berman (2009), in a preface to a translation of Winnicott's "Ego Distortion in terms of True and False Self", clearly formulates the two pathways to the development of the self that Winnicott describes – true vs. false:

> The first pathway is based on the ability of the good enough mother... to respond to the spontaneous gestures of the infant and child, to respond to him empathically and to give his experiences a meaning through her facial expressions and later on through her words as well... this process leads to a profound familiarity of the child with himself and to the formation of a unique true self. The other pathway is the one built upon the failure of the process of finding the personal meaning when... the incapability of the mother and the family to meet the child where he really is emotionally, and their expectations for obedience, of him to be "a good boy" by customary social norms, urges the child – should he wish to survive – to react with a submissive adaptation, with pleasing, with the formation of a false self.
>
> (pp. 199–200. my translation – H.Y)

The way the child experiences the very core of his soul, his subjectivity, does not receive validation. On top of that, the parent also attacks the child's perception of himself. The child learns to hide all that is real in him – needs, urges, desires, aggression, and feelings. All that is spontaneous and all that is creative is silenced and stifled and with it the experience of being alive.

Excessive criticism might also extract psychic elements and capabilities from the child, through the process of extractive introjection (Bollas, 1987). For example, if a child seeks to express himself and his opinions, but the adult doesn't allow it and reacts with excessive criticism and correction, the child will become "confused and perplexed...less articulate" (ibid, p. 105). In this case the adult might feel superior and knowledgeable in comparison to the child, but in the process he destroys the development of this ability in the child. The offender appropriates something that belonged to the offended-subject and the subject loses it. Bollas also links this to the formation of the false self:

> As a person takes from another person's psyche, he leaves a gap, or a vacuum, in its place. There he deposits despair or emptiness in exchange for what he has stolen. The situation is further complicated by the fact that a child who is the victim of consistent extractive introjection may choose to identify with the aggressive parent and install in his personality this identification, which then functions as a false self.
>
> (ibid, p. 108)

Sometimes, criticality serves the parent as a defense against envy.[3] The child is expected to react to the world and conduct himself in it just like the parent would, and knows that should he "get it wrong", the parent would react with criticism, contempt, and devaluation. Some of these children will become silent, voiceless. They can but echo the parent's voice, taking on positions, opinions, and a demeanor which constitute a false self. The child might grow to become a perfectionist whose experience of himself depends on the way he is perceived or believes he is perceived, at the moment, by others. He might become 'addicted' to achievements, although an achievement would bring about only a fleeting sensation of a cohesive self. Alternatively, he might fear criticism and failure to the extent that he would refrain from trying, all the while being submerged in grandiose fantasies of abilities and achievements that could have been his or have yet to be his. The parent's critical voice becomes a persecutory-sadistic super ego and the child might develop a profound lack of confidence, difficulties with decision-making, and an avoidant stagnation in his life.

Emotional Instability

The narcissistic parent's vulnerability along with his immature defense mechanisms leads to an emotional and a behavioral instability that the child will experience as Dr. Jekyll and Mr. Hyde. When the parent's narcissistic needs are fulfilled, all that is good in him is unhindered and he will be inclined to be placated and in good spirits and act benevolently. Once his narcissistic equilibrium is disturbed, he will evacuate the feelings of anxiety and fragmentation into the object in front of him. Narcissistic rage is the manifestation of such a disturbance to the equilibrium, brought about by the confrontation of the parent with reality. This reality might be the separateness from the object or the fact that the parent is not, in effect, omnipotently perfect. "The rigid preservation of the ideal self-image… is felt to be endangered by any insight and contact with psychic reality" (Rosenfeld, 1964, p. 336). Awareness to reality can be aroused by factors in the parent-child relationship, for example if the child resists the parent's control over him, or factors in the parent's relationships with others which have boiled the parent's narcissistic rage to the point where it spills over to the child. The parent would become strict, cold, critical, and hostile. The parent's aggressiveness might manifest itself through facial muscle tension, through the rigidity of the body, through an icy cold glance, through an icy tone of voice, or through a sudden outburst of rage. In all of the above the child might sense the desire to annihilate him. The signs might appear in an instant, a narcissistic rage that the child might possibly not understand what he did to give rise to it. Winnicott (1960) described that the false self develops in order to protect the true self, in some radical cases to protect it from annihilation. He wrote:

> If the True Self ever gets exploited and annihilated this belongs to the life of an infant whose mother was not only 'not good enough'... but was good and bad in a tantalizingly irregular manner. The mother here has as part of her illness a need to cause and to maintain a muddle in those who are in contact with her... There may be a degree of this which can destroy the last vestiges of an infant's capacity to defend the True Self.
>
> (Winnicott, 1960/1965, p. 147)

For the child, this is a chaotic world lacking in consistency. The object constancy is undermined. These children experience continuous anxiety regarding 'which parent' they would encounter. In trying to avoid the second, crazy version of the parent, they learn to develop antennas, "a special sensitivity to unconscious signals manifesting the needs of others" (Miller, 1979, p. 9). In the jargon that ensued, a person of such sensitivity is called an Empath.

The parent is inconsistent and his behavior is unpredictable. A door that now stands open within him might in a moment be closed shut. At times he will keep his promise, at other times he will not. A certain action the child takes might elicit a positive response one day, indifference or reproach the other. For the child, who fails to understand the change that took place in the parent's inner world, the link between cause and effect is severed. He might feel helpless or feel responsible and guilty about things he has no influence over. His capacity to trust is undermined. He cannot rely on long-term plans or on his ability to positively affect the outcome. On top of that, the child feels undeserving of anything from the world and does not trust he would obtain that which he needs, thus he might experience difficulties delaying gratifications, and act in a self-defeating way.

The following case depicts the three characteristics discussed thus far:

> Ariel grew with a father to whom turning could be met with warmth and containment or with alienation and aggression, according to his narcissistic equilibrium. When Ariel began therapy, a recurrent nightmare came up, in which she would get to my practice, but a woman whose face are a stranger's face opens the door. Ariel said that she had considered seeking psychoanalysis, but have rejected the idea since the thought of lying on a couch

without seeing the therapist's face was intolerable for her. She felt a need to make sure my facial expression remained benevolent, free from criticism and anger, and that she wouldn't be flipped on or abandoned. Sometimes she would phone me in between sessions saying: "I just wanted to hear your voice", making sure the voice-object does not disappear or change and relaxing somewhat. Ariel exhibited an almost supernatural sensitivity to slight changes in my mood and sometimes would even guess seemingly telepathically events occurring in my life. In that manner she tried to use the sensitive antennas she had had to develop, in order to defend herself from the loss of the object. Feeling excluded was intolerable and she tried to penetrate my life in order to know what transpires in it.

The Use of the Child to Fulfill Parental Needs/Parent-Child Role Reversal

A parent's identification with his child naturally arouses archaic infantile narcissistic needs. A narcissistic parent carries a deep wound inside which makes him all the more prone to regress to those needs. They are awakened in him intensely and the child is required to fulfill them in diverse ways. He is required to mirror the parent's idealized image of himself (while for the child receiving mirroring is conditioned upon pleasing the parent). It is common for a role reversal to take place, in which the child plays the parental role in the relationship, a process known in the jargon as parentification. The child is expected to take care of the parent, shower him with attention, and contain him. On the one hand, the child is required not to grow, and on the other hand, he is required to take care of his progenitor in a parental manner which requires that he exhibits a precocious (pseudo) maturity. The child might be required to lend an ear to the parent's plights, including those associated with couples' relations, to soothe the parent, to adjust his behavior and the environment to the parent's needs, to show interest in the parent, to remember birthdays when he is still but young of age, to put effort into making the parent happy, and so on. The parent may demand the child's time and investment in a manner which leaves the child deprived of an emotional space for other relationships. Being a parent is an endless source for the supply of narcissistic needs. Young children admire their parents, need them, are weaker than them, and accept without questioning that the parent knows best. Furman (1982) quotes Anna Freud's parting words to her, upon finishing her psychoanalytic training and leaving England: "A mother's job is to be there to be left" (p. 15). Furman wrote:

"The child's mastery of this developmental step [growth and separation from the mother] can occur only when the mother can allow herself to miss her child, to feel not needed, and to remain lovingly available for the moments when he chooses to return to her."

(ibid, p. 16)

With a narcissistic parent, the child is required to maintain the role of the smaller and weaker party and does not receive the 'permission' to grow and separate from the parent, since separation is experienced as abandonment. There is a well-known caricature depicting narcissism, in which a kitten looks at the mirror and sees a lion. The narcissistic parent looks at his child who has grown into a lion, and sees a kitten (here envy plays a part as well). What the narcissist is in need of from others, in order to maintain the narcissistic equilibrium, is termed, both in Kernberg's writings (1975) and in the popular jargon, narcissistic supplies. The authority and power inherent in the parent-child relationship satisfy narcissistic needs. The parent may "feed off his child" (Talia Saidel-Cohen – personal communication, 1.4.21). Manzano et al. (1999) liken the conflictual overload of the parent's (exaggerated and pathological) narcissistic scenarios on the child to a parasitic process. The parent holds on to his child for his own needs and molds him into being passive, pleasing and lacking the ability to protect himself in the face of abusive behavior. Such a child is habituated to identify with the parent's aggression, to deny or justify abusive behavior toward him, or to blame himself for it. He may become a pleasing adult who finds himself in abusive relationships with narcissists, both because he has become a 'magnet' for them, being adept as he is at satisfying their emotional needs whilst trampling over his own, and because these are the object relations he is familiar with and whom he tries to fix with repetition compulsion. Identification with the aggressor might also render the child abusive toward others, of course.

Need for Control, Manipulative Behavior, and Emotional Blackmail

The narcissistic parent has a need for an omnipotent control over his child and for enmeshment with him. The sense of control and the denial of separateness are defense mechanisms against anxiety and also serve to fill the sensation of emptiness and death in the parent's internal world. His anxieties may appear on the surface as neurotic, some of which may indeed be so, but in effect, his fundamental and profound anxiety is of a psychotic breakdown since he tends toward a paranoid-schizoid position where the dominant anxieties are of annihilation and disintegration. As a result, displays of independence, separateness, or maturation may trigger an intense reaction from the parent, along with the exacerbation of symptoms in an attempt to keep control over the child. The severely narcissistic parent is dogmatic, holding beliefs and principles that, in his perception, do not require proof and cannot be challenged, and expecting everyone to accept them and act upon them. Control is exercised through a variety of methods with varying degrees of severity – excessive involvement, conscious and unconscious manipulations, overt domineering, the use of threats, and intimidation. Should one refuse to submit to his control, the parent may attempt to reinstate it vindictively through punishment (withholding love, rights, or money). The punishment may include humiliation and belittlement of the child, ignoring the child, known in the jargon as 'the silent treatment', or ostracizing and shunning the child. In order to enforce his will and opinions, the parent may also evoke the child's fear by exploding in rage (screaming, aggressive gestures). In other words, he will employ violence. The parent acts like a bully or a tyrant. The child may become 'trained', so that a glance is enough to dissuade him from expressing himself.

Even when the parent's way with his child appears to convey love and caring, the motive, even if unconscious, may be control. The parent's will is conveyed to the child in an unconscious manner and manages to exert extreme pressure on him. A baby's attention is directed toward its mother, and her speech to him is enchanting, hypnotizing. Our parents are the ones who teach us about the world, name things, and give them meaning. They are the ones to tell us what is day and what night is, what is good and permissible and what is bad and forbidden. For this reason, when a parent defines his child in a certain way, the message will permeate and take hold in the child's psyche, and he will hardly be able to question it.

Cohen (2020) describes this as a suggestive influence of the parent on his child. He describes messages which define or label the child and in effect dictate the identity he should adopt.

> The messages… are consistently presented to the child authoritatively and judgmentally, creating a kind of hypnotic suggestion that exerts control over him and drives him towards helplessness, self-negation, or withdrawal and isolation… The child experiences within himself duplicity and conflict, between what he was told he is or should be, and the way he experiences himself. In fact, the child… experiences the parent's attitude towards him as an attack… an internal conflict is created in which the child is defeated either way, whether he accepts and internalizes the parental message or resists it.
>
> (ibid, pp. 151–157, my translation – H.Y.)

Another means that the parent may employ is economic control. Money is used as reward and punishment. Sometimes it serves as bait, a monetary Trojan horse – the child will receive financial assistance, but he who pays the piper calls the tune, and now the parent has taken the liberty to dictate what the child will purchase or where he will live. A common manifestation of financial control is the threat of, or de facto, vindictive disinheritance from the will.

Another tool for controlling the child is emotional blackmail, i.e., evoking the child's guilt in order to make him submit to the parent's will. The parent conveys a message that, should the child refuse, he is bad or unworthy, or that refusal hurts the parent. The guilt and shame that overwhelm the child, along with the accompanying anxiety, make submission to the parent's will the default. In addition, the child will fear resisting the parent because the parent's expected reaction to refusal is an attack comprised of belittling and hurtful words, a bursting narcissistic rage, devaluation and ridicule, and facial expressions conveying abysmal disappointment. The child may also refrain from responding out of "learned helplessness" (Miller & Seligman, 1975; Maier & Seligman, 1976). He knows that there is nothing he can do to avoid the pain-inducing agent and that in any case there is no chance of accepting his position as a legitimate one. Therefore, he may try to find some sense of control by taking the blame on himself. In her book *Emotional Blackmail*, Forward (1997) defines emotional blackmail not only as manipulating someone by guilt feelings but also in a broader sense, as "a powerful form of manipulation in which people… threaten, either directly or indirectly, to punish us if we don't do what they want" (p. x). She describes that a person who is being blackmailed thus doesn't realize it, because he is engulfed in a FOG made of Fear, Obligation, and Guilt (Ibid, p. xi).

The child is trapped in a reality that dulls his senses. *Gaslight* (Cukor, 1944) is a movie based on a play called 'Angel Street', written by Patrick Hamilton in the 1930s. It tells the story of a woman whose husband tries to make her believe she is losing her sanity through manipulations. The husband's manipulations include moving her objects and dimming the gas lights in the house, while telling her that she is imagining the changes her senses are picking up because she is unwell. Following the movie, the term 'gaslighting' was coined and became a common term to describe a manipulation intended to make someone doubt his perception of reality and his sanity. The manipulation may be done consciously or unconsciously. When a pathologically narcissistic parent tells a child 'it never happened' or *It's Just Your Imagination* (Horowitz, 2017), it evokes in him confusion, anxiety, and a doubt in his perception of reality. This manipulation is often accompanied by other manipulative tactics, such as changing the subject and refusing to address the child's claims, blaming the child (either for being cruel and hurting the parent or for being 'too sensitive' as a way of saying that his reality testing is flawed), and inducing feelings of guilt. These tactics are also used to deflect criticism and deny any possible fault in the narcissist or his actions. My impression is that in most cases these actions are unconscious, driven out of mechanisms that the parent employs to re-establish omnipotent control through eliminating reality. Gaslighting is a process of introjection in which the one undergoing the process internalizes the perception of the world the manipulator wishes to force upon him.

As for the feelings of guilt, these are also activated by the religious and social commandment that demands honoring parents. In her book *The Body Never Lies*, Miller (2005) addresses the commandment "Honor thy father and thy mother" (Exodus 20:12) and how the religious and social norm demands it be followed, thus preventing a person from acknowledging his true feelings, at a high cost. Miller notes that this is in fact the only commandment that includes a threat, or a clarification of the punishment for disobedience – early death – "that thy days may be long upon the land which the LORD thy God giveth thee" (Exodus 20:12). She emphasizes that emotions cannot be commanded and writes:

> Individuals who believe that they feel what they ought to feel and constantly do their best not to feel what they forbid themselves to feel will ultimately fall ill— unless, that is, they leave it to their children to pick up the check by projecting onto them the emotions they cannot admit to themselves.

(Miller, 2005, p. 16)

The narcissistic parent's manipulations steer the important choices in his child's life, including career and romantic relationships. The child may feel he is being operated like a marionette in a play called his life.

Noah recounted:

> He would say to me: "call grandpa, go visit your aunt, talk to your brother, apologize to your mother". I had to do it immediately. In addition, there were instructions on what to do in my free time, what a legitimate activity is, and what is a waste of time. I had to appear to be happy. My depression didn't suit him, it ruined his 'perfect' world. If I approached him with distress, it would irritate him. When I was a child and got wounded, he would yell at me for it. If the child of a friend of his wanted something of mine, he would pressure me to give it to him as a gift. I always agreed. I couldn't bear the guilt, his inversion of me into 'bad' and 'selfish' if I refused. I wasn't important, what was important is how I – and therefore he – appeared to his friend. I had to be as he needed me to be. There were incessant directing instructions and I knew I couldn't refuse. It was easier to swallow the bitter taste of affront and humiliation and do as he pleases, than to be subjected to his anger and vindictiveness. When I was little, I didn't understand what was happening, I just felt bad. I'd obey without thinking. If he was angry with me, I felt like the most malicious child in the world, and anything was better than feeling that way. When I became a teenager, I felt such emptiness that I actually felt like climbing the walls. I didn't understand why I felt that way, but now I understand. You were right when you told me, that his emotional disappearance and my becoming 'bad' would take me apart every time, and that even in his absence, these things kept happening again and again inside of me. I feel guilty all the time. Now I've started seeing him in my imagination as a puppeteer, playing with me, my brothers and my mother, constantly pulling our strings, putting words in our mouths, and enacting entire dialogues between us. My niece plays with her dolls that way – making one say something to the other and deciding what the other would reply.

The system of pressures and control that was described prevents the child from learning to set boundaries and teaches him to excessively and comprehensively fulfill the needs of others at the expense of his own. Unlike a child whose parents respect his feelings, he does not learn to express what he feels or needs, and he struggles to endure situations where others are not pleased with him. What is created is an obedient human shell, confused, and empty inside, operated by others from the outside, similar to the description in Dahlia Ravikovitch's poem, 'Clockwork Doll':

On that night I was a clockwork doll
And I turned to and fro, right and left

And I fell face down and became fragmented and cleft
And a deft hand attempted mending my fragments from my fall.

And then I was a clockwork doll once more
And my demeanor was all prudent and obedient
But by then I was a doll of a second rate.

Extract From: Clockwork Doll ("Bubba Memuchenet") by Dahlia Ravikovitch, [my translation from Hebrew – H.Y.].

Substantive Deficiencies in Empathy

Impaired empathy is a prominent feature of narcissism, which also appears as one of the diagnostic criteria in the DSM-V. The narcissistic parent may show empathy toward his child as long as the child lives up to his expectations and is perceived as a positive extension of himself, and as long as the child's emotional distress does not challenge the parent's defenses. I believe that feeling empathy threatens the parent's defensive split. Empathy is a bestowal needed by the child as much as oxygen for breathing, especially in areas of human vulnerability, areas that the narcissistic parent splits and denies. The parent who struggles to contain his child's pain may respond with various reactions that dismiss or diminish the child's experience – dismissal, anger, and anxiety. When something happens in the child's life, the parent focuses on the impact of these events on himself rather than on the child's feelings or needs. Thus, the child is deprived of the validating, comforting, and tranquilizing experience that one is bestowed upon when another person makes him feel deeply understood. Not only does the parent fail to give meaning of the child's difficulties and soothe him, but he also projects into the child his own anxieties and unprocessed primary areas. In Bionian terms, not only does the parent's alpha function fail in digesting and converting the child's beta elements, that are thrown back at the child, but the parent also throws his own beta elements into the child. The parent's thought process is concrete, lacking in symbolization (Bion, 1962a), unable to differentiate between objects, a thought process prone to collapse into a psychosis. By projective identification processes, the parent exerts pressure on his child to become so indistinguishable from him, to the point that the parent's thought processes are all the child knows. Furthermore, the parent fails to fulfill for the child the functions that enable linking (Bion, 1959). In fact, the parent attacks anything he cannot control, including the child's independent thinking, creativity, and ability to trust his perception of reality. The child remains with a 'nameless dread' (Bion, 1962a, p. 96, 1962b, p. 309), unable to think the pain or contain it, and incapable of seeing the parent and his abusiveness. When thinking is under attack and the child is deprived of validation, reality becomes distorted like a painting by Dali or a dream – things become disproportionate, oozing, fragmented into their components, or indistinguishable from one another. The child, who experiences himself as guilty of this, becomes lost in this experience of losing his mind and becomes even more dependent on the parent as a 'compass' to guide his way in 'reality'. The child's capacity for thinking, symbolization (Bion, 1962a; Segal, 1957), and mentalization (Fonagy, 1989) is compromised. He does not learn the words for what he feels and what he needs, does not know or understand himself, and does not attain the ability to grasp the psychic complexity of others.

> The capacity to conceive of the contents of one's own as well as the object's mind is an important prerequisite for normal object relations. In its absence, the patient is prone to experience meaninglessness, chaos, and nameless dread as others' feelings, intentions, and the expectability of certain behaviours, can only be represented at a primary… level.
>
> (Fonagy, 1989, p. 107)

According to Fonagy, the process is also adaptive because it protects the child from contemplating what is on the parent-object's mind, a contemplation that would be intolerable (Fonagy, 1989). The child learns to protect the parent from his feelings and to protect himself from the parent's reaction and 'manage on his own'. He learns that emotions are illegitimate and repulsive and he experiences a dissonance between what he feels and what he is told he should or should not feel. The child does not learn how to contain his own emotions and soothe himself. He may be ridiculed for expressing emotions which are uncomfortable to the parent, and he becomes confused in front of the parental empty well that he approaches in his distress. The child does not feel that his emotions are valid and learns to silence them. He navigates the world feeling misunderstood and that he cannot share his experiences and inner world with others and, worse, he is dissociated from his emotional experiences. "The absence of parental figures endowed with adequate empathy to react appropriately… may contribute to a permanent impairment of structuralization leading to the child's poor comprehension of his own and others' mental states" (ibid, p. 107).

Modell (1975) views avoidance of affects as a characteristic narcissistic defense. "[When] a specific narcissistic defence against affects… predominates it contributes to the formation of the personality structure that we associate with the narcissistic character disorder" (p. 275). He describes a 'narcissistic affect block' that arises from fear of closeness to the object and argues that when it is present, one can invariably see that it is based on a fantasy of grandiose self-sufficiency. This is because affects imply the presence of 'object hunger' and object seeking. Avoidance of affects allows the individual to maintain an illusion that he does not need anything from anyone. Modell wrote that "Winnicott understood that the experiencing and sharing of feelings helps to organize an early sense of self… Where there is a false self, what is shared and displayed is essentially false because it is based on compliance" (ibid, p. 278). Modell concludes with the speculation that narcissistic disturbances arise from an environmental trauma that "consists of the mother's failure to accept the child's separateness and autonomy", generating in the child a "fear of the mother's intrusiveness" (ibid, p. 281).

The child is accustomed to not receiving empathetic responses to his needs and is accustomed to the fact that his needs evoke discomfort, anxiety, and even aggression in others. When the child receives something from another person, familiar feelings arise that something forbidden was taken, stolen, given grudgingly and reluctantly. He may feel uncomfortable being the receiving party within a relationship and fear his own needs. Receiving something, whether it's praise, empathy, or something material, also constitutes an event outside the child's control, and therefore it arouses anxiety. Similar to the parent, intimate closeness and spontaneous expressions of needs and emotions are for the child something that is not under his control, and therefore is threatening. Thus, impairment is created in these domains. In addition, the child is accustomed to being expected to reciprocate for the things he receives and may prefer not to receive and remain uncommitted. Such children will aspire to self-sufficiency, but once an event occurs that disrupts the fragile balance they created, a flood of neediness and dependence may emerge, triggering feelings of fragmentation and terror.

Michael grew up under his mother's obsessive control. He sought treatment due to symptoms of anxiety and depression, which he believed stemmed from his son's desire to quit medical school. During the first month and a half of therapy, he spoke only of and through his son. He described campaigns of persuasion and pressure that he exerted on his son to make him comply with his wishes, including threats of financial punishment and even banishment from home. The son suffered from panic attacks, but Michael believed that his "cry-baby" son's behavior was manipulative and called for boundary setting. Time and again, Michael bent over backwards verbally to avoid referring to his son's condition as anxiety, and when I reflected this to him, he suddenly leaned forward violently and shouted, "I'm furious at him!" In that moment, his face contorted in rage, his eyes blazed, and I found myself pinned to the back of my chair by the intensity of the emotional hurricane. I felt I was seeing in him his mother's "crazy" and furious face she had when he did not do as she bids. Eventually, the son quit his studies, and only then did Michael speak about himself for the first time. It became clear between the lines that Michael projected his insecurity and feelings of failure onto his children, and that his preoccupation with his son, or rather with his own projected parts through his son, served as a means to avoid confronting his own painful parts or having to endure the anxiety associated with going through psychic processes himself. Over time, some space was formed between him and his son, which moderated the narcissistic injury that the son's difficulties constituted for him. This new space also enabled us to focus on the lonely and sad child that Michael himself once was, and on the way his mother's behavior undermined his belief in himself and in his decisions, which was manifest in his present-day insecure and self-defeating behavior.

Envy and Jealousy

Klein (1957) viewed envy as a direct derivative of the death instinct, a destructive, unconscious force initially directed against the nurturing object, which the infant not only needs but desires to possess and control. She defined envy as follows: "Envy is the angry feeling that another person possesses and enjoys something desirable—the envious impulse being to take it away or to spoil it" (p. 181). She described that projective identification serves both to implement the envious aim and to defend against envy, for instance, by getting into the object and taking control of its qualities. Segal (1983) wrote: "To me envy and narcissism are like two sides of a coin... narcissism could be seen as a defence against envy and therefore to be more related to the operation of the death instinct and envy than to libidinal forces" (pp. 271–270).

At the core of the narcissistic parent's psychic structure is a strong sense of deprivation and a feeling that what others have is denied from him and prevents him from filling the void that consumes him from within. As a result, he covets and aspires to destroy what is good in the object. The destructiveness of this trait does not pass over the child. Envy may manifest as devaluation, as reprimand or as an appropriation of the child's successes by the parent. The child may feel that his achievements and accomplishments are not truly his own, that he is an imposter (imposter phenomenon), destined to fail and be exposed (Clance & Imes, 1978). Such a child may feel uncomfortable with compliments or with extroversion of his gifts. A narcissistic parent may exhibit hostility toward the development of an independent thinking, of emotional and sexual maturity, and of creativity. Klein (1957) wrote: "The capacity to give and to preserve life is felt as the greatest gift and therefore creativeness becomes the deepest cause for envy" (p. 202). The child may feel that suppressing his creativity is a defense against the envy of the actual parent as well as that of the parent internalized in the superego. To the child, the occult message echoes loud and clear: "You must succeed enough to make me look good, but you must not surpass me". A common dynamic is that the parent continues to 'poison' the psych of his adult child with his envy, in a manner the child cannot contain, until eventually the child evacuates the poison into his own family. "Every time I am about to visit my parents, I become tense, anxious, and irritable, and I take it out on my wife and children", one of my patients told me.

Joseph Cedar's award-winning film 'Footnote' (Cedar, 2011), tells the tale of a father and son, both professors of Talmudic studies. The father, a stern persona full of self-importance, feels marginalized by the professional community. His greatest achievement is the mention of his name at a footnote in his mentor's important book. He is envious of his son's success and popularity. The son's wife aptly describes the personality differences between the father (the narcissist) and the son (the echoist): "Your father goes all the way with his truth and is willing to pay the price, while you are a nice guy who is afraid of confrontation". One day, the father receives a phone call informing him that he won the Israel Prize.[4] As the plot unfolds, it is revealed that a mistake occurred, and the son is the actual winner of the prize. The son pleads with the prize committee to give the award to his father. He says to the committee chairman: "I can't take it! ever since I became a professor, he stopped being happy for me. All my achievements come at his expense, and I know he blames me for ruining this world that was supposed to be his. Maybe he will survive this blow, maybe he will even relish it; for him, it will be yet another proof that everyone but him is an amateur, but he will hate me. If I tell him about this mistake, I will be burying my relationship with him for good". In the end, the committee agrees to award the prize to the father, and the son commits in return that he may never be able to accept the Israel Prize himself. In a newspaper interview celebrating the award, the father says of the son's research: "I wouldn't call the work he's engaged in Talmudic research... It has nothing to do with scientific truth... it's an empty vessel". Gradually, the father realizes that his son is the true winner, but the matter is not discussed between them, reality is denied, and that atmosphere lingers like a volatile acidic dark cloud surrounding the entire family. This story is an example of a relationship between a narcissistic father who envies his son's success, is hostile towards him, and projects his emptiness onto him, and a son whose efforts to gain his father's approval and love repeatedly fail. The son's fear of the expected outburst of narcissistic rage if the truth is revealed by the father drives him to give up professional recognition, fame and success, even in the face of an abusive and cruel treatment by the father. Another plotline in the film is the son's relationship with his own son, which vividly demonstrates the intergenerational transmission, as he repeats the mistakes made with him and lashes out at his son when he can no longer contain the aggression his father evacuates into him.

While one might discuss the experience of an envious and hostile persona as a projection, the example presented in the film demonstrates well the cases in which these are first and foremost real characteristics of the parental object.

The father portrayed in 'Footnote' is a rigid and emotionally stingy father. While the pathologically narcissistic parent may be absorbed in his own affairs and neglect his child emotionally and materially, in many cases, the opposite picture emerges. There is significant investment, but it is not necessarily adapted to the child's needs. Instead, it serves the desires and wishes projected onto the child by the parent, and it comes at a heavy price. In such cases, the characteristics of narcissistic parenting at hand create an exceptionally deluding and burdensome admixture. The parent's giving, which can be abundant, is accompanied by a message that the child should be grateful, and contradicts the child's elusive experience, that such giving entails something that does not see his true wishes and obligates him in a suffocating and binding manner. The child remains with inner sensations that something is wrong and with a free-floating anxiety and a burdensome sense of obligation, without understanding the source of these sensations. At a conscious level, he can only tell himself that his is a good and an exceptionally devoted parent, a message that the parent himself reinforces and needs. The child remains distressed and is unable to comprehend the cause. It strengthens the sense that something is wrong with him as well as his self-blame and created an experience that he is losing his mind.

The double edged sword of such a giving is well demonstrated in the poem 'An Ancient Melody' ('Niggun Atiq') by Natan Alterman:

> If your tears at night quiver,
> I will kindle my joy like a bundle of hay
> If your bones with cold shiver,
> I will cover you and on bedrock down myself lay
>
> If embarking on dance you desire
> With the last of my strings I will play for you
> If a birthday gift you require
> My life and my death I shall give you
>
> And if bread or wine you crave
> I will get, shoulders hunched, to my feet
> And I'll sell both my eyes and I'll slave
> And bring you wine to drink and bread to eat
>
> But should ever I find you laughing
> Without me, in your friends' company
> My jealousy will be silently passing
> And burn your house upon thee

> Natan Alterman, Ancient Meloddy
> [My translation from Hebrew – H.Y.].

Seemingly, in the poem, the lover's devotion and willingness to give are exceptional. However, a dark and chilling atmosphere lingers, ultimately clarifying itself with a distinct threat – the beloved has no right to be separate. The lover's giving grants him, in his mind's eye, the right to treat her as his property and do with her as he pleases.

Conditional Love

"All of us, whoever we are, have our breathable beings. If we lack them, we lack air, we suffocate. Hence we die. To die for lack of love is horrible! The suffocation of the soul!"

> –Victor Hugo, 1862. Les Miseerables, Quatrième partie, p. 226. [my translation – H.Y.]

Kernberg (1975) described that when there is a normal regulation of self-esteem, the increase in the normal and healthy narcissistic investment in the self is accompanied by an increase in the capacity to love, to give and to feel gratitude. "The charging of the battery of the self induces secondarily a recharging of the battery of libidinal investment in objects" (p. 320). In order to attain this ability, the individual needs to mature beyond more primitive mechanisms where there is no complete separation between self and object, and where there is no ability to grasp the object in a complex way, as one containing both positive and negative aspects. This maturation is a prerequisite for the establishment of healthy object relations and the cultivation of complex ambivalent feelings toward a whole object. It is implicit in Kernberg's words, that in order to love another with a mature love, the ability to be separate from them is necessary, and indeed, a few years later he wrote: "There can be no meaningful love relation without the persistence of the self, without firm boundaries of the self, which generate a sense of identity" (Kernberg, 1980, p. 290). According to Kernberg (1975), in borderline and in narcissistic conditions, a pathological fixation of the splitting processes occurs – splitting of good object representations and good self-representations from bad ones, hence also splitting of the love and hate toward the objects. The lack of integration, characteristic of narcissism, impairs, therefore, the capacity to love. Kernberg's words resonate with the writings of Klein (1946), who aptly described the processes of splitting and their influence on the way one relates to the object: "The frustrating breast... is felt to be in bits; while the gratifying breast... is felt to be complete" (p. 101). She described "the constant *interaction* of love and hate" (Klein, 1937, p. 306) and the lifelong struggle between these emotions. She wrote about the hatred and the aggressive feelings that can arise when an object we are dependent on frustrates us and of our phantasized retaliation of destroying it. If the depressive position is successfully worked through, along with a complex view of the others and ourselves as containing both good and bad aspects, then this process brings forth a concern for the object, an attempt at reparation, and the capacity to love, to feel gratitude, and to show generosity toward the object. However, if the paranoid-schizoid position dominates, as in narcissistic pathology, then the bad and frustrating aspects are attributed to the object, and the object remains split and persecutory, with the need for and love for the object denied. As long as there is no capacity to recognize the other, as well as ourselves, as separate and complex subjects, love toward the other will be but projected love for ourselves, and hate toward the other will be self-hatred projected onto them.

To a narcissistic parent, a child that pleases is a child who enables everything that has been described so far – a lack of separateness, omnipotent control, gratification of the parent's needs, and so on. If the child frustrates, fragmentation is quick to occur. A vicious cycle is generated, in which the aggression aroused in response to the frustrating, split, negative object is reintrojected as a persecutory object, thereby reinforcing aggression and so forth. The parent's ability to love is lost in these situations, as he experiences the child as bad object parts. If the child is not quick to toe the line and become a pleasing object once more, the vicious cycle may become irreversible, and the child may be branded by the parent as a 'bad child'.

The message that the narcissistic parent conveys to his child is that receiving love is conditional upon obedience and performance. 'Failure' leads to criticism and rejection. Love and relationships are conditioned on the erasure of differences between the parent and the child. In order to survive, the child sacrifices his authentic core, developing a split, people-pleasing, false self (Winnicott, 1960). The child is poised to learn that he cannot be truly loved, that closeness comes at a high cost of self-erasure, that receiving anything is accompanied by a demand to meet the giver's expectations. Such a child is expected to develop attachment difficulties (Bowlby, 1988) that may manifest on a spectrum ranging from avoidance of relationships to an anxious attachment pattern accompanied by clinging to the love-object.

Segal (1983) described a patient with a severe narcissistic pathology – in an association to a dream he spoke of the film 'The Third Man', which depicts a man who steals penicillin causing children to receive defected, diluted penicillin which harms and deforms them. Referring to that she wrote:

> The 'diluted love', in this case the narcissistic love, is poisonous because it separates one from real love… the blind and deaf person in the dream is also himself…it is himself he is feeding the diluted penicillin which destroys his senses, his sanity, ultimately his life, and it is himself that he deprives of love.
>
> (pp. 271–272)

Davies (2004) describes a patient who, in her childhood, had to adapt to her depressive mother's moods and take care of her. Davies describes the lived experience of such a child through her own counter-transferential feelings: "Something toxic and untrue, something malignant in a psychotic sense, is being forced inside me" (p. 720). She explains: "The presence of a psychotic parent—of one who forced the acceptance of an insane reality as the precondition for a loving relationship onto and into a vulnerable child—hovers around the consulting room, exuding a malignant and sulfurous stench" (ibid, p. 719). She describes the discrepancy between the mother's expectations of the child and the child's experience of her 'innermost core' (ibid, p. 720). The outcome is destructive: in order to feel sane, the child must recognize that the significant other is insane, but then she is left alone, unprotected in a hostile world, forced to give up love. In order to feel safe and loved, she must accept a psychotic reality and live in her mother's world, namely rendering herself insane.

Most children will choose the second option, in the spirit of the Fairbairn's 'moral defense' (1943) – "It is better to be a sinner in a world ruled by God than to live in a world ruled by the devil" (p. 66–67). In other words, the child would rather believe himself to be 'bad' and 'guilty' than believe that the parent he depends on may harm him and does not provide him with protection. In continuation of her article, Davies (2004) writes, "The child/patient must blind herself to many of the negative aspects of the other, thus rendering herself 'crazy' in terms of her capacity to judge reality" (p. 722). Like Miller (1979), Davies emphasizes the exceptional sensitivity that children like these exhibit: "The child who internalizes and identifies with parental abusiveness in such a way must also maintain simultaneously and in dissociated form an accurate capacity to read the interpersonal emotional landscape with clarity and sensitivity to nuance" (Davies, 2004, p. 722).

The Narcissistic Parenthood as a Traumatogenic Agent

The Recurring parental failures constitute a relational-developmental trauma (Stolorow & Atwood, 1992).

In his paper *Confusion of the Tongues between the Adults and the Child*, Ferenczi (1933/1949)[5] went back to the model of actual trauma and childhood seduction that Freud had abandoned.[6] The paper discusses trauma resulting from sexual abuse and incest, but Ferenczi's observations are also applicable in their absence. The essence of the trauma arises from the lack of recognition that a violation has occurred, from the denial of the child's emotional experience, and from the absence of validation. The response to the traumatic reality, to which the child is forced to blind himself, and that his psyche cannot bear, is dissociation and splitting. Ferenczi writes that he had begun to listen to patients who "reproached me with being selfish, heartless, conceited" (p. 225) and for whom expressions of anger of this sort were exceptional. In sessions, these patients mostly manifested an "almost helpless compliance" (ibid). He began to suspect that "even these apparently willing patients felt hatred and rage" (ibid). Ferenczi describes children who were traumatized time and again, who are constantly vigilant, and whose personality has formed around the efforts to avoid the parent's next outburst and to survive it. Hence they:

> have an exceedingly refined sensitivity for the wishes, tendencies, whims, sympathies and antipathies of their analyst, even if the analyst is completely unaware of this sensitivity. Instead of contradicting the analyst or accusing him of errors and blindness, the patients identify themselves with him; only in rare moments of an hysteroid excitement, i.e. in an almost unconscious state, can they pluck up enough courage to make a protest.
>
> (ibid, p. 226)

Ferenczi speaks of identification with the aggressors and the development of defensive splits:

> These children feel... helpless, their personalities are not sufficiently consolidated in order to be able to protest, even if only in thought, for the overpowering force and authority of the adult makes them dumb and can rob them of their senses. The same anxiety, however, if it reaches a certain maximum, compels them to subordinate themselves like automata to the will of the aggressor, to divine each one of his desires and to gratify these; completely oblivious of themselves they identify themselves with the aggressor. Through the identification, or let us say, introjection of the aggressor, he disappears as part of the external reality.
>
> (ibid, p. 228)

Thus, the child can attempt to control the aggressors, which has now become an internal reality. Ferenczi also notes that the child introjects the perpetrator's guilt feelings and describes a precocious maturity among these children:

> The fear of the uninhibited, almost mad adult changes the child, so to speak, into a psychiatrist and, in order to become one and to defend himself against dangers coming from people without self-control, he must know how to identify himself completely with them.
>
> (ibid, p. 229)

According to Balint (1969), the trauma occurs within the framework of object relations, and he refers to the objects that induce the trauma as traumatogenic objects. These are objects to whom the child is attached with an intense emotional bond and is dependent upon, and toward whom the child's feelings, even if ambivalent, are feelings of love and trust. The adult "does something highly exciting, frightening, or painful" (p. 432) and subsequently denies the occurrence and denies the child the recognition of the experience and the comfort for it.

Stolorow (1999) describes a "profound sense of estrangement and isolation" (p. 464) that forms the basis for the development of psychic trauma. Stolorow argues that the essence of psychic trauma lies in the experience of an unbearable affect. The affect is unbearable not due to its intensity but due to the relational system in which it occurs. It becomes traumatic because the child lacked the attunement he needed from the parent to assist him in tolerating, containing, and modulating the affect. According to Stolorow, when the child's emotional and perceptual experience massively and consistently encounters invalidation and denial from the parent, his belief in reality becomes unsteady. Stolorow further adds that this situation renders the child prone to delusional ideas whose purpose is to transform an endangered psychic reality into a reified one, i.e. it makes the child more vulnerable to a psychotic disease proper. In their book, Stolorow and Atwood (1992) wrote:

> Parents who repeatedly rebuff primary selfobject needs are usually not able to provide attuned responsiveness to the child's painful emotional reactions [for being rebuffed at the first place]. The child perceives that his painful reactive feelings are unwelcome or damaging to the caregiver and must be defensively sequestered in order to preserve the needed bond... these walled-off painful feelings become a source of lifelong inner conflict and vulnerability.
>
> (p. 53)

Stolorow and Atwood explain that the dissociation the child is forced to make between his painful affect and his ongoing experience often results in the development of psychosomatic states or to a withdrawal from attachments to others, as these attachments may lead to injury. They add that even if the child remembers his traumatogenic experiences, he will remain plagued by doubts about their occurrence and even doubts about his reality altogether. This is an inevitable consequence of the lack of a validating attunement, a lack which is the very core of the psychic trauma. "The traumatized child... may 'conclude' that his own unmet needs and emotional pain are expressions of disgusting and shameful defects in the self and thus must be banished from conscious experiencing" (ibid, p. 55). The concept of prohibition on affects also appears in another book (Orange, Atwood & Stolorow, 1997), where it is described how the absence of a steady and attuned responsiveness to the child's needs makes him feel that his developmental yearnings and emotional reactive feelings are a loathsome defect in his personality or a manifestation of an inner badness. As a defense mechanism, the child establishes a self-ideal devoid of those affective states that were perceived to be intolerable to his early environment. Living up to this self-ideal becomes a condition for maintaining the relationships with the caregivers and the self-esteem. As a result of this process, the emergence of forbidden affects is experienced as a failure, as an exposure of his defective and bad essence, and it will be accompanied by feelings of shame, isolation, and self-loathing.

The process of suppressing affects comes at a heavy price. According to Stolorow and Atwood (1992), the child fails to develop the capacity to tolerate his affects or the ability to use them as signals which provide information, which only makes him more susceptible to recurring traumas.

In his book *Descartes' Error*, neuroscientist Antonio Damasio (Damasio, 1994) demonstrated how "emotions are not a luxury" (p. 130), but rather they play an essential and central role in our ability to make decisions and comprehend social situations. Descartes' error is the separation between body and mind. It appears one should not say: "I think therefore I am", nor "I feel therefore I am", but rather both processes combined are necessary – "I think and feel therefore I am". Paraphrasing the subject at hand – without feelings, it is impossible to feel one's own existence.

The attempt to deny emotions, to deny the subjective experience of the child, is a traumatic threat to his psychic existence.

Khan (1963) described a 'cumulative trauma' that occurs due to repeated failures of the mother to serve as a protective shield for the child and to manage his environment. Such cumulative failures result from the intrusion of the mother's personality in a manner which is maladaptive to the infant's needs. This leads to the formation of a collusive relationship between the mother and her child. As a result, the development of the child's 'self' is impaired. Khan added that "What Winnicott calls 'the false self' is a characterological consequence of the disruption and distortion of ego autonomy. What Winnicott calls 'impingements' are the failure of the mother in infancy to dose and regulate stimuli—both external and internal" (p. 296). A provocative, tantalizing overstimulation is formed, which according to Khan is "of the most pathogenic genetic elements in cumulative trauma" (p. 297). Khan notes several outcomes of cumulative trauma: the child's self develops prematurely, precociously, and partially to adapt to the mother's expectations and needs and to cope with the deficiencies. The child develops heightened sensitivity or a special responsiveness to the mother's mood, splits and conceals his own aggression, and becomes compliant. Alongside parts that function precociously and a concern for the mother, the child becomes dependent and struggles to develop separateness. The child is forced into a precocious cathexis of the external and the internal reality, which "leaves out a very important function of the ego's subjective awareness and experience of itself as a coherent entity" (ibid, p. 299). Khan adds that all subsequent developmental experiences are affected by that interplay between the mother and the infant and that the 'incorporative and projective' identification that arises between them "confuses a proper differentiation and growth of internal psychic structures" (ibid, p. 501) and also creates distortions in the psychosexual development. Khan emphasizes that cumulative trauma has treacherous aspects since it "operates and builds up silently throughout childhood right up to adolescence" (ibid, p. 301). He warns that due to this treacherous nature of the trauma, the therapist may not recognize how internal pressures, as well as environmental ones, i.e. reality, shaped the adult character. Identifying this subtle, almost invisible, trauma is crucial for the success of the treatment. Thus, he wrote in the conclusion of his paper: "It is important for us to be able to chart out clearly the earliest nature and role of these failures, because only thus can we organize our clinical expectancy and arrive at true diagnosis" (ibid, p. 303).

The recurring emotional trauma makes the child susceptible to the formation of post-traumatic symptoms at the very least, if not a complex post-traumatic stress disorder (cPTSD) – a type of PTSD which results from recurrent exposure to traumas in childhood, that detrimentally affect the formation of the personality (Hermann, 1992). The child may suffer from symptoms of hyper-arousal such as difficulty sleeping, heightened reactivity to noise, and an exaggerated startle response, from avoidance (of reminders of traumatic events, of relationships, of self-disclosure), from dissociative symptoms (inability to remember aspects of the traumatic events, emotional detachment), from intrusive memories of traumatic experiences, from difficulties in interpersonal relationships, from accompanying depressive symptoms, from somatic symptoms, and more. These symptoms may be exacerbated during periods of distress and in the course of therapy.

Notes

1 These are two of the mechanisms Rosenfeld (1964) mentions as characteristic of narcissistic object relations.
2 These representations are identical to the narcissistic object-choices described by Freud (1914).
3 See 'envy and jealousy' below.
4 The prize is regarded as the state of Israel's highest cultural honor.
5 The paper was read by Ferenczi at the Twelfth International Psycho-Analytical Congress, Wiesbaden, September 1932 and was published in German in 1933. The English translation was published in 1949.
6 The paper was the blow that severed the last thread in the emerging tear between Ferenczi and Freud. It ended their years-long relationship. Freud was furious at Ferenczi's refusal to scrap the paper.

Bibliography

Balint, M. (1969). Trauma and Object Relationship. *The International Journal of Psychoanalysis, 50*: 429–435.

Berman E. (2009). Preface to D.W. Winnicott's 'Ego Distortion in terms of True and False Self'. In: E. Berman (Ed), True Self, False Self: Essays, 1935–1963 (pp.199–201). Am Oved Publishers, 2016 (In Hebrew).

Bion, W. R. (1959). Attacks on Linking. *The International Journal of Psychoanalysis, 40*: 308–315.

Bion, W. R. (1962a). *Learning from Experience*. Basic Books Publishing Company.

Bion, W. R. (1962b). The Psycho-Analytic Study of Thinking. *The International Journal of Psychoanalysis, 43*: 306–310.

Bollas, C. (1987). *The Shadow of the Object*. Routledge, 2018.

Bowlby, J. (1988). *A Secure Base: Clinical Applications of Attachment Theory*. Basic Books.

Britton, R. (1989). The Missing Link: Parental Sexuality in the Oedipus Complex. In R. Britton, M. Feldman, E. O'Shaughnessy, & J. Steiner (Eds.), *The Oedipus Complex Today: Clinical Implications* (pp. 83–101). Karnac Books.

Britton, R. (2004). Subjectivity, Objectivity, and Triangular Space. *The Psychoanalytic Quarterly, 73*: 47–61.

Cedar, J. (2011). *Footnote* (film). United King Films.

Clance, P. R., & Imes, S. A. (1978). The Impostor Phenomenon in High Achieving Women: Dynamics and Therapeutic Interventions. *Psychotherapy: Theory Research and Practice, 15*(3): 241–247.

Cohen, M. (2020). *The Figure Behind the Mirror: The Unseen Other in Narcissistic Relations*. Resling (In Hebrew).

Cukor, G. D. (director). (1944). *Gaslight* [film]. MGM.

Damasio, A. (1994). *Descartes' Error: Emotion*. Reason and the Human Brain. Penguin, 2005.

Davies, J. M. (2004). Whose Bad Objects Are We Anyway? Repetition and Our Elusive Love Affair with Evil. *Psychoanalytic Dialogues, 14*: 711–732.

Eigen, M. (1999). *Toxic Nourishment*. Routledge, 2018.

Fairbairn, W. R. D. (1943). The Repression and the Return of Bad Objects (with Special Reference to the 'War Neuroses'). In: *Psycho-analytic Studies of the Personality* (pp. 59–81). Routledge & Kegan Paul, 1994.

Ferenczi, S. (1933, translation published 1949). Confusion of the Tongues Between the Adults and the Child—(The Language of Tenderness and of Passion). *International Journal Psycho-analysis, 30*: 225–230.

Fonagy, P. (1989). On Tolerating Mental States: Theory of Mind in Borderline Personality. *Bulletin of the Anna Freud Centre, 12*: 91–115.

Forward, S., with Buck, C. (1989). *Toxic Parents: Overcoming Their Hurtful Legacy and Reclaiming Your Life*. Bantam Books.

Forward, S., with Frazier Glynn, D. (1997). *Emotional Blackmail: When the People in Your Life Use Fear, Obligation, and Guilt to Manipulate You*. Harper, 2001.

Forward, S., with Frazier Glynn, D. (2013). *Mothers Who Can't Love: A Healing Guide for Daughters*. Harper-Collins.

Freud, S. (1914). On Narcissism: An Introduction. In: J. Strachey (Ed.), *The Standard Edition of the Complete Psychological Works of Sigmund Freud* (vol. 14, pp. 67–102). The Hogarth Press, 1957.

Furman, E. (1982). Mothers Have to Be There to Be Left. *The Psychoanalytic Study of the Child, 37*: 15–28.

Herman, J. L. (1992). *Trauma and Recovery.* Basic Books/Hachette Book Group.

Horowitz, R. S. (2017). *It's Just Your Imagination: Growing Up with a Narcissistic Mother - Insights of a Personal Journey.* Horowitz Publishing.

Hugo, V. (1862). *Les Miserables.* Quatrième partie. https://beq.ebooksgratuits.com/vents/Hugo-miserables-4.pdf

Kernberg, O. (1975). *Borderline Conditions and Pathological Narcissism.* Rowman & Littlefield Publishers, 2004.

Kernberg, O. F. (1980). *Internal World and External Reality: Object Relations Theory Applied.* Aronson.

Khan, M. R. (1963). The Concept of Cumulative Trauma. *Psychoanalytic Study of the Child, 18*: 286–306.

Klein, M. (1937). The Writings of Melanie Klein Volume I. *Love, Guilt and Reparation and Other Works 1921–1945.* The Free Press (1975).

Klein, M. (1946). Notes on Some Schizoid Mechanisms. *International Journal of Psychoanalysis, 27*: 99–110.

Klein, M. (1957). *Envy and Gratitude.* In: *The Writings of Melanie Klein Volume III Envy and Gratitude and Other Works 1946–1963* (vol. 104, pp. 176–235). The Free Press (1975).

Kohut, H. (1971). *The Analysis of the Self.* The University of Chicago Press, 2009.

Kohut, H. (1977). *The Restoration of the Self.* The University of Chicago Press, 2009.

Maier, S. F., & Seligman, M. E. (1976). Learned Helplessness: Theory and Evidence. Journal of Experimental Psychology: General, 105(1): 3–46.

Manzano, J., Espasa, F., & Zilkha, N. (1999). The Narcissistic Scenarios of Parenthood. *The International Journal of Psychoanalysis, 80*: 465–476.

Miller, A. (1979). *The Drama of the Gifted Child: the Search for the True Self.* Translated from the German by Ruth Ward. Basic Books, 1981.

Miller, A. (2005). *The Body Never Lies: The Lingering Effects of Hurtful Parenting.* W. W. Norton & Company.

Miller, W. R., & Seligman, M. E. (1975). Depression and Learned Helplessness in Man. *Journal of Abnormal Psychology, 84*(3): 228–238.

Mitchell, S. A., & Black, M. J. (1995). *Freud and Beyond: A History of Modern Psychoanalytic Thought.* Basic Books, 2016.

Modell, A. H. (1975). A Narcissistic Defence Against Affects and the Illusion of Self-Sufficiency. *The International Journal of Psychoanalysis, 56*: 275–282.

Orange, D. M., Atwood, G. E., & Stolorow, R. D. (1997). *Working Intersubjectively: Contextualism in Psychoanalytic Practice.* Analytic Press, 2009.

Rosenfeld, H. (1964). On the Psychopathology of Narcissism: A Clinical Approach. *The International Journal of Psychoanalysis, 45*: 332–337.

Segal, H. (1957). Notes on Symbol Formation. *The International Journal of Psychoanalysis, 38*: 391–397.

Segal, H. (1983). Some Clinical Implications of Melanie Klein's Work—Emergence from Narcissism. *The International Journal of Psychoanalysis, 64*: 269–276.

Stolorow, R. D. (1999). The Phenomenology of Trauma and the Absolutisms of Everyday Life: A Personal Journey. *Psychoanalytic Psychology, 16*: 464–468.

Stolorow, R. D., & Atwood, G. E. (1992). *Contexts of Being: The Intersubjective Foundations of Psychological Life.* Routledge, 2002.

The Bible (2017). 21st Century King James Version. Cambridge University Press. (Original work published 1769).

Winnicott, D. W. (1953). Transitional Objects and Transitional Phenomena—A Study of the First Not-Me Possession. *International Journal of Psychoanalysis, 34*: 89–97.

Winnicott, D. W. (1965). Ego Distortion in Terms of True and False Self (1960). In: M. Khan (Ed.), *The Maturational Processes and the Facilitating Environment: Studies in the Theory of Emotional Development* (vol. 64, pp. 140–152). Karnac Books.

Chapter 4

The Narcissistic Family Dynamics

In a household where a parent is narcissistic, the dynamics revolve around that parent. The child feels obligated to tend to the parent's needs, desires, and emotions. Should the child fail to do so, he will be met with anger and blame, and feel guilty and 'bad'. The oppressive figure of the parent is constantly held on the rim of the child's awareness. In severe cases, the experience is akin to that of an individual living under a tyrannical regime, fearful and deprived of rights and personal autonomy. The child channels great emotional resources into the attempts to please the parent. Since the parent uses the child as a mechanism for evacuation from his own inner world and fails to recognize the actual child in front of him, criticisms and demands persist, and the parent will not be pleased. Much of the narcissistic parent's communication is passive-aggressive, wherein any adverse thing he says or does is deniable. The parent's supposed 'good intentions' or the child's 'over-sensitivity' can justify retrospectively any remark, as critical and insensitive as it may be. In a narcissistic family, there is a pattern of communication, behavior, and roles aimed at preserving the familial narcissistic equilibrium. This equilibrium depends on the family's image; a dichotomy of success versus 'shame'.

Communication in the Narcissistic Family

The communication in a narcissistic family is indirect and malfunctional, as the parent's omnipotent sense of control is challenged by dealing with emotions, intimacy, flaws, and pain. The inability to retort, speak of, and change abusive behavior, as well as the lack of authenticity, manifest in repetitive and rigid behavioral patterns.

There exists an idiosyncratic language unique to the family wherein words and idioms contain a hidden message. While the child understands the message all too well, it also confuses him by contradicting the explicit message. Praising the child may conceal an underlying criticism or an expectation for the child to keep 'improving'. The praising of others may serve as a well-aimed arrow of disguised criticism directed at the child. If the parent says that the child doesn't need to do something for him, the hidden message might be that the parent very much expects it, thus he successfully conveys the expectation to the child while relieving himself

DOI: 10.4324/9781032625393-4

of the guilt and presenting himself positively. Facial expressions, subtle changes in the tone of speech, exchanging glances with the other parent, and so forth can also be used to convey or emphasize the message. The child may defensively grasp onto the idea that the parent genuinely only meant well. "Your mother tongue is not Hebrew", I said to a patient, "it is Hebrew with a subtext". To outsiders, the family's language of communication (both verbal and non-verbal) is always a foreign language, and so even if the patient recognizes the hidden message, the therapist may think the communication was naive. In processes that have already been described, the child learns to hide his emotions from others and even from himself, learns that intimacy exposes him to rejection and criticism, and detachment and estrangement between the family members ensues.

Pardess (2013) wrote about 'the multiple faces of shame':

> The very need for reassurance in distressing situations may give rise to shame in individuals who have not received an attuned and validating responsiveness from their environment. In order to defend against the scorching experience of shame, individuals can completely deny their distress and their need for acknowledgement and support... In an intimate relationship, there... are [many] moments when one party recognizes the other's needs past the defensive ideal... **Intimacy avoidance is thus a hallmark of relationships that are based on shame.**
>
> (ibid, under the subheading 'Inter-Subjective Approach',
> my translation – H.Y.)

Shame is therefore established as a consequence of traumatogenic responses to the child's experiences and emotional needs, and it becomes an obstacle to interpersonal relationships and self-realization. One might say that "the abuse of the past... exists as the shame of today" (Fossum & Mason, 1986, p. 87).

Fossum and Mason (1986), who come from the field of family therapy, described the family dynamics from a perspective that might be overlooked in an individual therapy. Their book focuses on families dominated by a malignant shame. Such families can vary greatly from one another and may include individuals struggling with addiction or compulsive behaviors. Although Fossum and Mason did not specifically address narcissistic parents, the familial patterns presented in their book align precisely with those found in narcissistic families. According to their definition, a shame-bound family is one in which there is a set of rules reflecting a demand for control and perfectionism. The rule system perpetuates itself across generations. The patterns created by these rules:

> Inhibits or defeats the development of authentic intimate relationships, promotes secrets and vague personal boundaries, unconsciously instills shame in the family members, as well as chaos in their lives... It does so regardless of the good intentions, wishes, and love which may also be part of the system.
>
> (ibid, p. 8)

The authors enumerate eight rules that constitute a recurring behavioral pattern in such families:

1 Control: Control is the fundamental rule from which all other rules are derived. One or more family members have a need for controlling all the behavior and interactions of the other family members either tyrannically or through manipulations. In cases of tyranny, family members without power live in anxious fear of the controlling family member. In cases of manipulations, their indirect nature allows the manipulator to evade accountability for his actions.

> How can you challenge someone who is only trying to be helpful? Spontaneous and authentic responses seldom emerge in family interaction following this rule... We see a family of images, eternal strangers to one another. People hold tenaciously and unconsciously to a narrow range of repetitive responses or games that serve to conceal rather than reveal themselves to each other. After years, everyone in the family knows each other's next lines in the relational dialogue... Where communication is heavily loaded with indirect motives... each person's individual subjectivity stays undeveloped... all attention going to deciphering the messages of others.
>
> (ibid, p. 89)

In some families, the control rule manifests as "a primitive drive for domination and submission. The satisfaction is in experiencing the power to impose one's will upon others" (ibid, p. 87). Fossum and Mason add that in such family systems, domination-submission roles also serve as primitive means of establishing relatedness or closeness with others since the parties involved lack basic interpersonal skills. "Both the tyrant and the victim... have a very limited sense of themselves as persons, inadequate development of relationship skills and no understanding of the nuances of intimacy" (ibid, p. 88).

Fossum and Mason do not use the term specifically, but in these cases, the relationship is tinged with a sadomasochistic hue, a common occurrence between a narcissistic parent and his child.

2 Perfection – The 'right' thing must be done in accordance with the family's value system, whether it is dressing in the latest fashion, striving for academic achievements, or upholding righteous moralistic positions. Family members are required to conform themselves to an ideal which may shift on the go. They may appear 'well put together' externally while experiencing suffering and shame internally. Fossum and Mason observe that it is an axiom that there would be a family member who meets the criteria of 'perfection' and is considered 'good' while another family member is considered 'bad', neither of them possessing an authentic self-confidence or a developed identity.

3 Blame – Someone to blame is required when something does not happen as planned. Blame projects the shame felt by one family member onto another.

Blame may be activated when the control rule fails in order to restore an illusion of control.
4 Denial – of feelings, especially those expressing neediness.
5 Unreliability – The relationships are unpredictable or unstable. Mood swings and emotional disappearances of at least one family member are common. An experience of closeness and rapport may disappear for no apparent reason.
6 Incompleteness – Interactions between the parties involved do not reach a conclusion. Conflicts are not resolved but are instead dropped.
7 No talk – An embarrassing or abusive behavior will not be discussed directly.
8 Disqualification – If embarrassing or abusive behavior occurs, it is denied or concealed, undermining the perception of reality of the persons involved.

Even after deeply hurting each other, family members will not discuss it but rather will eventually behave as if nothing happened. There is an unspoken prohibition on discussing feelings or mentioning that something abusive actually took place, preventing a proper resolution of the conflict.

Fossum and Mason note that such interaction-rules may generate:

A dehumanizing, shame-bound regime in any human system, whether a nuclear family, a staff work group [and so forth. Cults and despotic regimes fit under this depiction as well – H.Y.]… The interaction flowing from these rules insidiously nullifies or voids one's experience as a person. Relationships in the system… undermine the faith that "I am a person" and inhibit the growth of a self-accepting outlook.

(ibid, page 87)

The difficulties managing emotions are also associated with an impaired capacity for mentalization (Fonagy, 1989, 1991), which is noticeable in the parent and, consequently, in the child. Another reason for the difficulty with emotions is that the parent is focused on image. It can be said that this focus is also driven by shame. Since authentic emotions often contradict the desired image, the parent does not express such emotions and he will also suppress the expression of emotions in his children, along with other parts that he perceives as undesirable and inconsistent with the image.

Due to all the reasons described, the child is deprived of the opportunity to experience his true emotions and to get to know himself through them. Thus, a family is formed in which the individuals are emotionally detached, not truly knowing themselves or each other. It is a family whose members leave each other empty and isolated. Children in such a family learn that it is forbidden to talk about emotions and are left lacking basic skills for managing conflicts and lacking basic skills for interpersonal communication overall. The language of intimacy remains a foreign language.

When Gabriel, a 30-year-old single man with sparse social relationships, sought therapy, he and his three brothers were still living with their parents. He felt lonely, full of self-criticism, and suffered from social phobia. He described a dominant, critical, and controlling mother who lived through her children, power struggles between the parents, and his own experience of constant stress, as well as a sense of detachment and lack of meaning. While he detachedly described the difficult day-to-day interactions with his parents, he explained that he was unable to leave home because he felt that his family did not know him, and only when they know him would he be able to do so. Unable to verbalize it, he yearned for an emotional connection with his parents and an emotional closeness to them. Knowing that it is rare for the parent to change, I found myself contemplating the high price he would have to pay to achieve personal growth and freedom. When a child's emotional 'battery' is charged, he feels secure and capable of distancing himself from the parent and free to live his own life. If, however, his emotional needs are not met, he is likely to return time and again to the barren well, hoping to quench his thirst this time. Like many of my patients with a narcissistic family background, Gabriel described a tormenting, decades-long experience of emptiness, depression, anxiety, and a sensation that he is losing his mind, without having the slightest of insights as to its source. In other words, Gabriel, too, did not know himself.

Roles, Relationships, Behavioral Patterns in the Narcissistic Family and Their Ramifications

I observed that three general coping mechanisms can be identified for a child growing up in a narcissistic family: (1) Identification with the aggressor accompanies by submission to the parent's will and self-effacement. (2) Rebellion – The child fights to save his mind and soul, refusing to comply with the parent's demands and paying the price with a genuine experience of losing the parent's love. In this scenario, the child essentially rejects the parent's projections. A process of estrangement between the parent and child occurs, since the parent experiences separateness as alienation and rejection, feels attacked, and distances the child even further. Often, such a child is labeled 'the black sheep of the family' (in the jargon – the scapegoat child), while the compliant child becomes the successful or 'golden child'. In therapy, the rebellious child stands out as the identified patient within the family, i.e., the family member representing the familial pathology which is projected onto him in order to deny its existence. (3) Detachment – The child develops mechanisms of emotional detachment from the guilt the parent strives to instill in him. He may find psychic equilibrium that includes introjecting aspects of the narcissistic parental-object and experiencing certain demands as ego-syntonic. In this way, the child gains certain approval from the parent without completely sacrificing himself. The price for this coping mechanism is emotional numbness. It is possible that in some families, this coping mechanism is more accessible to older children who may be granted certain freedom and a space for growth by the narcissistic parent, who turns to the younger child for the fulfillment of his narcissistic needs.

The negative vibe that permeates the household, the various roles assigned to the children, and the distorted modes of communication often hinder the possibility of creating close bonds and friendships among siblings. It is not uncommon to find a sibling who, due to identification with the aggressor, the desire to please the parent, jealousy toward a favored sibling, or an attempt to redirect his own unbearable experience, becomes abusive toward a weaker sibling.

A common phenomenon in the dynamics of narcissistic abuse generally, and particularly when it transpires within a family, is abuse by proxy. This involves the narcissist using another person who believes in the image and narrative presented by the narcissist. The proxy is usually manipulated without being aware and acts under the internal pressure generated by the manipulation or with good intentions to 'get the black sheep to toe the line' and conciliate. The proxy could be the other parent, a sibling, a friend, etc. The proxy may reprimand and preach, tug on feelings of guilt, and exert pressure. Sometimes, there is a series of proxies or multiple proxies who come together, increasing the pressure. These proxies were aptly designated 'flying monkeys', named after the winged monkeys who carried out the biddings of the wicked witch of the west in 'The Wizard of Oz'.

A child who is motivated by the need to please the parent above all others, who has internalized a distorted pattern of object relations, is likely to pay a high social price. An idiosyncratic language and the absence of a model for empathy lead to impaired social skills. The fear of forming an attachment, combined with the covert prohibition on the child to grow, impair his capacity to form age-appropriate social relationships. Additionally, the child's enforcement to be 'parentified' and behave maturely beyond his age, along with the introjection of the parent's critical attitude toward others, can also hinder the child's ability to socially integrate among peers. This impairment creates a gap between the (split) adult part in him and other children, through making him critical toward the 'infantilism' in others and through leaving a split childish part who seeks parental nourishment and approval in others in a way that may deter them.

The fear of the parent and the inability to dispute him turns into internalized rage, accompanied by a sense of helplessness. These factors are a fertile ground for the development of depression and anxiety. Such a child may feel attacked merely by being approached by others, wear an armor made of defenses and mistrust, and may even avoid relationships altogether. He would experience chronic stress and anxiety and a sense of loneliness that he cannot explain, even when among people and even when among loving people as an adult. Children like these may try to numb emotional pain using psychoactive substances or act out through engaging in a constant search for excitement. Such a child may be alone in a defensive manner, but without the capacity to truly be alone. Winnicott (1958) wrote about the capacity to be alone, which depends on the presence of a good object in the individual's psychic reality. He described this state as ego-relatedness, a state where the experience of the connection between two people is preserved even when they are apart. According to Winnicott, only when a person can be alone in this way can the id experiences occur, in which he can authentically experience sensations and impulses. When a child experiences narcissistic parenting, he does not get to experience an attuned gratification of his needs and to feel assured that the other person will be there once needed. If the mother herself is incapable of separateness, it is likely that she will fill the infant's world with her own anxiety and needs (either the need that he will need her or the need that he would not burden her with his needs). Without the introjection of the mother as a good object in the psychic structure, the absence is perpetuated as a psychic void. As a result, the capacity to be alone and, with it, the capacity to experience authentic feelings, will not evolve, leading to an experience of profound loneliness and emptiness.

Many times, the child retreats into a pseudo-autistic world or a world of 'psychic retreats' (Steiner, 1993). It is a hiding place both from the paranoid-schizoid position and the depressive position, a necessary retreat for a child with narcissistic parents, as the experience of being persecuted by the parent (both the internalized and the realistic one) may be excessively menacing, and the necessary mourning for the recognition of the realistic parent for who he is, is difficult to bear. In these psychic retreats, the child finds refuge from the real world and from the need to engage in real relationships, which are extremely painful and frightening for him. In this world, the child's object relations will be fantasized. The child will engage in relationships with fantasized characters, animals, areas of interest, socio-political positions, or psychoactive substances, all of which can serve as objects. If the child forms a close relationship with another person, that relationship may be revealed on deeper examination as a relationship with a fantasized figure projected onto that person. This world is constructed through processes of projective identification, while losing parts of the self in the process of projection, and dwelling in these retreats hinders the child's development. This internal world can be so rich and real for the child and is so necessary for him as a defense, that it may border on the edge of reality testing. The reality testing of such a child can be likened to a pencil drawing that has been arbitrarily wiped by an eraser back and forth – lacunas are formed, borderline areas where reality testing is blurred and psychotic areas where reality testing is absent. Accordingly, the child may experience himself as perforated, undefined, and unreal.

> Only the True Self can be creative and only the True Self can feel real… the existence of a False Self results in a feeling unreal or a sense of futility… [The true self] does no more than collect together the details of the experience of aliveness.
>
> (Winnicott, 1960, p. 148)

Oedipus in the Narcissistic Family

Britton (1989, 2004) wrote about the Triangular Space – when the recognition of the parental relationship, from which the child is excluded, serves as a boundary to the inner world and a foundation for the ability to witness object relations that he does not participate in. The capacity to imagine ourselves as seen by others, the ability for self-reflection and the awareness of the other's point of view evolve from this space. Britton states that he regards the 'borderline syndrome' as a particular from of narcissistic disorder in which what is missing is the third position at hand. He writes of 'thin skinned' and 'thick skinned' narcissistic patients, as Rosenfeld (1971) named them, and states that in the relationships of these patients, as well as in therapy:

> Instead of there being two connected, independent minds, there are either two separate people unable to connect or two people with only one mind... In one group, *the other* is treated as of no significance; in the second group, the patient cannot commune without making *the significant other* an extension of him- or herself.
>
> (Britton, 2004, p. 52)

My impression is that with a narcissistic parent, the Oedipal boundaries dissolve in a way that prevents the formation of the triangular space, which affects the child's self-awareness and interpersonal abilities. It is common for a narcissistic parent to demonize and belittle the other parent in their child's presence. Combined with disharmony at home, this situation makes the child perceive couples' relationships as negative and painful. As described, it is not uncommon to see cases in which the parent turns his child into an alternative partner (for example, if the parent projects his own introjected parental object onto the child in order to create a scenario of a relationship with that object). In such cases, the child may struggle even more with establishing relationships, especially romantic ones, since it would be perceived as an abandonment of the parent, both by the child, who may carry a heavy burden of guilt, and by the parent, who may react by emotionally withdrawing from the child.

Loewald (1979) wrote about an Oedipal conflict surrounding the separation from the parent:

> It is no exaggeration to say that the assumption of responsibility for one's own life and its conduct is in psychic reality tantamount to the murder of the parents, to the crime of parricide, and involves dealing with the guilt incurred thereby. Not only parental authority is destroyed by wresting authority from the parents and taking it over, but the parents, if the process were thoroughly carried out, are being destroyed as libidinal objects as well... What will be left if things go well is tenderness, mutual trust, and respect—the signs of equality.
>
> (pp. 757–758)

The following case demonstrates how this process does not take place in a family with a narcissistic parent. The parent will not come to respect the child nor treat him as an equal fellow adult, and the child will endure unbearable feelings of guilt for natural processes of growth and separation:

23 years old Tom commuted daily to his job located far from his parents' house because he felt unable to leave home. Eventually, he rented an apartment with roommates in the city he worked at. The move evoked feelings

of emptiness and gloom that Tom did not understand. The incentive for the move was a romantic relationship that Tom concealed from his parents, because the woman he was involved with did not meet the criteria of appearance and socio-economic status that he knew they expected. When he set to buy a double bed for the apartment he rented, his mother pushed him to take the single bed from his childhood room and asked in wonderment why he needed a new bed. Several months after leaving home, he became involved in another, overt and positive relationship. When he went on a romantic weekend trip with his girlfriend, he kept feeling a heavy sense of unexplained sadness and restlessness, and he struggled to enjoy himself. In the subsequent therapy session, he realized that his mother was on his mind most of the time, and that he was riddled with guilt for leaving her 'all alone' on the weekend, with his father and sisters. In therapy, we could contemplate how his depressive reaction was a result of the 'unthought known' (Bollas, 1979, 1987), that the object-mother withdrew her love in retaliation to his distancing from her, both real and fantasized, and of the guilt he felt for 'abandoning' her. Shortly thereafter, his mother told him that she had a dream in which she gave birth to a baby, and an anonymous hand appeared and severed the umbilical cord.

Why does the child continue to be emotionally trapped in a reality of such a toxic and suffocating family dynamic? The image in the dream that Tom's mother had had was that the umbilical cord between her and her son was severed violently. Woe to the baby whose umbilical cord was severed before he could develop and mature into a separate-independent existence.

Natalie's dream vividly conveys the almost unavoidable confinement of the child to what harms him:

Natalie grew up with a narcissistic father. As a child, she found him strong and impressive, but also intimidating. Reaching adulthood, he continued to treat her like a little girl in many ways and did not allow her to grow. During therapy, recurring dreams about a lion appeared. In one of the dreams, she wanted to reach a place that symbolized a place of healing. Suddenly, a lion emerged on her path. At first, she admired it, but then she realized it wanted to attack her and she escaped it at the last moment. Later in the dream, she arrived at her destination, of which she told the following: 'There was a double bed on an elevated stage, like a hotel room that has everything, except the shower was not separated from the rest of the room, and the room was not a private one. I looked at the bed and thought to myself that it was not appropriate in such a place. I took a shower, and suddenly someone entered the shower because it was a public shower. Suddenly, there was this hyperbaric pressure chamber, and I entered it. I understood that the hyperbaric pressure chamber was harming me, and that I needed to get out. I was afraid that I was trapped there because you can't open the door all at once, and I realized I would have to wait and be subjected to more damage". In another dream, she dreamed she was walking with her partner on a narrow path flanked with chasms on both sides. 'The path was full of overgrown vegetation, very neglected, and there was suddenly a point where one couldn't keep going because there was a dead white lion on the floor. It was very aesthetic, like a rug made of fur only artificial. It was dead, and I was afraid to step on it, it disgusted me. We couldn't pass. We looked around, seeking to bypass it, but the ground around it was decaying and muddy". Natalie continued to tell that in the dream, her partner "simply stepped on the lion and went on". She couldn't remember if she followed suit or rather needed him to carry her over the lion in order to pass it, or perhaps she didn't manage to pass at all. I thought that at different moments in her life all three possibilities alternately occurred because, according to her associations to the dream, the lion represented her father. We understood these dreams as conveying the sense that her impressive and also 'artificial' father didn't allow her to grow and move forward in her life's path. If she tried, she would stumble upon his narcissistic rage and be attacked, but if she did not try to move forward, she would be caught in his psychic death and it would adhere to her. She could not move forward with her life without wading in the swamp of depression and mourning for the loss of the parental object, a loss that would inevitably occur should she dare to grow. Over the years, Natalie indeed endured major depression proper. The act of walking over the dead lion also reflects a depressive position (Klein), a position that bears the guilt for the destruction of the object. Natalie knew that for her father, her growth was tantamount to abandoning him, and in her unconscious fantasy, growing up was tantamount to killing him. Thus, the dream also presents an Oedipal conflict — in order to move forward on the path of life, one must kill the parent and leave him behind, walk over the dead lion. The unresolved Oedipality is also manifested by the bed on the stage — the primal scene exposed to Natalie's eyes and the intrusive, boundaryless atmosphere of the hotel room-bathroom in the dream. The image of the hyperbaric pressure chamber demonstrates the impossible situation in which children growing up in a narcissistic familial 'pressure chamber' find themselves — they need the relationship with their parents like oxygen; without it, they ail (experience psychic death). However, the excessive oxygen is toxic, the relationship itself makes them ill as well, and they are trapped in the relationship and keep being harmed.

The Tale of Rapunzel: the Archetype of the Narcissistic Parent

A quintessential archetype of the pathologically narcissistic parent is portrayed exceptionally in the film *Tangled* (Greno & Howard, 2010), demonstrating the variety of manipulations the parent employs to control his child and continue receiving the narcissistic supply he depends on. The film tells the story of Rapunzel, the girl with the long hair, who was imprisoned in a tower by a witch. In the film, Gothel, the witch, uses the power of an enchanted flower to preserve her youth. Reality, time, and aging are denied, a denial which is a universal narcissistic defense. When the pregnant queen falls ill, the flower is found and an elixir is extracted from it, which heals her. The magical powers are transferred to the enchanted hair of the newborn baby girl, Rapunzel (the name 'Rapunzel' arises from the flower, whose name is specified in the Grimm Brothers' version of the story). Gothel kidnaps the infant princess. She locks her up in a tower and raises her as her own, forbidding her from venturing out into the world for fear of losing her and her life-giving hair. To an outsider, 'Mother Gothel' may appear to be a loving mother nurturing and protecting her daughter from all harm. She calls her 'flower' and 'pet' and expresses words of love, however a deeper understanding of the forces at work within Mother Gothel's psyche leads to a different conclusion altogether. When Mother Gothel calls Rapunzel 'flower', she sees her as an object to fulfill her needs. In the film, whenever she says "I love you", either her gaze is on the hair or she touches it, and her words are actually directed toward the hair as a representation of the original object, the flower. She loves what Rapunzel provides her, and if Rapunzel were to cease doing so, she would not receive 'love'. To keep Rapunzel to herself, Mother Gothel utilizes various manipulations, including instilling fear of the outside world (describing it as filled with ruffians, 'men with pointy teeth' and diseases) and promising protection by 'Mother'. The manipulations also include belittling Rapunzel in order to cut her wing, by means of direct insults or ones masked as jokes, and by labeling her autonomous desires and her yearning for growth as selfish, forbidden, and harmful to the 'mother', all the while evoking feelings of guilt. Mother Gothel projects and accuses Rapunzel of treating her cruelly or of engaging in 'dramatic' (i.e., histrionic) behavior, which she herself exhibits. She does all this while presenting herself to Rapunzel as a loving and devoted mother, who therefore cannot be presented with complaints or demands, and while caring first and foremost for herself and for her external image in the world (her beauty).

When a young man named Eugene breaks into the tower, Rapunzel finally dares to escape, a getaway she responds to with an emotional roller coaster of exhilaration-freedom and depression-guilt. This is the rather comic sequence of things she says after setting foot on the grass for the first time in her life: in a frightened, guilt-ridden tone she says that she can't believe she did this. She immediately repeats the same words, only this time with an exited, happy tone. Contemplating how furious her mother would be when she finds out, she tells herself that what her mother doesn't know won't kill her, only to be filled with anxiety the next moment saying to herself that this will kill her mother. She continues with alternating exclamations of elation and of a defeated, guilt-ridden anxiety, saying how much fun this is, that she is a horrible daughter, that she is going back, that she is never going back, that she is a despicable human being, that it is the best day ever. As she sits sobbing, overwhelmed by the burden of guilt and anxiety, Eugene tells her that he couldn't help but noticing that she seemed a little at war with herself. Indeed, she is at war with herself, with the internalized mother within her. Here, we have a weakening internal struggle, where living means killing the parent, and succumbing means loss of vitality and depression. Yet this is not solely an internalized mother – there's also a real, vengeful mother with an unequivocal threat of losing maternal love and protection if she dares to disobey the mother.

The reason that entices Rapunzel to dare and escape from the tower is the life instinct itself – she wants to fulfill her dream of seeing 'the lights' that appear once a year, which are actually floating lanterns released by her parents, the king and queen, every year on her birthday. This desire to see 'the lights' symbolizes her desire to live her own life and embrace her authentic identity, her true self. When Mother Gothel tracks Rapunzel down and discovers of her love for Eugene, she uses every manipulation in the book to sow discord between them: she tells Rapunzel the thought Eugene likes her is demented and that she has invented this whole romance, which proves that she is naïve and that she never should have left. She goes on to tell Rapunzel that there's no reason he would like her or be impressed with her, calling her 'dummy' and urging her to come back with her to the tower. When Rapunzel refuses, Mother Gothel shows her the crown which Eugene stole from the palace and left behind in Rapunzel's tower. This is Rapunzel's crown, but only Mother Gothel and the spectator know that. The crown is a symbol of her true identity and in this part of the story, her virginity as well. Mother Gothel goes on to tell Rapunzel to go ahead and give him what he wants [the crown] and behold how fast he'll leave her once he gets what he came for. After that, Mother Gothel abducts Rapunzel back to the tower. Upon arriving back at the tower, Gothel declares that "it never happened!". At this point, flashes of memory arise in Rapunzel, and she suddenly realizes that she is the lost princess and confronts her 'Mother' for the first time. During the quarrel, the mirror in the room breaks, symbolizing Rapunzel's refusal to be a mirror for Mother Gothel's narcissistic use anymore. At this moment, Gothel informs her that from now on, she is going be 'the bad guy' and restrains Rapunzel with (now actual) chains. When Eugene comes to rescue Rapunzel, Gothel stabs him with a knife and projects the blame, saying, "look what you've done!". Rapunzel pleads with Gothel to let her heal Eugene with her enchanted hair and offers to stay with Gothel in return, essentially remaining the little girl so that Mother Gothel can stay young and in control. Rapunzel promises it will be the way it was, just like Gothel wants. Indeed, that is the parent's wish – that nothing changes, that the child does not grow up. Thus, he can continue to fulfill his narcissistic needs in the various ways described, placating the parent's anxiety of separateness and of a psychotic breakdown that the loss of the defense, i.e., the recognition of separateness, may bring. As Eugene refuses to let Rapunzel make this Faustian bargain, she tells him that she can't let him die. He replies that if she did this she would die. That is the choice facing the child who does not have the right to a life of his own – to live and 'kill' the other, or sacrifice himself. Rapunzel approaches Eugene to heal him, but he cuts her hair with a shard from the mirror, abruptly ending Mother Gothel's narcissistic nourishment and taking her out of Rapunzel's life. As the ravages of age seize hold of Gothel in a fast-forward, she falls out of the tower window and disintegrates into dust – an embodiment of the psychotic breakdown she so feared, the disintegration that is the terror of the pathologically narcissistic parent and the deep motive for his abusive behavior. The tear Rapunzel sheds over Eugene contains one last drop of magic that saves him, just as he saved her, and she returns to the palace and to her true identity as a mature woman.

To the innocent spectator, Mother Gothel is a caricature of a narcissistic personality-disordered mother, but for children of such a parent, her behavior pattern and Rapunzel's experience are painfully familiar.

The example given also illustrates a common reaction of the narcissistic parent when the child finds a partner (something that often will not come to pass, due to guilt feelings and impaired social skills). The partner becomes a threat that seeks to take the child away from the parent and becomes another factor that reflects on how the parent is perceived in society, thus the partner may become a subject of criticism, ranging from conveying the message that no one is good enough for the child to a poisoning of the relationship by the parent.

Bibliography

Bollas, C. (1979). The Transformational Object. *International Journal of Psychoanalysis, 60*: 97–107.

Bollas, C. (1987). *The Shadow of the Object*. Routledge, 2018.

Britton, R. (1989). The Missing Link: Parental Sexuality in the Oedipus Complex. In: R. Britton, M. Feldman, E. O'Shaughnessy, & J. Steiner (Eds.), *The Oedipus Complex Today: Clinical Implications* (pp. 83–101). Karnac Books.

Britton, R. (2004). Subjectivity, Objectivity, and Triangular Space. *The Psychoanalytic Quarterly, 73*: 47–61.

Fonagy, P. (1989). On Tolerating Mental States: Theory of Mind in Borderline Personality. *Bulletin of the Anna Freud Centre, 12*: 91–115.

Fonagy, P. (1991). Thinking About Thinking: Some Clinical and Theoretical Considerations in the Treatment of a Borderline Patient. *The International Journal of Psychoanalysis, 72*: 639–656.

Fossum, M. A., & Mason, M. J. (1986). *Facing Shame: Families in Recovery*. W. W. Norton & Company.

Greno, N., & Howard, B. (2010). *Tangled* [film]. Disney.

Loewald, H. W. (1979). The Waning of the Oedipus Complex. *Journal of the American Psychoanalytic Association, 27*(4): 751–775.

Pardess, E. (2013, June 4). *On Shame: Perspectives in Psychodynamic Thinking*. Pardess. info. Retrieved March 1, 2021, from https://www.pardess.info/category/articles/

Rosenfeld, H. (1971). A Clinical Approach to the Psychoanalytic Theory of the Life and Death Instincts: An Investigation into the Aggressive Aspects of Narcissim. *The International Journal of Psychoanalysis, 52*: 169–178.

Steiner, J. (1993). *Psychic Retreats: Pathological Organizations in Psychotic, Neurotic and Borderline Patients*. Routledge.

Winnicott, D. W. (1958). The Capacity to be Alone. *The International Journal of Psychoanalysis, 39*: 416–420.

Winnicott, D. W. (1965). Ego Distortion in Terms of True and False Self (1960). In: M. Khan (Ed.), *The Maturational Processes and the Facilitating Environment: Studies in the Theory of Emotional Development* (vol. 64, pp. 140–152). Karnac Books.

Chapter 5

The Echoism

In this chapter, I will attempt to delineate the contours of the echoist. As mentioned, I perceive echoism as a subtype of narcissism that can be distinguished and named, thus constituting a clinical entity in its own right. The use of separate terminology may contribute to the understanding of intricacies and to achieving a greater depth of understanding and may provide valuable hints when faced with a patient who exhibits echoistic features, concerning his dynamic-genetic history and object relations. The echoist presents a false self (Winnicott, 1960/1965), and, as Miller noted (1979), tracing the origins of this false self leads to narcissistic injuries experienced in childhood, often at the hand of a parent demonstrating narcissistic pathology.[1] Just as the repetitive erosion by water leaves marks on a rock, the persistent pressure on the child to echo the parent's needs chisels the echoistic child's personality, subtracts from it, and leaves its marks. Modell (1975) believed that the false self described by Winnicott is similar, if not identical, to the narcissistic disorder outlined by Kohut. The echoist, therefore, grows in the shadow of narcissism and is shaped in its image, although I argue that the former is a mirror image of the latter.

In chemistry, there exists a phenomenon of enantiomers[2] – a term describing two molecules identical in their chemical composition that constitute mirror images of each other. Like the left hand to the right hand, they appear to be identical until we place one on top of the other. Their physical properties are identical (boiling point, density, etc.), but if we shine through them a special light, called 'plane polarized light', one will deflect the light rays to the right, while the other will deflect them to the left (see Figure 5.1). I believe that the narcissist and the echoist were formed of identical components of narcissistic injury, but they are enantiomers, mirror images of each other. Thus, the narcissist will deflect the rays of injury toward grandiose-manic defenses, while the echoist will deflect them toward the opposite direction, depression (see Figure 5.2).

I believe that every person possesses numerous narcissistic and echoistic enantiomers, in a highly individualized mixture that varies over time within the same person. The narcissist is situated at one end of the spectrum, and the echoist at the opposite end, but there may be an oscillation between states, a change in the ratio between the quantity of narcissistic enantiomers and echoistic ones,

DOI: 10.4324/9781032625393-5

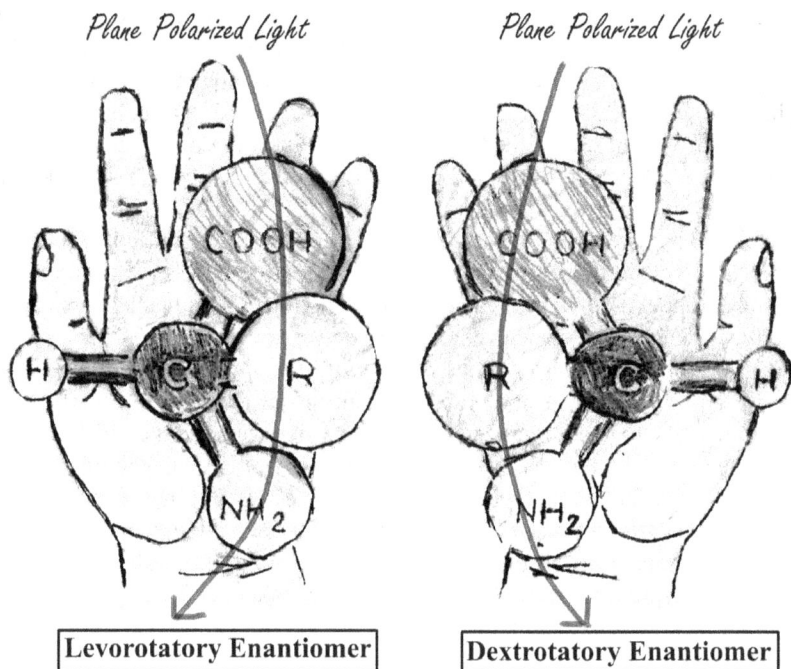

Figure 5.1 Enantiomers. Illustration by the author.

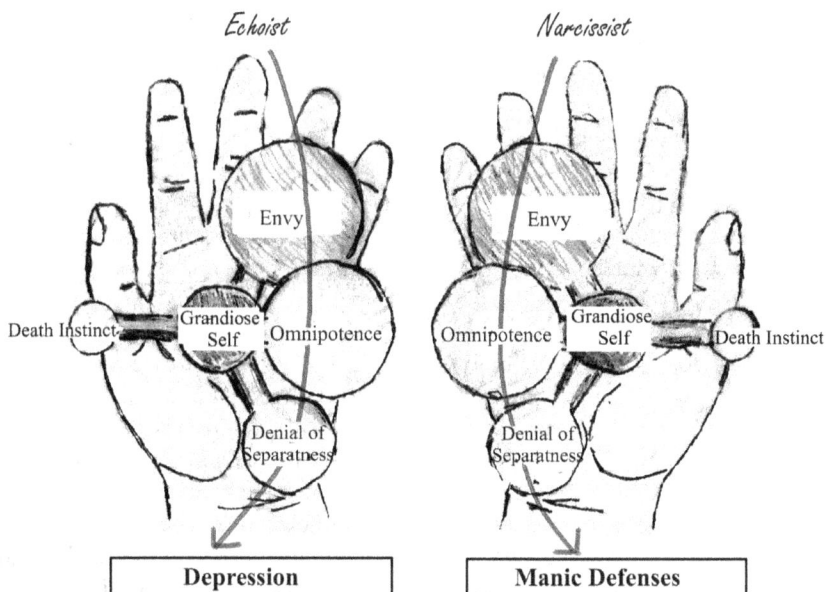

Figure 5.2 The narcissist versus the echoist. Illustration by the author.

or twinkling, when alternatingly certain characteristics are expressed and others are not. These changes occur in response to environmental factors and to intra-psychic processes. In chemistry, when a mixture contains equal amounts of right-handed and left-handed enantiomers of the same molecule,[3] the plane polarized light will not be deflected in any direction. In relation to our subject, when there is a balance between the narcissistic and echoistic enantiomers in the psyche, there will be no prominent psychological symptoms. I believe that the degree of narcissistic pathology and the pattern in which the child's personality develops, that is, his dominant position on the continuum between narcissism and echoism, depend on various factors, including the coping mechanisms available to him – identification with the aggressor versus rebellion or detachment. I believe that those individuals that identify with the aggressor tend to be more pleasing and to exhibit a lesser degree of splitting of their sense of worthlessness, because they have internalized the critical voice well and they identify with it. For this reason, the pattern of behavior that will emerge will manifest covert grandiosity. Other factors that will influence the direction of development are the nature of parental projections on the specific child (which depend on the scenario in the parent's inner world, projected according to the child's gender and order of birth), and the child's temperament, which generates a specific interaction with the parental projections.

Who is the echoist then, and what distinguishes him from his relative, the familiar narcissist? Is the echoist the covert narcissist (Akhtar, 1989)? I tend to think it is a subtype of this condition, but one entailing distinctions that require further theoretical exploration. Akhtar (2000) specifies, among the characteristics of the covert narcissist, a morose self-doubts, envy, and chronic boredom. Delving further into the description of this type of narcissism, Akhtar chose to call it the shy narcissist. He described the shy narcissist as follows:

> Like the ordinary narcissist, the shy narcissist is ambitious, omnipotence-seeking, involved with fantasies of glory and fame, lacking in empathy for others, and defective in his capacity for deep object relationships... Unlike the usual narcissist, however, the shy narcissist keeps his grandiose beliefs and aspirations tightly under cover. He appears modest.
>
> (pp. 115–116)

I argue that we are facing an echoist when the aforementioned covert and shy narcissism is accompanied by an intense need to merge with an idealized figure and to dedicate oneself to that figure. As long as the symbiosis with this figure is maintained, it supports the psychic structure like scaffolds and is perceived by the echoist as an inseparable part of himself. The lack of empathy that Akhtar describes in the shy narcissist is manifested partially with the echoist. The echoist grew up as an object of the narcissist and is therefore wired to perceive the feelings and needs of others and to adapt to them. For the echoist, this capacity is vital as a means of adjustment and survival. In the object relations that he is familiar with, that is what was required of him and therefore that is the only way he knows how to be in a relationship. The empathic failure of the echoist exists, as in any type of narcissism, but it is more restricted and is characterized by fluctuations between abundant empathy toward another whom he idealizes and empathic failures when he defensively withdraws from relationships. Empathy may be exaggerated, lacking in separation, but it may also dissipate easily should a narcissistic injury occurs by the hand of the idealized figure.

Kohut (1971, 1977, 1984) described a type of narcissistic personality with a prominent low self-esteem and a noticeable tendency to experience shame. He wrote that these patients experience a horizontal split, which is a repression of the grandiose needs. This split is a defense mechanism against an early injury to the sense of self-worth. Another type of split described by Kohut is the vertical split, in which dissociation occurs between the grandiose part of the personality and the part that feels worthless, so that the individual feels either grandiose or worthless. Kohut viewed the vertical split as more severe and pathological than the horizontal split (Kohut, 1971, 1977). Akhtar (2000) associated the horizontal split with the shy narcissist. I believe that the mechanism of vertical splitting is dominant in overt narcissists, while horizontal splitting is dominant in shy/covert narcissists and in the echoist.

The echoist can be outlined using behavioral characteristics which are prevalent amongst these patients. We may observe an intense need to please, an excessive need for validation and approval from others, difficulty relying on their own feelings, perception of reality and judgment, which manifests as ambivalence and indecisiveness. Additionally, we may observe a lack of assertiveness and a tendency toward a pleasing, apologetic demeanor, underneath which lie hidden feelings of anger and aggression, which are intense and unconscious. Their exaggerated politeness is but a reaction formation to that aggression. They exhibit self-effacement, but beneath it lies grandiosity, unconscious as well. These patients have difficulty identifying emotions and needs. They are ridden with guilt and tend to assume responsibility for negative events that are beyond their control, while positive occurrences are perceived as chance or luck, even if they result from their own talents and hard work. Weather out of fear of envy, out of masochism, or out of a dialog with an internalized persecutory object, they feel the need to downplay their achievements and have great difficulty experiencing satisfaction from them. This self-flagellation may serve as a preemptive move, stemming from the expectation that a blow dealt by the other will be more painful, and it is also a way to maintain a relationship with a sadistic object. They struggle to trust others, to the point of paranoia, but if they do form a relationship, this fear may lead to a counter-phobic response, and they may injudiciously expose their soft underbelly, meaning they expose themselves and share without judgment and inappropriately. They harbor a sense of victimhood and may unconsciously evoke exploitation, mistreatment, and even danger. However, they remain silent in the face of real or perceived injustice and carry a pent-up resentment. Alternatively, their tendency to please and to jus-tify the other often blinds them to the fact that they are being mistreated. Depres-sion is like a second nature for these patients, and anxiety in its various forms is prevalent as well. A unique characteristic of their depression is the prominent correlation between exacerbation in the psychological state of the offender and the severity of the depression, as well as an inverse correlation between the distance from offender and the severity of the depression. This distance can be physical, such as going on vacation or moving to a distant place, or emotional. It leads to a dilution of the relationship with the offender and a reduction in the emotional burden and toxicity associated with it. Whereas a physical distancing which is not accompanied by an emotional distancing may initially generate feelings of guilt and gloom, these are usually replaced over time with relief. This unique charac-teristic of the depression may assist in identifying the echoist and discerning the underlying etiology.

One might speculate that the echoist would be more receptive to treatment than the grandiose narcissist, whose grandiose defenses are more fortified, and whose need for the other is more effectively denied. The echoist tends to project his grandiose self onto the other – the therapist or another idealized figure – and then re-introject it through identification. He perceives all that is good as residing in the other and projects onto the other what is good in himself as well, thus tending to idealize rather than devalue the therapist, although this state may change during the therapeutic process through the activation of other primitive parts of his psyche.

As mentioned, I believe that there is an oscillation between the degrees of narcis-sism and echoism in the same individual during different periods and circumstances in their life, with a general tendency to be around a certain area on the spectrum. This oscillatory movement is similar to the movement between the Kleinian 'posi-tions'. "Position describes the state of the ego, typical anxieties, object relations and defences which persist at every level" (Segal, 1983, p. 270).

As for the Kleinian positions proper, the paranoid-schizoid position dominates in both narcissist and echoist, but I believe the echoist will shift more easily to the depressive position, which "is characterized by an ambivalent relation to whole loved objects, a budding sense of psychic reality, with the accompanying anxieties about guilt and loss. The move from the one to the other is a move from predomi-nantly psychotic to neurotic functioning. Omnipotence lessens and the ego grows in strength" (ibid, pp. 269–270). I believe that feelings of guilt – their existence, intensity, and quality – can help distinguish between the narcissist and the echoist. Freud (1931) wrote about the narcissistic libidinal type: "There is no tension be-tween ego and super-ego (indeed, on the strength of this type one would scarcely have arrived at the hypothesis of a super-ego)" (p. 218). Britton added to this: "No tension, [between the ego and the superego], I would suggest, because the individ-ual is of the opinion that he is what is wanted" (p. 76). The denial of limitations and mistakes is a central defense mechanism for the narcissist, therefore awareness that he has erred or harmed another, and feelings of guilt associated with it, will be rare or quickly repressed. In contrast, the echoist is plagued by intense feelings of guilt, a punitive superego that is the introjection of a critical and reprimanding parent.

Kernberg (1975) emphasizes the pathology of the superego amongst those with narcissistic personality disorder and indicates that the presence of antisocial traits is a negative prognostic factor. I believe that the prognosis is more positive for the echoist who, as a general rule, exhibits less severe superego pathology and a lack of antisocial traits, in comparison to what is familiar with the narcissist. Akhtar (2000) notes something similar regarding the shy narcissist – that he has a stricter conscience than the 'ordinary narcissist', is more prone to remorse, and is capable of gratitude. He is also capable of feeling guilt and a need to offer reparation if he had hurt another. The echoist is in the opposite end to the narcissist in this sense, as his inability to bear the sense of guilt or to harm others leads him to lose the ability to protect himself and hence to harm himself in a masochistic manner. An example of this can be seen in the case of Gabriel, who continued to date a girl he did not like because he was unable to deal with the guilt he would feel for rejecting her, or in the case of Ariel, who volunteered at a nursing home and allowed an elderly and sick stranger with pneumonia to give her a kiss. The elderly woman lay in her sickbed, attached to an oxygen mask and a catheter, reeking with the stench of illness. Ariel approached her room to give her water when the elderly woman said to her: "I want to give you a kiss". In the most fundamental way, Ariel could not say no. From her description, it appeared that the elderly woman, who made the strange request, was delirious due to her illness, but Ariel did not stop to ask herself if the request was legitimate and, in fact, she did not concern herself with the person making the request at all. She could not bear the thought of offending and was never given the permission to refuse.

The echoist would usually be anxious and shy, reacting to criticism with shame and cowardice (as opposed to the anger and deflection of the grandiose narcissist), tending to dismiss himself in the presence of authority figures and fear them, haunted by feelings of guilt, having difficulties safeguarding himself in relation to others, and seeking to please. This does not mean that the echoist does not need and seeks narcissistic reinforcements. On the contrary, he depends on the approval of others to maintain a sense of self-worth and stability. Maintaining these depends on what happens in relation to others, especially within a relationship with a significant other. However, unlike the narcissist, he is inclined to be tormented by feelings of self-loathing, diminished self-worth, and a conscious experience of impotence, which are akin to what is seen in borderline patients. Additionally, the echoist may express a hunger for objects and become dependent on them out of an illusion that they can serve as a buffer, shielding him against the outside world. Modell (1975) described similar distinctions between the narcissistic patient and the borderline patient. Modell added his assumption that the environmental trauma leading to severe narcissistic disorders is less severe than that leading to borderline conditions. It is worth examining further the extent of the damage endured by the echoist compared to that endured by the narcissist, the developmental stage in which it occurs, and its relationship to innate sensitivity. Regarding the echoist's self-hatred, the question arises as to whether this hatred is truly directed toward himself or whether it is more accurate to say that it is directed toward his introjected object (also as a way to deflect forbidden feelings toward the real object). In any case, it is an ego-destructive superego (Bion, 1959), or what Fairbairn (1943) called the "internal saboteur" (p. 101) and later changed to "anti-libidinal ego" (Fairbairn, 1956, p. 58). Fairbairn sees the internal saboteur as a split-off part of the ego that is linked to a rejecting object. Consequently, the echoist will be haunted by a sense of impairment and will have difficulty recognizing his own abilities, and the internal saboteur may cause him to behave in a self-defeating manner. Freud (1923) wrote: "To the ego, living means the same as being loved—being loved by the super-ego" (p. 58). If we reverse the statement, it seems that not being loved by the superego is akin to death. If so, here we have an explanation for the tyrannical power of the superego and the extent of sabotage it can carry out, as well as the degree of sacrificing of parts of the self that the echoist will sacrifice in order to gain approval and recognition from the parental objects and their derivatives throughout his life. Kohut (1971) wrote:

> Persons who have suffered such traumas are... forever attempting to achieve a union with the idealized object since, in view of their specific structural defect (the insufficient idealization of their superego), their narcissistic equilibrium is safeguarded only through the interest, the responses, and the approval of present-day... replicas of the traumatically lost self-object.
>
> (p. 55)

Britton (2004a) relied on Rosenfeld's (1971) division into destructive narcissism and libidinal narcissism and wrote about two types of narcissistic disorder – one primarily destructive and the other primarily libidinal. Both are intended for "the production, by projective identification, of a narcissistic relationship with an ego ideal in order to evade a relationship with a destructive parental super-ego" (p. 477). In destructive narcissism, the relationship with an external object is attacked, and the need for a relationship is denied. In libidinal narcissism, the patient invests the superego's power in a narcissistic object and becomes dependent on its approval and love. Britton proposed that destructive narcissism is formed when the prominent element in the etiology is an excess of aggression toward the object in the child, while libidinal narcissism is formed when the prominent element is parental failure. In the case of destructive narcissism, the parental object is experienced as persecutory and murderous. In the case of libidinal narcissism, the internalized mother-object is absent, a void which is "not simply an absence but a negating presence" (ibid, p. 486). I believe that the degree of narcissism and echoism found in a patient is related to these factors. In the case of the echoist, the narcissism is primarily libidinal, and the more we approach the other end of the spectrum, grandiose narcissism, the narcissism becomes primarily destructive. Britton illustrated destructive and libidinal narcissism through the case studies of two patients and implies that the patient with destructive narcissism is more disturbed and ego-centric than the patient with libidinal narcissism. He also emphasized the differences in the transference. In the case of destructive narcissism, the feeling of exclusion is projected into the analyst, who feels excluded from the patient's mental space and in addition, the relationship that is formed has perverse, sadomasochistic characteristics. In the case of libidinal narcissism, the transference is adherent, and the patient colonizes the analyst's psychic space.

The echoist needs an idealized other to serve as an auxiliary ego that supports his incomplete psychic structure and strength, the relationship with whom allows him to escape from a persecutory and loveless superego. This does not mean that the echoist will be voiceless and submissive in every relationship and at all times. Usually, the echoist will be introverted and distant, and while submission to authority figures is the rule, idealization and dependence will be reserved for selected few in his life. I believe that many adults who are in a narcissistically abusive relationship are in effect the children of parents who had such a relational pattern. These are echoistic children who are dependent on a strong connection to the parent, a connection without which they experience a disintegration originating in their unfinished psychic structures. Even as adults, these individuals tend to be approval-seeking and reliant on the acceptance of others, seeking to experience themselves as a part of an idealized figure perceived as greater and stronger than themselves (for example, in couple's relationships).

I will use a segment from the comic opera 'L'elisir d'amore' (the elixir of love) by Donizetti (Donizetti & Romani, 1832), to further clarify the distinction between the echoist and the narcissist as well as their commonalities. The opera is comic, and the depiction of the characters in it is stereotypical and superficial, but nonetheless, in the lyrics of the duet 'Una parola, o Adina' (A word, oh Adina), we can see the need of the echoistic character, the simple village boy Nemorino, to merge with another character, Adina, a sophisticated and narcissistic landowner with whom he is in love. Nemorino's echoistic needs stands in contrast to Adina's manic narcissistic defenses, defenses that do not permit loving. In his first aria, Nemorino demonstrates how he perceives himself and his love object: "She reads, studies, learns. There is nothing she does not know / I am always an idiot, I only know how to sigh". These words of Nemorino's are the words of a child who feels small in the shadow of a narcissistic parent. Adina, on the other hand, does not feel small or impotent. She is proud, wooed, toys with the men around her, aware of her power over them, and derives pleasure from the sense of power it gives her.

Adina rejects Nemorino's advances, and he pleads before 'Doctor' Dulcamara, a charlatan selling potions, to sell him an elixir of love. The Bordeaux wine sold as a love potion frees Nemorino from his persecutory superego, and he is convinced that Adina is to fall in love with him 'tomorrow', as promised by the doctor (who mutters to himself that it leaves him plenty of time to escape). The wine that Nemorino drinks can be seen as a metaphor for the internalization of a good, validating, and reinforcing parent. Confident in himself, he ceases to be 'adhesive' and clingy and displays indifference toward Adina, who, in revenge, agrees to marry a narcissistic sergeant who pursues her. Nemorino's 'confidence' (and the rumor of an inheritance he inherited) makes all the village girls desire him and makes Adina jealous and angry that he dared, seemingly, to get over her.

Through the lyrics of the duet, we can analyze the inner world of the characters:

Nemorino:
A word, oh Adina!
Adina:
The routine nuisance, the usual sighs!
You would do better to go to town to your uncle
Who is said to be ill, and gravely so!
Nemorino:
His suffering is nothing next to mine
I cannot leave
A thousand times I have tried
Adina:
And what if he dies and leaves another as heir?
Nemorino:
What does is matter to me?
Adina:
You will die of hunger and with no one to support you
Nemorino:
Of hunger or of love, is all the same to me
Adina:
Listen to me, you are good, you are modest
Unlike that sergeant
You are not certain you can inspire affection in me
That is why I speak frankly to you
And tell you that in vain you hope for love
That I am capricious
And there is not a desire that will not die in me
As soon as it awakens
Nemorino:
Oh, Adina, and why ever is that?
Adina:
A fine question!
Ask the flattering breeze
Why she flies without pose
One moment over the lily, one moment over the rose
One moment over the meadow, one moment over the brook
She will tell you that it is her nature
To be fickle and unfaithful
To be fickle and unfaithful

Nemorino:
Then what must I do?
Adina:
Renounce your love for me, flee me
Nemorino:
Dear Adina, I cannot
Adina:
You cannot? Why?
Nemorino:
Why?! Why?
Ask the river why, lamenting
From the cliff where he sprang to life
He rushes to the ocean which beckons him
And in the ocean goes to die
He will tell you he is being pulled
By a force he cannot explain
A force he cannot explain
Adina:
Then what do you want?
Nemorino:
To die like him, but to die following you
Adina:
Love elsewhere, you're allowed to
Nemorino:
Ah it is impossible
No, no, impossible
Adina:
In order to be cured from that madness
For loyal love is madness
Follow my example
Change a lover every day
Just as a nail drives out a nail
So does love drive love away
In that way I enjoy myself
In that way my heart remains free
Nemorino:
Ah! Only you I see, I hear
Day and night in everything
I have tried in vain to forget you
Your face is engraved in my heart
You can replace, as you do
Every other love
But you can not

You cannot ever
Uproot the first one from the heart
Adina:
Yes! Yes! Yes!
I laugh and enjoy myself
In that way my heart remains free
Nemorino:
No! No! No!
[You cannot] uproot from the heart
From the opera L'elisir d'amor (Donizetti & Romani,
1832), first act [my translation – H.Y]

The first love, the first object, indeed cannot be uprooted from the heart, but sometimes this object leaves such a great void that, like Nemorino, the grown-up child will forever feel an overwhelming force driving him to be assimilated in a 'greater' other and calm the feelings of smallness and impotence within him, or perhaps more than that, to contain him and pacify the experience of disintegration. Freud (1930) described the 'oceanic feeling[4]'. It is a feeling of "limitlessness and of a bond with the universe" (p. 68), of "oneness with the universe" (p. 72), of inseparability from the object, an experience that is also related to religious spiritual transcendence. "Originally the ego includes everything, later it separates off an external world from itself" (p. 68). Freud regarded the oceanic feeling as a regressive experience of primary narcissism that provides a sense of defense against the danger of being hurt by the external world. Sometimes, like in the case of Nemorino, the need would be to immerse oneself in a monumental and great other. Other times, like in the case of Adina, the child would identify with the grandiose aspects of the archaic object and, through narcissistic defenses of omnipotence, denial of the need for others and self-sufficiency, would regard the other as a generic 'flower'. Whether it is the lily or the rose that satisfies his needs does not matter, as long as there is no awareness of needing something from another or of a dependence on an irreplaceable other. Nemorino and Adina, the echoist and the narcissist, are two parts of the same whole. This whole is composed of grandiose, omnipotent, and devaluative defenses that cover up an experience of smallness and dependence. We see before us an echoist or a narcissist depending on which part of that whole is the personality standing out on the surface and which is submerged in the unconscious. However, I hope that this excerpt demonstrates that despite the similar dynamic-genetic etiology, clinically the personality is so different that it may justify a distinction between the two, both in diagnosis and in treatment.

Using Meltzer's theory, I would like to propose a possible explanation for the clinical difference, based on the assumption that the echoist's impairment is rooted in a more primary injury than the narcissist's, following more severe failures in primary maternal care, greater innate sensitivity, or a combination of both.

Meltzer (1975) presents a developmental theory that identifies four dimensions of psychic development: (1). One-Dimensionality – States of mind where there is no experience of space and time. The individual reacts by stimuli and response, attraction and repulsion, and thinking is absent. Time and space are indistinguishable from each other. (2). Two-Dimensionality – Objects and self are experienced as surfaces with sensual qualities. There is no ability to construct in thought things different than what the individual has already experienced because there is no internal space for phantasy. This self has impaired memory and desire, without the ability to introject objects. It is a state of changelessness, where any threat is experienced as a break-down of the surfaces. Time is perceived circularly, without a sense of development or progression. (3). Three-Dimensionality – The object is no longer experienced as two-dimensional, with the self on one of its sides or the other. There is an awareness of orifices in both the object and the self, and an experience of the object and the self as having potential spaces and a container capacity. Time acquires directionality, but the continued operation of omnipotent projective identification results in an experience that time is moving in oscillation and that the separation between object and self is reversible. Only relinquishing projective identification can lead to the next stage. (4). Four-Dimensionality – A perception of a four-dimensional world, where time flows in one direction. Now there is a perception of the possibility for development and therefore hope (rather than being arrested by attempts to control the object in response to the envy triggered by needing it). Now introjective identification is possible, a precondition for which is the ability to relinquish control over the object. Meltzer refers to the importance of Klein's paper 'Notes on Some Schizoid Mechanisms' (1946) in the understanding of mechanisms of identification and mentions the prevalent conception that followed – that projective identification is the very mechanism of narcissistic identification. Meltzer mentions another, more primitive mechanism of narcissistic identification: adhesive identification.[5] I shall argue that adhesive identification characterizes the echoist and distinguishes him from the narcissist. Projective identification is the narcissist's way of relating, while adhesive identification is the echoist's way. Meltzer links adhesive identification to a primitive developmental stage, the two-dimensional stage, as opposed to the projective identification of the three-dimensional stage. Adhesive identification involves identification with external attributes of the other, expressed through superficial imitation, such as imitating the object's dressing style. Bick (1986) proposed that the infant experiences the different parts of his personality as lacking an inherent binding force and not yet differentiated from the body, thus entirely dependent on the object for a sense of containment and of being held together. The object (primary caretaker) generates this containing 'primal skin' experience through the infant's caretaking. If the parental-skin container is adjusted and the infant is capable of introjecting it, a sense of envelopment and of self-containment develops, crucial for ongoing healthy psychic development. If this primal skin function fails to develop, a defensive 'second skin' may form (such as relying on innate talents or on a rich internal world into which the child 'autisticly' retreats). I believe that the shedding of this second skin in therapy exposes just how thin and vulnerable the patient's real skin is, as well as the ease with which he may be subject to experiencing disintegration, due to the absence of a true integration of the personality parts. An individual living in a two-dimensional world such as that cannot see the other as a whole subject, and adhesive identification may become the primary way in which he may attempt to sense cohesion of his own parts and establish a relationship with another. My impression is that if such a person becomes attached to another, a highly regressive and primitive dependency may develop, and he would desire to be the river engulfed by the ocean, not only willing but longing to lose himself inside the other, just so long as he does not feel skinless and scattered in space. I believe that it was about such patients that Kohut (1971) wrote:

> The personality will throughout life be dependent on certain objects in what seems to be an intense form of object hunger. The intensity of the search for and of the dependency on these objects is due to the fact that they are striven for as a substitute for the missing segments of the psychic structure.
>
> (p. 45)

Kohut noted that during the regression that takes place in therapy, patients like these become "addicted to the analyst or to the analytic procedure" (p. 46). Indeed, in therapy, echoistic patients will exhibit patterns different from the familiar narcissistic alienation and devaluation. Echoistic patients will appear cooperative, engage in idealization of the therapist, and exhibit intolerance of reminders of the separateness from the therapist, such as vacations, weekends, or innuendos about the therapist's private life. Transference may include feelings of love and gratitude alongside childish demandingness and guilt. Bollas (1987) described what, in my opinion, characterizes echoistic patients in therapy, writing that in analysis:

> The person who has been emptied by the active violation of the Other, his internal life having been extracted from him…will seem almost incapable of projecting into the analyst. More likely, the analysand will develop a parasitical transference in which he assumes that all that is life-enhancing…is inside the analyst, thus inspiring him to live as close to the analyst as possible.
>
> (p. 107)

One may find in this conduct, both in relationships and in therapy, the distinction between the echoist and the narcissist. The transference will be experienced differently, as the former would tend to be pleasing and openly dependent on the therapist, while the latter would feel resentment due to his own neediness. The narcissist will devaluate in an attempt to deny needing something that he lacks while the Other possesses. If the therapist is idealized, it occurs during periods when the therapist is experienced as an inseparable part of the narcissistic patient. Separation anxiety revolving vacations will be absent or at least denied with the narcissist.

Meltzer's writings suggest another possible and significant difference between what I call an echoist and the narcissistic. As mentioned, I believe that similar to the Kleinian positions and the transition between them, the echoist and the narcissist move between different psychic regions that have characteristic object relations patterns and defense mechanisms. At the more primitive extreme, the echoistic one, there is a two-dimensional world where adhesive identification is the dominant mode of relating, while at the other extreme, there is the narcissistic projective identification, seeking control over the object and penetration into it. Meltzer (1966) further clarified and spoke about a specific type of projective identification characteristic of the narcissistic disorder – intrusive identification. It is a delusional identification with the object. There is an attempt to escape the dependency on the object and the envy by penetrating the object in phantasy, becoming the object, an attempt to 'hasten' the slow and painful growth processes with their accompanying anxiety through this means. According to Meltzer, this process leads to the development of a pseudo-adult personality, similar to Winnicott's (1960/1965) false self or Deutsch's (1942) 'as if' personality.

The denial of the dimension of time and of separateness constitutes a rich substrate for perversion, which I will expand upon later.

From all that was previously mentioned, another dimension of injury emerges, related to primitive mental states. When the pathologically narcissistic parent is the infant's primary caretaker (usually the mother), the injury may be double. First, there is a very primary injury through failure in the infant's treatment, which would register in the body, but lacking conceptualization and words, would fail to register in the memory. Then there is an injury which arises from the failures already described in detail. Indeed, many mothers with narcissistic traits would be devoted and loving (it is common for difficulties to emerge only once the child begins initial natural steps of separation); however, when the narcissistic pathology is severe, and especially if the infant's temperament challenges the mother, there may be significant failures from the very first moments of life. I tend to think that the echoist expresses such a 'double injury'. The initial injury leaves him 'skinless', more vulnerable to the second injury. Since the initial injury comes from a pre-verbal period that is inaccessible to memory and conceptualization, we must look for clues to it in somatic symptoms, in our experience in the countertransference, and in the adhesive identification patterns of the patient. These patients may imitate the external characteristics of the object/therapist, such as his dress style, and use the therapist's voice, image, smell, and the clinic itself as an alternative skin. A change in these characteristics may lead to a severe reaction in the patient.

Ariel, who was mentioned earlier as an example of the ramifications of the lack of separation and lack of emotional stability of the narcissistic parent, also expressed adhesive identification and a lack of primal skin. As I described, during the initial phase of therapy, sometimes she would telephone me between sessions "just to hear" my voice, and she had nightmares in which a woman with a different face opened the practice's door to her, or in which while we were talking, my appearance changed right before her eyes and I became uninterested and impatient. A change in the office's furniture or a change in my hairstyle led to a catastrophic anxiety response because the object that changed its external characteristics was no longer the same object for her. Ariel's father was subjected to mood swings and outbursts depending on his narcissistic equilibrium, and I, too, sometimes turned into a persecutory object, capable of transforming from a Dr. Jekyll into a Mr. Hyde in an instant. Ariel's mother also had a narcissistic disorder, due to severe deprivation of her own in her childhood. She related to Ariel through forceful intrusion into her life. The mother would compulsively and ceremoniously rummage through Ariel's belongings, touch her body intrusively in an objectifying manner, and scrutinize her with invasive looks, as if she was trying to read her thoughts. Not only did the mother fail to serve as an enveloping skin and a container for Ariel, it seemed that the mother was seeking gratification for her own infantile needs from Ariel. Ariel expressed a feeling as if her mother was attempting to get under her skin and colonize her from within. The mother knew no other way of relating other than intrusive identification. Once, the mother caressed Ariel in a way which was disturbing and repugnant to her. Ariel described feeling as if she was skinless and the touch was unbearable. When Ariel aversively recoiled, the mother angrily hissed: "This is my body!" I mentioned in the previous description[6] that Ariel rejected the idea of psychoanalysis because of her need to see the therapist's face, fearing it would change from Dr. Jekyll into Mr. Hyde. We understood the reason for this shortly into the treatment, but there was another reason, a more hidden and primary reason, which led me to think that Ariel's injury was a "double injury" (from the 'classical' narcissism of the father, but before that, from the more primitive and covert narcissism of the mother). The mere thought of lying on a couch, exposed to an examining and unseen gaze of the analyst, evoked an intense aversion in Ariel, which over time we came to understand as an outcome of the perverse maternal treatment she received, possibly in a pre-verbal and unremembered period.(see the concept of "idolization" by Khan in Chapter 6)

Ariel sought to engulf herself in surrogate mothers and surrogate skins. The perfume she used was the perfume of a previous object-figure. The use of the perfume was an attempt to wrap herself in a different skin-identity. In association with that, she recounted a memory from her early childhood, perhaps around the age of three, of her mother, all made up and dressed up to go out with the father, applying perfume. She remembered being enchanted by these feminine attributes and remembered her mother's refusal to let her use the perfume. The refusal was symbolic of the, as aforesaid, deeply injured mother, refusing to allow Ariel identification and connection, meaning to experience herself as part of the mother and to serve as an enveloping skin for her. This is not the place to delve into the Oedipal components of the situation presented, but the refusal also symbolizes a refusal to allow Ariel identification with the parental figure of the same sex and to internalize the mother in this domain, which subsequently led her to desperately search for female figures to identify with throughout her life. The office itself and the setting became an enveloping skin. When the couch and one of the pictures in the office, which had warm color tones, were replaced with ones with cooler color tones, the place suddenly felt foreign and I was perceived as distant and cold. In her anger toward me, she said, "You've taken all the warmth out of the office" and during that period, she often complained of feeling physically cold. The office itself was an enveloping skin that preserved the warmth of her body.

Unable to Throw Up, Unable to Swallow: The Void in the Mind Occupied by the Other

The narcissistic parent's pathology is one of parts of false self that the child cannot truly internalize, alongside the projection of poisonous and aggressive self-parts whose internalization arouses in the child feelings of shame and self-loathing.

> That a relationship with a bad object should be shameful can only be satisfactorily explained on the assumption that in early childhood all object-relationships are based upon identification. This being the case, it follows that, if the child's objects present themselves to him as bad, he himself is bad...However much he may want to reject them, he cannot get away from them. They force themselves upon him; and he cannot resist them because they have power over him, He is accordingly compelled to internalize them in an effort to control them. But, in attempting to control them in this way, he is internalizing objects which have wielded power over him in the external world; and these objects retain their prestige for power over him in the inner world. In a word, he is 'possessed' by them...also, and above all...he *needs* them.
>
> (Fairbairn, 1943, pp. 64–67)

While the real parent may possess good qualities and good intentions in abundance (the quantity and quality of which may determine the extent of the pathology that will develop in the child), in the end, the child goes out into the world with an internalized bad object that he has "either to embrace or else remain objectless and deserted" (ibid, p. 72).

One of my patients often described a feeling of wanting 'to vomit something' out of himself. I understood it as a wish to throw up and expel the internalized bad object. Another patient, at a point in therapy where she was aware of the dynamics with her internalized objects and with those in her real world, explicitly expressed a desire to throw her parents up and out of herself. I fathom the narcissistic parent as an object that the child is 'unable to throw up, unable to swallow'[7] – if he threw up, he would be left empty and starved. If he swallowed, he would be controlled and poisoned. An internal world devoid of objects is the embodiment of a psychic death.

The very nature of the narcissistic parent's pathology impairs the child's ability to internalize a whole parental figure with both positive and negative components. The splitting in the parent leaves the child no option but to split both self and object's bad aspects from good ones. In other words, the child lacks the capability of maintaining a depressive position and preserving internalized good objects while in conflict with the parent (and not yielding to the parent means conflict). The splitting places the good components in the parent and the bad components in the child. The child can then experience goodness as a part of himself just as long as enmeshment with the parent is maintained and he receives approval from the parent (and subsequently from other external sources in his life). This goodness is not internalized, and the child does not deeply experience it as his own, nor as something sustainable. It is therefore a passing experience completely dependent on the presence of another; similar to the way Echo did not exist without Narcissus and needed his words to echo them. The child's internalized experience, the parts he experiences as his own, are 'bad' parental parts which were projected onto him. Without the enmeshment with the parent, what is left are 'bad' self-parts alongside a lack of a regulating and soothing factor. Kohut's term, selfobject, explains well what that regulating and soothing factor is: "objects which are themselves experienced as part of the self" (Kohut, 1971, p. xiv). According to Kohut, in a healthy trajectory, the archaic narcissistic structures and needs, as well as the idealized parent imago, are transmuted and internalized into the psychic structure (into the ego and the superego respectively). If the child experiences traumatic disappointment in the parent, the internalization of the idealized parent imago into the superego and its transformation into a tension-regulating psychic structure would be compromised. The idealized parent imago that was not internalized would remain an archaic, transitional selfobject which is required in order to maintain the narcissistic equilibrium of the child (i.e., he is in need of an external figure); that is the reason why, as Kohut points out, it is common for the initial complaints of the patient to revolve around "subtly experienced, yet pervasive feelings of emptiness and depression which...are alleviated as soon as the narcissistic transference has become established – but which become intensified when the relationship to the analyst is disturbed" (ibid, p. 16). Kohut suggested that what accounts for the vagueness of these complaints is the "nearness of the pathologically disturbed structures (the self) to the seat of the self-observing functions in the ego... The eye, as it were, cannot observe itself" (ibid, p. 16).

I would like to propose an additional reason. The vagueness, the fact that the eye does not observe, is related to the internalization processes of the parental object along with his stances, to the gaslighting, to the FOG (Fear, Obligation and Guilt – see Chapter 3 or Forward, 1997), to the dependence upon the parent and the defensive splitting, which, as previously described, disconnect the traumatogenic factor from the suffering caused, thus intensifying the suffering and creating the blindness which is characteristic of such relationships. Many of my patients who have experienced narcissistic parenting described these very same vague feelings of emptiness and depression that lasted for years without being able to understand them. Often, this is the initial complaint that leads the individual to seek treatment.

A few of them dreamt recurrent dreams in which there were motifs of an unfinished, dilapidated, or falling apart building which represented their psyche. During sessions, they describe a desperate attempt to build their lives on shaky foundations. In therapy, these patients manifested in varying ways dependency and difficulty with separateness, which alternated with rage over the dependency and separateness. Just like Kohut described, they experienced aggravation and responded with depression and anxiety whenever disruption occurred in the therapeutic relationship. Kohut described the ways in which the (parental) objects cause a narcissistic disequilibrium in the child through threats of punishment, withdrawal of love, or disappearance (Kohut, 1971). The narcissistic equilibrium of the child, which was interwoven with the parent, is undermined, and the sense of self-cohesion and self-worth is compromised. I believe that the experience of an undermined self-cohesion, of that disintegration, arises from the loss of the object that the child is dependent on, an object that serves as a supporting structural part for him. The withdrawal of love by the object is tantamount to pulling the rug out from under his feet. The disintegration leads to that very experience of 'psychic death' that looms over the child, an experience of the loss of the self. However heavy the price of succumbing oneself to the parent's whims and to being enmeshed, opposite it lies the unbearable choice of a psychic desert. The intensity of anxiety that this threat evokes is great and intolerable, and the range of things that children would accept in order to prevent or stop this anxiety is inconceivable for an outside observer, especially when, in many cases, this situation persists in 'adult' children.

Dana was raised in a household in which her mother ruled with a firm hand over all family members. She sought therapy due to depression, anxiety, and difficulty forming social and romantic relationships. She described a conflict between her desire for relating and the feeling that within a relationship she is engulfed by another which takes control over her. As our relationship deepened and her perceived threat of needing me became greater, I increasingly felt that the content she brought up seemed to revolve around pseudo-philosophical topics that appeared unrelated to therapy. When I attempted to explore the deeper meaning behind the things she brought up, she experienced it as if I disagreed with her, and in response, she became furious and felt that I was undermining her sense of reality. I felt that the content was repeated compulsively and reflected Dana's attempt to trample me as a therapist and sterilize my ability to provide therapeutic interventions. She could not tolerate the separateness between us and the triangulation (Britton, 2004b), my relationship with anyone and anything other than her, whether it be people, my thoughts that were perceived as different from hers or the psychoanalytic theory. As this situation persisted, I had an intensifying feeling that Dana was attempting to press something into me, not just her opinions but herself, her essence. I felt that my ability to think was compromised, and I was unable to extricate us from the place we were in. Finally, I said: "I feel we're trapped in these discussions and are reenacting something. It feels like you're imposing something on me that I don't want, forcing me to participate in a debate that I experience as something vague that covers up some truth, and that you won't let go of it until you force me to agree with your opinion". In response, Dana exclaimed: "Yes! My mother forced herself down my throat all my life!" Afterwards, we were able to discuss the harsh ways in which her mother's tyranny and intrusiveness manifested, which often included a perverted violation of her privacy and bodily autonomy.

Notes

1 Other situations in which the needs of the parent overshadow the needs of the child, such as a parent with borderline personality disorder, depression, or addiction to psychoactive substances, may lead to a similar but not necessarily identical outcome. The outcome will be similar if the parent exhibits strong narcissistic traits in the form of exaggerated projections on the child that erase the child's existence as an individual in his own right and in the form of intrusive behavior by the parent. These traits not only injure the child's psych and create mental health symptoms but also bind the child to the parent in a Gordian knot.
2 A pair of enantiomers are optical isomers to one another.
3 In chemistry, this situation is named a 'racemic mixture'.
4 The term was coined by the author Romain Rolland in his correspondence with Freud.
5 A concept he drew from Bick's work.
6 See Chapter 3.
7 As the Hebrew saying goes.

Bibliography

Akhtar, S. (1989). Narcissistic Personality Disorder. Descriptive Features and Differential Diagnosis. *Psychiatric Clinics of North America, 12*: 505–529.

Akhtar, S. (2000). The Shy Narcissist. In: J. Sandler, R. Michela, & P. Fonagy (Eds.), *Changing Ideas in a Changing World: The Revolution in Psychoanalysis. Essays in Honour of Arnold Cooper* (pp. 111–119). Karnac.

Bick, E. (1986). Further Considerations on the Function of the Skin in Early Object Relations: Findings from Infant Observation Integrated into Child and Adult Analysis. *British Journal of Psychotherapy, 2*: 292–299.

Bion, W. R. (1959). Attacks on Linking. *The International Journal of Psychoanalysis, 40*: 308–315.

Bollas, C. (1987). *The Shadow of the Object*. Routledge, 2018.

Britton, R. (2003). *Sex, Death, and the Superego: Updating Psychoanalytic Experience and Developments in Neuroscience* (2nd Edition). Routledge, 2021.

Britton, R. (2004a). Narcissistic Disorders in Clinical Practice. *The Journal of Analytical Psychology, 49*(4): 477–490.

Britton, R. (2004b). Subjectivity, Objectivity, and Triangular Space. *The Psychoanalytic Quarterly, 73*: 47–61.

Deutsch, H. (1942). Some Forms of Emotional Disturbance and Their Relationship to Schizophrenia. *Psychoanalytic Quarterly, 76*(2): 325–344, 2007.

Donizetti, G., & Romani, F. (1832). *L'elisir d'amore: An opera in Two Acts* [Musical score].

Fairbairn, W. R. D. (1943). The Repression and the Return of Bad Objects (with Special Reference to the 'War Neuroses'). In: *Psycho-Analytic Studies of the Personality* (pp. 59–81). Routledge & Kegan Paul, 1994.

Fairbairn, W. R. D. (1956). A Critical Evaluation of Certain Basic Psycho-Analytical Conceptions. *The British Journal for the Philosophy of Science, 7*(25): 49–60.

Forward, S., with Frazier Glynn, D. (1997). *Emotional Blackmail:* When the People in Your Life Use Fear, Obligation, and Guilt to Manipulate You. Harper, 2001.

Freud, S. (1923). The Ego and the Id. In: J. Strachey (Ed.), *The Standard Edition of the Complete Psychological Works of Sigmund Freud* Vol. 19, Hogarth Press. 1964

Freud, S. (1930). Civilization and Its Discontents. In: J. Strachey (Ed.), *The Standard Edition of the Complete Psychological Works of Sigmund Freud* (vol. 21, pp. 57–146). Hogarth Press and Institute of Psycho-Analysis, 1968.

Freud, S. (1931). Libidinal Types. In: J. Strachey (Ed.), *The Standard Edition of the Complete Psychological Works of Sigmund Freud* (vol. 21, pp. 215–220). Hogarth Press and Institute of Psycho-Analysis, 1968.

Kernberg, O. (1975). *Borderline Conditions and Pathological Narcissism.* Rowman & Littlefield Publishers, 2004.

Klein, M. (1946). Notes on Some Schizoid Mechanisms. *International Journal of Psychoanalysis, 27*: 99–110.

Kohut, H. (1971). *The Analysis of the Self.* The University of Chicago Press, 2009.

Kohut, H. (1977). *The Restoration of the Self.* The University of Chicago Press, 2009.

Kohut, H. (1984). *How Does Analysis Cure?* The University of Chicago Press.

Meltzer, D. (1966). The Relation of Anal Masturbation to Projective Identification. *The International Journal of Psychoanalysis, 47*: 335–342.

Meltzer, D. (1975). Dimensionality as a Parameter of Mental Functioning: Its Relation to Narcissistic Organization. In: D. Meltzer, J. Bremner, S. Hoxter, D. Weddell, & I. Wittenberg (Eds.), *Explorations in Autism: A Psycho-Analytical Study* (pp. 223–238). Clunie Press.

Miller, A. (1979). *The Drama of the Gifted Child: the Search for the True Self.* Translated from the German by Ruth Ward. Basic Books, 1981, pp. 73–74.

Modell, A. H. (1975). A Narcissistic Defence Against Affects and the Illusion of Self-Sufficiency. *The International Journal of Psychoanalysis, 56*: 275–282.

Rosenfeld, H. (1971). A Clinical Approach to the Psychoanalytic Theory of the Life and Death Instincts: An Investigation into the Aggressive Aspects of Narcissism. *The International Journal of Psychoanalysis, 52*: 169–178.

Segal, H. (1983). Some Clinical Implications of Melanie Klein's Work—Emergence from Narcissism. *International Journal of Psychoanalysis, 64*: 269–276.

Winnicott, D. W. (1965). Ego Distortion in terms of True and False Self (1960). In: M. Khan (Ed.), *The Maturational Processes and the Facilitating Environment: Studies in the Theory of Emotional Development* (vol. 64, pp. 140–152, 144–145). Karnac Books.

Chapter 6

The Narcissistic Perversion

Many of my patients described an experience of being violently trampled, consisting of qualities typical of rape – a sense of being penetrated accompanied by disgust, rage, and the activation of dissociative defenses. I believe this experience stems from a perverse pathology that is an inseparable part of a severe narcissistic disorder. It is not coincidental that the myth of Narcissus and the concept of narcissism first appeared in the field of psychology specifically in papers on sexual perversions (Ellis, 1898; Näcke, 1899). Seemingly subtle things may in fact be manifestations of an essentially perverse lack of separation and of the narcissist's desire to enter the object, to dwell beneath its skin, and to erase the separating boundaries that lie between them. This is an obsessive need to control the narcissist's self-parts that have been projected onto the object. A parent who reacts with exaggerated excitement to any scratch or minor bruise of the child and meticulously investigates its meaning may be dwelling in the perverse areas. A clearer case, though hidden from the child's eyes, was that of a father who described the strong impulse he felt to peep through the keyhole every time his adolescent daughter locked herself in her room with her boyfriend. One of my patients described how his mother used to grope his buttocks, seemingly in affection, until he turned 17, and the difficult feelings of revolt, rage, and helplessness it would evoke in him. The perversion is evident in Abigail,[1] who was, as was described, preoccupied with her son's male organ to the extent she burst into his room to check it. All of the parents I have described here exhibited severe narcissistic personality pathology.

The narcissistic perversion usually manifests in a non-sexual manner, which resides in the less severe side of a spectrum, whose other end includes sexual perversions proper and sexual abuse.

Paraphrasing Segal (1983), who maintained that: "Envy and narcissism are like two sides of a coin" (ibid, p. 270), I shall argue that perversion and narcissism are two sides of a coin and that the narcissistic object relations are perverse by their very nature.

Psychoanalytic thinking on perversions can be divided into two main frameworks – the first views perversions through the drive model and the second views it as a pathology of object relations with "pathological ego or self development" (Eshel, 2005, p. 1073). I shall argue that one might also divide perversions into sexual

DOI: 10.4324/9781032625393-6

perversions versus perversions of the personality. While sexual perversions appear in individuals who have a perverse personality, not everyone with a perverse personality will exhibit sexual perversions.

Individuals with pathological narcissism act with the aim of avoiding pain, depression, psychotic anxieties, and a sense of psychic death. They lack the ability to see the Other as a whole and separate subject, objectifying him and disintegrating him into parts instead. In this sense, it is not different from what occurs in sexual perversions, even if the actions are non-sexual. The perverse act seeks to overturn ('per-verte' in Latin), subvert, or negate distinctions (between generations, between individuals, between sexes, and between self and other). Furthermore, the thought process of an individual with a severe narcissistic disorder is perverse, in the sense that its (unconscious) purpose is to implant doubts and confusion in others, to compel them to act the narcissistic scenario out, and to bring about their obliteration as individuals. In this sense, it is an action rather than a thought (Racamier, 2014), a thought-action parallel to the sexual perverse action that uses the Other to fulfill the pervert's scenario.

Freud's writing on perversion was within the framework of the drive theory, but it encompassed much more than that. In it, one may find hints at the connection between perversion and object relations and between perversion and the attitude toward reality. When Freud (1914) described individuals who choose a narcissistic libidinal object, meaning an object of love in their own image, he included among them the perverts: "people whose libidinal development has suffered some disturbance, such as perverts…that in their later choice of love-objects they have taken as a model not their mother but their own selves" (p. 87). In his article on fetishism, Freud (1927) described a mechanism in which the reality (of the absence of a penis in women) is simultaneously disavowed and accepted by the child, out of fear of losing his own penis. One may apply Freud's understanding more broadly, to perverse situations, in which a similar defense of both disavowing and accepting reality occurs simultaneously.

Rosenfeld (1971) linked narcissism with perversions in the classic-sexual sense of the word, placing them in the context of the drives. He wrote:

> In many of these patients the destructive impulses are linked with perversions. In this situation the apparent fusion of the instincts [the libidinal instinct and the death instinct] does not lead to a lessening of the power of the destructive instincts; on the contrary the power and violence is greatly increased through the erotization of the aggressive instinct.
>
> (ibid, p. 174)

In Steiner's view (1993), perversion is a pathology whose manifestations are broader than sexual perversions proper and he suggests "seeing sexual perversions as a special instance of a more general perverse attitude" (p. 89). He described perversion as a state of mind of the pervert's, in which reality is simultaneously accepted and disavowed, distorted by the attempts to hold contradictory versions of it. This allows for an escape from anxiety. Steiner described psychic retreats the patient uses in order to withdraw from unbearable psychic pain. These retreats are constructed from defensive, pathological personality organizations, and from object relations that involve an exaggerated amount of projective identification. He noted that these processes play a central role in perversions and that "A perverse relation to reality is consequently a feature of most, if not all, psychic retreats" (ibid, p. 100). Among those with pathological personality organization as described by Steiner, the processes of projective identification are one-directional and parts of the self which were lost through projection into the object cannot be retrieved. This creates rigidity (both behavioral and of the personality). In such instances, the only way to maintain contact with parts of the self that were lost through projection is by an omnipotent and domineering possession of the object into which they have been projected. The anxiety evoked by contact with reality or separation from the object is annihilation anxiety, a dread of death, since the parts of the self that were projected into the object and cannot be retrieved are to be lost along with the object. It is also an anxiety of a schizo-paranoid fragmentation, meaning a fear of a psychotic disintegration.

Perversion, therefore, can be seen as a consequence of the afflicted individual's object relations. It arises from the pervert's need to control his objects in order to avoid facing a reality of psychic pain, of neediness, and of mourning and loss, which are inherent aspects of human existence. It involves weakness of the ego and the superego – weakened psychic structures that necessitate reliance on the Other in a dependent or even parasitical manner. If these characteristics strongly resonate with what was previously described about narcissism and narcissistic object relations, it is not coincidental. Steiner noted that "all pathological [personality] organizations are basically narcissistic in structure" (ibid, p. 130). He suggests the concept of "narcissistic perversion" (ibid, p. 96) as an analogous concept to 'sexual perversion'. It is a manifestation of a distortion of reality, created in order to avoid acknowledging that the source of the needed goodness lies outside of one-self and to avoid acknowledging separateness. It serves as a defensive retreat into a destructive narcissistic world where distinctions between good and bad dissolve and distinctions between sexes and generations do not exist. Several authors have described similar situations in which differences between the sexes are annulled in a perverse manner (Chasseguet-Smirgel, 1974, 1981, 1984; McDougall, 1972; Meltzer, 1966). Reality itself is a narcissistic injury.

Kohut (1972, 1977) regarded perversions as a "disease of the self" (Kohut, 1977, p. 122) and accordingly self-psychology regards perversions as reflecting a pervasive narcissistic disturbance. According to Kohut (1977), perversion is a behavioral expression which only appears to stem from a drive, while in fact the drive is mobilized in an attempt to "regain possession of the idealized omnipotent self-object... and then to internalize it" (p. 126), an attempt at healing the self. Kohut (1972, 1977) regarded perversion as a sexualization of structural defects and maintained that the unique intensity of the perverted urge is accounted for when it is fathomed as a fusion of the need to fulfill a structural defect and a pregenital drive.

Meltzer (1973) wrote of a perverse object world and regarded perversion as a kind of addictive behavior in which the narcissistic organization of the infantile structures weakens the control of the adult part of the personality over behavior. According to Meltzer, in this addictive structure, "'good' child parts...turned their dependence away from the parental figures toward the 'bad' part of the self" (p. 141). This occurs as a result of an inability to tolerate the pain inherent to the depressive position, the separation from the object, and the possessive jealousy the subject feels toward the object. Meltzer emphasized that in this way, any relationship or human activity can become perverted. He suggested using the word 'perverse' as an adjectival form related to the impulse, as in perverse sexuality, and to distinguish this use from the use of the noun 'perversion' which is to be used as a nosological term that describes an organization of behavior stemming from the narcissistic structure described. He wrote, "There is no human activity which cannot be perverted, for the essence of the perverse impulse is to alter good into bad while preserving the appearance of the good" (p. 142).

Khan (1979) wrote:

Spatially it [the pervert's object] is suspended half-way between external reality and inner psychic reality. The narcissistic magical exploitation of the object is patently visible... Anna Freud... has emphasized this crucial lack in the pervert's object-relations in terms of the incapacity to love and the dread of emotional surrender...It is my contention here that through the technique of intimacy the pervert tries to *make known* to himself and *announce* and *press into* another something pertaining to his inmost nature as well as to discharge its instinctual tension in a compulsive and exigent way.

(pp. 21–22)

Khan further wrote: "The ego of the pervert acts out his dream and involves another person in its actualization...No human being can do very much in ordinary life for a pervert because he can be...'only a sort of thing in his dream'" (ibid, p. 30). According to Khan (1979), even the physical care of the infant can be perverse when the mother's attitude is boundaryless and her touch stimulating, while she refers to the infant as her "thing-creation" (p. 12). Khan refers to this attitude as "idolization" (ibid). The child experiences objectification, which continues throughout life, alongside the mother's cathectic investment in him, leading to a dissociation in his experience of self and to an internalization of himself as someone's object. Later, during the Oedipal stage, the mother withdraws from the child, and he experiences abandonment. Khan, too, describes perversion as a defense which involves an idealized self-image aimed at preventing depression and psychotic disintegration. He wrote:

Elements of play, make believe, omnipotence and manipulation of the object are all guarantees against regression to ego-dependence or investment in true object-cathexis or surrender to emotional experience... If we examine the fantasy content and general defensive function of the technique of intimacy in terms of manic defence then we can see how it is exploited by the pervert to avert an in-trapsychic trauma or crisis by eroticized flight to reality and an external object. In this way what would have been overwhelming for the ego in terms of pas-sivity, guilt and anxiety is reversed into a predicament for the *external object*. This enables the ego to avoid abject helplessness and threat of dissolution and disintegration as well as depression... The typical anxiety affect of the pervert is the dread of ego dissolution and disintegration... In no other character disorder do we meet such a consistent idealization of the reactive defensive self-image as in the pervert.

(pp. 27–29)

A Perversion of the Personality

The non-sexual perversion is primarily discussed in the French psychoanalytic lit-erature. It is referred to as a 'perverse structure', meaning a psychodynamic struc-ture or a personality organization which are characteristic of perversion.

Even though Lacan emphasized sexuality and drive, he also saw perversion as a broader phenomenon. Swales (2012) writes: "Lacan's psychoanalytic take on what makes a pervert a pervert is not the fact of habitually engaging in specific "abnor-mal" or transgressive sexual acts, but of occupying a particular structural position in relation to the Other. Perversion is one of Lacan's three main ontological[2] diag-nostic structure, structures that indicate fundamentally different ways of solving the problems of alienation, separation from the primary caregiver and castration, or having limits set by the law on one's jouissance" (p. xii).

Chasseguet-Smirgel (1984) wrote that perversion is "a man's attempt to escape from his condition. The pervert is trying to free himself from the paternal universe and the constraints of the law. He wants to create a new kind of reality" (p. 12).

Mormont (1990) wrote:

The perverse personality is characterized by constant manipulation of others, transgression of laws and disrespect of limits. Perversity does not refer to the presence of a sexual perversion... but to a fact that the same basic principle underlies the organization of the perverse personality and of the perverse sexu-ality. Both forms could thus be understood as two different manifestations of intolerance to disappointment... To be able to discuss a perverse personality, it is necessary to admit the existence of a perverse principle, that is to say, a general 'law' capable of organizing certain aspects of psychic life and not only explaining the specific modalities of sexual behavior.... The perverse personal-ity transcends the different types (sadistic, masochistic...) in which it manifests itself... Its absence from classifications attests to the fact and reflects that many clinicians are unfamiliar with it... the means to attain enjoyment[3]... for the per-vert is the control and violence he imposes on others, with the explicitly desired object often being just a pretext.

(pp. 278–280, my translation – H.Y)

The individual with a perverse personality relishes the sense of power he obtains when he gains something or imposes his will. He seeks a sense of control, the ability to change the other and subdue him, rather than to obtain something specific which he desires. That is what, according to Mormont, differs him from the psychopath. Mormont elaborated:

> It seems that rather than the transgression of the law, it is intolerance to limitations that is essential [to motivate the pervert's actions] with the law being just a particular agent of restriction among others… The pervert always exerts a violence on the other that appears twofold: first the pervert does not allow the other the freedom to respond (refusal, compromise…); second the pervert imposes the modalities of the relationship (assigning roles necessary for the development of the perverse scenario). This violence… [is] an act that only holds value if it contradicts the other in some way and provides the opportunity to overpower him, to degrade him to the level of an object.
>
> (pp .280–281, my translation – H.Y.)

Racamier (2014) wrote:

> A particular kind of disavowal operates in the non-erotogenic manifestation of narcissistic perversion, in which the object is treated not as a person… but as a tool… narcissistic perversion is characterized for an individual by the predominant need to assert, and the pleasure of asserting, oneself at someone else's expense… As to the need underlying this perversion, its unconscious sources… are fundamentally counter-depressive and anticonflictual… *narcissistic perversion is an active system of eviction from the subject's inner life…* everything that serves the purposes of mastery is necessary to perverse narcissism…Narcissistic perverts never apologize and never say "thank you"… apology and remorse would invalidate an infallibility that must remain unassailable… gratitude would betray a dependence that is unbearable to them… these subjects impose a heavy burden on anyone who comes close to and concerns himself or herself with them. It is precisely in this respect that their narcissism touches on perversion.
>
> (pp. 119–124)

Racamier continues to discuss perverse narcissism's ways of communication, which, in his view, aim to undermine the other's ego and healthy narcissism. Thus, those are weakened while the subject's narcissism is strengthened and validated at the expanse of the object.

> We are all familiar with the techniques of subversion. They are relational techniques – nothing physical or bodily is involved in them – such as the imposition of insoluble dilemmas, either complex, such as paradoxical communications, or

relatively simple, such as active dismissal of the value and relevance of other people's thoughts and perceptions.

(ibid, p. 126)

Racamier gives an example of a joke about a man whose mother buys him two ties. He wears one, and she complains that he doesn't like the other. He wears the other, and she complains that he doesn't like the first one. He wears them both together, and she complains that he has lost his mind. Children of pathologically narcissistic parents regularly find themselves navigating through impossible conflicts like the one presented here. Racamier continues:

> The object of a narcissistic pervert will be disavowed not in its existence, but in its importance; it is admittedly bearable only if it is dominated, ill-treated, and sadistically attacked – and above all mastered. In a word, it is an object whose narcissistic autonomy is actively denied... The preferred medium and principal instrument of narcissistic perversion... is language.

(ibid, p. 127)

According to Racamier, perverse thinking is the opposite of psychoanalytic thinking:

> Perverse thought, for its part, seeks only to envelop and enclose, to confuse and seize its prey in a tightly drawn net of countertruths and unsaid propositions, allusions, and lies, insinuations and calumnies. It is a thought intended to intrude into the concerns of others, a poisonous thought, a thought that aims to dementalize, devalue and subvert the other – a thought made up entirely of action and manipulation, which fragments, divides and disorientate. Perverse thought... is in fact merely a disguised form of action.

(pp. 130–131)

McDougall (1995) views sexual symptoms as an infantile solution to conflicts and psychic pain which are related to object relations, similar to any mental symptom that is non-sexual. She writes:

> Perhaps in the last resort, only *relationships* can aptly be termed *perverse*; this label would then apply to sexual exchanges in which the perverse individual is totally indifferent of the needs and desires of the other... I propose that individuals who, in the service of libidinal and narcissistic homeostasis, create a neoreality and neoneeds in terms of sexual acts and objects, have short-circuited the elaboration of phallic-oedipal castration anxiety. At the same time, by disavowing the problems of separateness and infantile sadism, they have also circumvented what Melanie Klein termed the "elaboration of the depressive position".

(pp. 178–182)

Other authors have written that perversion is related to an objectifying misuse of the other and is a part of characteristic narcissistic defenses.

Filippini (2005) speaks of a 'relational perversion', which she also refers to as narcissistic perversion. It is a perversion that manifests in relationships and stems from the pathology in object relations characteristic of narcissism. The relationship becomes a system of power relations and control, and the offender does not recognize the rights and separateness of the other and uses the other for his own needs. Regarding psychological maltreatment, she writes, "What is happening is mainly an attempt to control the object through denigration, devaluation, reproach and sarcasm" (ibid, p. 760). She views perversion as a personality trait. She adds that the influences of the (relational) perversion are "truly *specific* and are the brand which perversion burns into the victim's existence" (ibid, p. 770). She concludes that further research is needed to understand "the way in which perversion penetrates and erodes the personality of its object" (ibid).

Coen (1992) wrote about perversion in the sense of misusing another. In his description, perversion is a defensive structure resistant to change and a kind of pathological dependence that involves exploiting the other to avoid internal conflict. The other in the perverse relationship undergoes dehumanization and is degraded into object-parts and serves as a container for the pervert's projective identification, with the goal being an omnipotent control over the other while denying separateness. Coen states that such relationships are perverse regardless of the presence or absence of a sexual aspect in them.

Sadism and Masochism in Narcissistic Perversion

Kernberg (2009) distinguishes perversity from sexual perversion.[4] According to Kernberg

> Perversity involves the recruitment of love at the service of aggression, the effort to seduce another person toward love or helpfulness as a trap that will end with the destruction, symbolic or real, in a social and sometimes even in a physical sense of the person so seduced.
>
> (p. 1014)

Kernberg explains that perversity may manifest as mild forms of sadomasochism. He notes that such forms of sadomasochism can be observed in patients who experience unconscious guilt that leads them to destroy what they receive. He believes that the underlying reason for this unconscious guilt is rooted in forbidden oedipal urges or unconscious aggression toward an early object toward whom they directed their dependency needs. Elsewhere, Kernberg (2004) discusses the more severely pathological level of perversion, which according to him appears in two major personality organizations – narcissistic and borderline. He mentions sadistic and masochistic features that, in the case of the 'ordinary borderline personality organization', appear both in the personality structure and in the sexual behavior. In the case of 'narcissistic personality structure', there is a fusion of aggressive drive aspects of the oedipal and pre-oedipal conflict that become condensed and infiltrate the 'perverse scenario'. He wrote:

> In the case of the syndrome of malignant narcissism,[5] the aggressive drive derivatives are integrated into the grandiose pathological self with consequent dangerous sadistic deterioration of the perversion. In the psychoanalytic literature concerning perversion, narcissistic features have been suggested as a general characteristic... Their anal-sadistic regression involves an attack on and destruction of object relations, while the oral regression is reflected in their oral-sadistic expression of envy and destructive greed... Because the syndrome of perversity appears with particular frequency in patients with severe narcissistic personality structure who, at the same time, may present a sexual perversion in a narrow sense, both syndromes may go together.
>
> (pp. 80–83)

De Masi (1999) argued that the primary goal of the pervert individual is to control the object, and that in order to understand the pathogenesis of sadomasochistic perversion, it is preferable to examine manifestations of aggression in the relationship rather than manifestations of sexuality.

McDougall (1995) discussed the mother who regards her child as a narcissistic libidinal extension of herself, as a means to repair a sense of internal damage in her internal world. The mother prevents the child from developing and solidifying a separate identity. The child, on his part, learns to link the aggressive actions with expressions of love and relationship with the object and thus develops a yearning to give himself to the object. This accounts for the masochistic component in the relationship with the parent, as well as in future relationships of such a child. As a defense mechanism, the child reacts by splitting the negative aspects of the object and internalizing them whilst turning a masochistic aggression against himself (and against his internalized bad object).

A vicious cycle is formed. The more the child succumbs to the parent (allowing a domineering intrusion into his psyche and even into his bodily autonomy), the more he receives closeness and gratification of infantile needs from the parent. Refusal of the parent's will and resistance to his actions, perverted as they may be, will lead to reactions ranging from inducing guilt for 'hurting' the parent, whose request is presented as legitimate, to psychological violence – the parent lashes out at the child for daring to behave this way, punishes him with silence or withdrawal of affection, and so on. In this process, aggressive parts of the parent are projected onto the child, eliciting a paranoid reaction from the parent, who then attacks those parts. In such cases, "What Freud describes under the category of 'death instincts' would thus appear to represent for the most part masochistic relationships with internalized bad objects" (Fairbairn, 1943, p. 79).

The manifestation of perversion in narcissistic relationships in general, and in the relationship between the pathologically narcissistic parent and his child in particular, is essentially sadomasochistic. In the parent, the sadistic side stands out, characterized by "The desire to control the object, the sadistic gratification of overcoming and humiliating it, of getting the better of it, the *triumph* over it" (Klein, 1940, p. 133). In the child, a complementary perverse and primarily masochistic image may develop. The child receives reinforcement and gratification of emotional needs when allowing the parent to treat him as an object, therefore for him the experience of a relationship involves being used. Additionally, as Kernberg (2009) described, there is an unconscious need for punishment for the aggression that arises in the child toward the object-parent as a result of the frustration of his needs. Steiner (1993) described a similar cause for masochism and wrote about patients who use self-punishment as a way to avoid perceiving the damaged state of their internal objects, which were attacked and destroyed in phantasy. Suffering serves as a kind of expiation for harming the object, but it prevents the reparation and restoration of the attacked objects. Self-punishment is but another attack on the objects that triggers additional guilt.

Kohut (1977) wrote: "The masochist attempts to fill in the defect in the part of the self that should provide him with enriching ideals through a sexualized merger with the rejecting (punishing, demeaning, belittling) features of the omnipotent parental imago" (p. 127).

In Kohut's story, 'The Two Analysis of Mr. Z', one may find the story of a narcissistic and perverse abuse of a child who was caught in "his enmeshment with the pathological personality of the mother" (ibid, p. 12) and who himself developed a narcissistic and perverse pathology. Upon changing the theoretical perspective, during the second analysis, Kohut began to realize that Mr. Z's self was "desperately—and often hopelessly—struggling to disentangle itself from the noxious selfobject, to delimit itself, to grow, to become independent" (ibid). Mr. Z's mother controlled her only son and his father with an iron fist.

The image which she portrayed successfully to people outside the family [was completely different from the one known to] those intimately involved with her... even though they were not able to raise this knowledge to a level of awareness which would have allowed them to share it with each other. They knew that the mother held... attitudes and actions which emotionally enslaved those around her and stifled their independent existence... the mother's emotional gifts were bestowed on him under the unalterable and uncompromising condition that he submit to total domination by her, that he must not allow himself any independence, particularly as concerned significant relationships with others... she had by no means been in empathic contact with the needs of his self... she had always taken totally for granted that... their relationship would never be altered, he would never leave her... [She had a] need to retain her son as a permanent selfobject.

(ibid, pp. 13–14)

The mother manifested a perverse behavior which included inspecting Mr. Z's feces until he was six years old and ceremoniously inspecting 'blemishes' in his skin.

She was not interested in *him*. Only his faeces and her inspection of them, only his bowel functions and her control over them fascinated her—with an intensity, a self-righteous certainty... that allowed no protest and created almost total submission.

(ibid, p. 15)

Mr. Z. reacted with depression, had difficulties forming romantic relationships, portrayed somatic symptoms, and developed a masochistic sexual perversion which manifested as masturbatory fantasies in which he would serve domineering women and be humiliated by them and in which he was "like an object that had no initiative, no will of its own" (ibid, p. 6).

Eshel (2005) describes a patient with a severe masochistic perversion which endangered his life. She views perversion "*as a defence organisation—through splitting, externalisation and compulsive sexualisation—against a violent, devastating, unbearable, deadening early past situation*" (ibid, p. 1080). According to Eshel, at the basis of the perversion is the child's desperate attempt

to overcome the intrusion of brutal situations, of unbearable psychic or psycho-physical violence and abuse, which could be neither endured nor escaped... since the significant other on whom it depends introduces terror or reacts to him with indifferent, sadistic imperviousness.

(ibid, p. 1078)

Eshel likens the perversion to the biological mechanism of autotomy, which is the ability of an organism, such as the gecko to sacrifice the wholeness of its body in order to survive. She describes the perverse solution thus:

Not all of me shall die!... massive dissociative splitting into two disconnected parts, alien to each other, as a means of psychic survival. One part continues functioning in the world, surviving by inertia, emotionally impaired, lacking and dull, lifeless and alienated from the inner core of its experiences. At times, it seems as if only a husk remains... The other part—the self that was offered to be devoured—is stuck in that devouring state, suicidally attracted to whatever wounds and preys, to whatever embodies and actualizes... the dark violence, the devastation, devourment, sadism and imperviousness, both within the psyche and in self–other relations.

(ibid)

Notes

1 See Chapter 3.
2 Lacan's view of human suffering is ontological, meaning it pertains to the nature and existence of human beings in relation to language, the world, and jouissance (enjoyment). Lacan delineates three main ontological diagnoses that represent subjective ontological positions in relation to the symbolic Other – neurosis, perversion, and psychosis.
3 Jouissance.
4 Kernberg reserves the term perversion for the strict psychiatric definition of the sexual perversion, meaning a significant restriction of sexual behavior to a specific, atypical pattern or interest that becomes a condition for sexual excitement and climax.
5 A type of narcissistic personality disorder accompanied by a severe pathology of the superego, antisocial behavior, prominent ego-syntonic aggressiveness, and paranoid tendencies. Kernberg views malignant narcissism as an intermediate syndrome between the narcissistic personality disorder and the antisocial personality disorder (Kernberg, 2004).

Bibliography

Chasseguet-Smirgel, J. (1974). Perversion, Idealization and Sublimation. *The International Journal of Psychoanalysis, 55*: 349–357.
Chasseguet-Smirgel, J. (1981). Loss of Reality in Perversions-With Special Reference to Fetishism. *Journal of the American Psychoanalytic Association, 29*: 511–534.
Chasseguet-Smirgel, J. (1984). *Creativity and Perversion*. W. W. Norton & Company.
Coen, S. J. (1992). *The Misuse of Persons: Analyzing Pathological Dependency.* The Analytic Press.
De masi, F. (1999). *The Sadomasochistic Perversion: The Entity and the Theories*. Karnac Books, 2003.
Ellis, H. (1898). Auto-Erotism: A Psychological Study. *Alienist and Neurologist, 19*: 260–299.
Eshel, O. (2005). Pentheus Rather Than Oedipus: On Perversion, Survival and Analytic 'Presencing'. *The International Journal of Psychoanalysis, 86*: 1071–1097.
Fairbairn, W. R. D. (1943). The Repression and the Return of Bad Objects (with Special Reference to the 'War Neuroses'). In: *Psycho-Analytic Studies of the Personality* (pp. 59–81). Routledge & Kegan Paul, 1994.
Filippini, S. (2005). Perverse Relationships: The Perspective of the Perpetrator. *The International Journal of Psychoanalysis, 86*(3): 755–773.
Freud, S. (1914). On Narcissism: An Introduction. In: J. Strachey (Ed.), *The Standard Edition of the Complete Psychological Works of Sigmund Freud* (vol. 14, pp. 67–102). The Hogarth Press, 1957.
Freud, S. (1927). Fetishism. In: J. Strachey (Ed.), *The Standard Edition of the Complete Psychological Works of Sigmund Freud* (vol. 21, pp. 147–158). Hogarth Press and Institute of Psycho-Analysis, 1968.
Kernberg, O. F. (2004). *Aggressivity, Narcissism, and Self-Destructiveness in the Psychotherapeutic Relationship: New Developments in the Psychopathology and Psychotherapy of Severe Personality Disorders*. Yale University Press.
Kernberg, O. F. (2009). The Concept of the Death Drive: A Clinical Prespective. *International Journal of Psychoanalysis, 90*: 1009–1023.
Khan, M. M. R. (1979). *Alienation in Perversions*. Routledge, 2018.
Klein, M. (1940). Mourning and Its Relation to Manic-Depressive States. *International Journal of Psychoanalysis, 21*: 125–153.

Kohut, H. (1972). Lecture 1 (January 7 1972): Perversions. In: P. Tolpin & M. Tolpin (Eds.), *The Chicago Institute Lectures* (pp. 1–11). The Analytic Press, 1996.

Kohut, H. (1977). *The Restoration of the Self.* The University of Chicago Press, 2009.

Kohut, H. (1979). The Two Analyses of Mr Z. *The International Journal of Psychoanalysis, 60*: 3–27.

McDougall, J. (1972). Primal Scene and Sexual Perversion. *International Journal of Psychoanalysis, 53*: 371–384.

McDougall, J. (1995). *The Many Faces of Eros: A Psychoanalytic Exploration of Human Sexuality.* Free Association Books.

Meltzer, D. (1966). The Relation of Anal Masturbation to Projective Identification. *The International Journal of Psychoanalysis, 47*: 335–342.

Meltzer, D. (1973). *Sexual States of Mind.* The Harris Meltzer Trust, 2018.

Mormont, C. (1990). Le Personnalité Perverse. *Acta Psychiatrica Belgica, 90*: 278–288.

Näcke, P. (1899). Die Sexuellen Perversitaten in der Irrenenstalt. *Psychiatriche en Neurologische Bladen, 3*: 122–149.

Racamier, P. C. (2014). On Narcissistic Perversion. *The International Journal of Psychoanalysis, 95*(1): 119–132.

Rosenfeld, H. (1971). A Clinical Approach to the Psychoanalytic Theory of the Life and Death Instincts: An Investigation into the Aggressive Aspects of Narcissim. *The International Journal of Psychoanalysis, 52*: 169–178.

Segal, H. (1983). Some Clinical Implications of Melanie Klein's Work—Emergence from Narcissism. *International Journal of Psychoanalysis, 64*: 269–276.

Steiner, J. (1993). *Psychic Retreats: Pathological Organizations in Psychotic, Neurotic and Borderline Patients.* Routledge.

Swales, S. (2012). *Perversion: A Lacanian Psychoanalytic Approach to the Subject.* Routledge/Taylor & Francis Group.

Chapter 7

Clinical Implications

The alternative to the narcissistic-perverse enmeshment is, in many cases, experiencing psychic death. Without the unraveling of the pathological enmeshment there is no life, whereas its unraveling may lead to death. This is why in treatment, a profound and stubborn resistance is common, since 'to see', to acknowledge reality, carries the loss of the object, disintegration, and death. "I wish him absent whom I most desire" (Ovid, 8 AD, 3:584). Woe to the lover who desires for his beloved to abandon him!

Likewise in Ovid's masterpiece, the acknowledgment of reality led to death, and he weaves this equation at the beginning of the story and at its end. At the beginning, when Narcissus's mother inquires with a sage whether her child should reach old age, the sage replies: "If e'er he knows himself he surely dies" (Ovid, 8 AD, 3:455). At the end of the story, just before his death, Narcissus realizes that the image he is in love with is his own reflection. Even in death, Narcissus's ordeal does not end: "To the cold shades his flitting ghost retires/And in the Stygian[1] waves it self admires" (Ovid, 8 AD, 3:623–624). A prolonged process of mourning, an emotional purgatorial hell, is required so that at its end a flower may bloom in the swamp of death.

Ogden (1989) wrote: "Not knowing deprives us of our sense of who we are, and yet to know is to see that which we cannot bear to see" (p. 3). Treating the wounds caused by narcissistic parenting requires descending into the abyss' depth, facing things that cannot be borne, and coping with the patient's intense resistance on his way to discovering who he is. "For in much wisdom is much grief: and he that increaseth knowledge increaseth sorrow" (Ecclesiastes 1:18).

The patient, if he increases knowledge, will resemble that animated cartoon that begins to plummet only once it looks down and realizes it is walking on thin air. He will no longer be able to hold onto old defenses, to blindness, but will plunge and break up into fragments before being able to be rebuilt. In my view, this is the cause of the resistance that such patients manifest in therapy, while they continue to present themselves and their therapist with the illusory life-scenario written by their parents, which they have internalized.

The abyss into which the 'cartoon'-patient plummets is the absence of representations of good internal objects to rely on in difficult moments. Thus, the ground gives way beneath the feet and disintegration occurs.

DOI: 10.4324/9781032625393-7

This is the 'fear of breakdown',[2] as Winnicott (1974) described it in an article by that name, "A failure of a defence organization... a breakdown of the establishment of the unit self.... it is the ego organization that is threatened" (p. 103). Winnicott described a fear of various types of anxieties that he termed 'primitive agonies', explaining that "anxiety is not a strong enough word here" (p. 104). Among these agonies, he listed a return to an unintegrated state, falling forever, loss of a sense of real and more. According to Winnicott, this breakdown has happened in the past – it is the failure of the parents' 'holding' of the child and serving as a facilitating environment, but it has happened at a time when the child was too immature to experience it, and therefore he must experience it at the present. Kolker (2009) wrote:

> The pursuit of breakdown is not only the psych's path to healing; it is also its path to itself. The gravitation toward breakdown is also the strength of the core of the self, because precisely in midst of his breakdown, in a brief moment of the implementation of being, despite endless pain, the individual feels that he is himself.
>
> (p. 291, my translation - H.Y.)

During the breakdown phase, the patient may experience profound depression, severe panic attacks, and an overall exacerbation of his clinical symptomatology, whatever it may be. And yet, only then can the truth, precious and healing, be found. As Victor Hugo wrote: "Diamonds are found only in the dark depth of the earth; truths are found only in the depths of thought" (Les Miserables, 1862, Première partie, p. 573. my translation – H.Y.).

Healing from these abysses involves decathexis of the libido from the internalized bad parental objects. Fairbairn (1943), who wrote that the child is possessed by his internalized bad objects, added:

> There is now little doubt in my mind that the release of bad objects from the unconscious is one of the chief aims which the psychotherapist should set himself out to achieve... the psychotherapist is the true successor to the exorcist.
>
> (pp. 69–70)

Fairbairn also notes that the libidinal aim is contradictory to the therapeutic aim. The libido 'refuses' to renounce its repressed object. Fairbairn found that this process leads to an "extreme stubbornness of resistance" (p. 73). He points out that it is common for patients to talk about death when their defense weakens and they face such a release of the bad object from the unconscious. He emphasizes that it should be remembered that from the patient's perspective, preserving the resistance is experienced literally as a matter of life and death.

Steiner (1993) also describes the patient's struggle:

He has to let go of an object upon whom he continues to believe his survival depends. At this primitive level separation is indistinguishable from death, and if the object is to die and if it contains too much of the self which has been split off and projected into it, then the patient is afraid of losing himself in the process... The situation seems to him to be unfair because he cannot take back the projections unless he can mourn, and he cannot let the object die and mourn it without taking back the projections.

(p. 63)

Steiner views mourning as a precondition to healing:

In order to regain parts of the self lost through projective identification it is necessary to relinquish the object and mourn it. It is in the process of mourning that projective identification is reversed and the ego is enriched and integrated.

(ibid, p. 59)

Steiner proposed a different perspective on the gradual processes of libidinal decathexis from the lost object that Freud described in 'Mourning and Melancholia' (1917), writing:

Today, as we recognize the central role of projective identification in the creation of pathological object relations, we can review Freud's formulation while thinking more in terms of detachments of parts of the self from the object rather than in terms of detachment of libido. It then becomes clear that, as reality is applied to each of the memories of the lost object, what has to be faced is the painful recognition of what belongs to the object and what belongs to the self. It is through the detailed work of mourning that these differentiations are made, and in the process the lost object is seen more realistically and the previously disowned parts of the self are gradually acknowledged as belonging to the self.

(Steiner, 1993, p. 61)

The resistance to therapy will be manifested both by the patient and the parent. When the child of a pathologically narcissistic parent begins a healing process, one might anticipate an exacerbation of the parent's behavior. The parent experiences the healthy psychological changes in the child, which include separateness, as a loss of control over the child, and reacts with rage, panic, and dread. It is common for the parent to try to tighten his grip over the child by intensifying the abusive behavior, often resulting in a deterioration of the child's mental state, as the toxic behavior of the parent makes him increasingly sick. Sometimes, the patient's intensifying pain may lead to a discontinuation of the therapy and a return to the familiar status quo in which defenses that numb the pain are utilized. Additionally, the parent may respond with efforts to bring about the discontinuation of the therapy.

Another factor which fortifies the defenses is the unconscious notion that separation from the object-parent would bring about the parent's death. Modell (1965) wrote:

> I would like to suggest that the belief that one does not have the right to a life is a derivative of what I would like to call separation guilt. For the right to a life really means the right to a separate existence... [For those individuals with separation guilt] separation is unconsciously perceived as resulting in the death of the object.
>
> (p. 328)

Surely everyone is familiar with that parent who guilt trips his child – 'you're killing me'? The fact that a detachment of the libido from the object, or a detachment of parts of the self according to Steiner (1993), is necessary in order to heal, means that indeed "The object has not perhaps actually died, but has been lost as an object of love" (Freud, 1917, p. 245).

An extraction of the internalized bad object from the patient's psychic structure is required according to Britton (2003) as well. He wrote that removing the bad object from its position of power and authority leads to the ego's emancipation from the superego. Britton uses the story of Job to illustrate the process of freeing the patient's ego from an internalized bad object that has become a persecutory superego. Although Job refuses to renounce God, he questions his motives, becomes separate, and challenges him:

> Is it good unto thee that thou shouldest oppress,
> that thou shouldest despise the work of thine hands,
> and shine upon the counsel of the wicked?
> Hast thou eyes of flesh? or seest thou as man seeth?
> Are thy days as the days of man? are thy years as man's days,
> That thou enquirest after mine iniquity, and searchest after my sin?
> Thou knowest that I am not wicked;
> and there is none that can deliver out of thine hand.
>
> (Job, Ch. 10, vs.3–7)

Britton interprets:

> Taking Job to be the ego and God to be the superego in this story, it represents a crucial moment in development when the ego takes the superego to task and, whilst still afraid of its power claims, the right to question its judgement and to doubt its motives. This is I think also a crucial moment in some analyses when the individual can question the authenticity of the inner voice of adverse judgement.
>
> (pp. 80–81)

In my view, the process described by Britton represents an especially crucial therapeutic stage for the echoist.

Hence, the healing process goes through breakdown and mourning, and a depressive reaction is prevalent at this stage. The required mourning is not over what was and is there no longer (a good object that will remain internalized), but rather over what never was and what can never be. For this reason, the depression can be particularly severe and it constitutes a bewildering experience, unrelated to the present-day reality of the patient's life. "This would suggest that melancholia is in some way related to an object-loss which is withdrawn from consciousness, in contradistinction to mourning, in which there is nothing about the loss that is unconscious" (Freud, 1917, p. 245). The patient must be able to 'throw up' the injured and injurious parts of the parent from within himself, remaining, for a substantial soul-tormenting period of time, with painful voids inside, with an inner world depleting of objects and with psychic death. Eigen (1999) depicted how avoiding the consumption of the toxic nourishment is starvation. I believe that in the case of severe parental narcissistic pathology, the patient must endure the hunger in order to heal. In the words of Victor Hugo (1862): "Saving yourself through what is destroying you is the masterpiece of great men" (Les Miseerables, Quatrième partie, p. 683, my translation from French – H.Y). The patient must recognize the extent of the parent's pathology and the reality of object loss, realize the repetition compulsion in the relationship and let go. Miller viewed this repetition compulsion of patients as "the only manifestation of their true self" (Miller, 1979, p. 79), as it expresses the unfulfilled authentic infantile wishes and needs. A paradox emerges here. The patient must renounce the only way he knows to express his true self in order to be able to truly express it. In the jargon, recognition of this pattern and relinquishment of the repetition compulsion is termed 'radical acceptance'. This concept was originally coined by Marsha Linehan (1993) and serves as a tool in the Dialectical Behavioral Therapy (DBT) method she developed. It means "letting go of a fight with reality" (p. 417) and "to radically accept that which cannot be changed" (Lynch, Trost, Salsman, Linehan, 2007, p. 185). The goal is not to give up on change but rather to open up the opportunity to of seek it out of a profound recognition of reality. According to Linehan (1993), "Acceptance of reality… is the only way out of hell" (p. 420). She wrote the following:

> The bottom line is that if you are in hell, the only way out is to go through a period of sustained misery. Misery is, of course, much better than hell, but it is painful nonetheless. By refusing to accept the misery that it takes to climb out of hell, you end up falling back into hell repeatedly, only to have to start over and over again.
>
> (ibid, p. 461)

Winnicott (1974) described a similar situation in 'Fear of Breakdown': "but alas, there is no end unless the bottom of the trough has been reached, unless *the thing feared has been experienced*" (p. 104).

When implementing the concept of radical acceptance in the realm of narcissistic parenthood, the implication is recognizing that we cannot change the parent or his behavior; that a significant process of mourning it took place, and that out of this process of disillusionment, a change in the patient's response pattern becomes possible. Such a change holds the power to minimize the parent's ability to injure and hurt. If the patient ceases to repeatedly approach the empty trough in hopes of quenching his thirst, the shattering disappointment is diminished, and it becomes possible to allocate resources to seek another water source. Additionally, this involves the patient 'radically accepting' himself, meaning the ability to accept oneself as imperfect. This allows for self-compassion as well as compassion for others, opening up opportunities for the patient to create relationships based on perceiving the other as a separate subject rather than a persecutory object. While Linehan perceives radical acceptance as a cognitive-behavioral tool for emotional regulation that enables the patient to better tolerate difficult situations, I have observed that this acceptance naturally occurs in analytically oriented therapy as well, once therapy succeeds in promoting growth and profound change. I believe this process is the only way to break free from the grasp of the conflictual relationship with the parent.

Ruth described the process as follows: "There was no arguing with Mom and there was no compromising. She would simply start yelling right away and could keep yelling for hours, and she always knew how to yell louder than anyone else. She exerted as much force as necessary to make me do her bidding. It had to be just the way she wanted it to be. When I was a little girl, she forced me to apologize to the neighbors' daughter, who had actually wronged me. I stood by their front door for a whole hour. A whole hour of torment. Eventually, my fear of Mom overcame and I apologized. Once, she did something and suddenly I could take it no longer. I refused. She did not speak to me for months. I have to admit that during those months, my mental state improved significantly, just like it always did whenever I traveled abroad and distanced myself from her. Whenever I didn't give in to her, I had to apologize in the end. It never ended differently. If I did not do it immediately, my father and my sister would talk to me, begging for me to understand her, to pity her and to reconcile. This time, I couldn't ask for forgiveness. Eventually, we met at a family event and started talking again, but things were never the same. I understood that I must not tell her anything. She used everything I shared with her, either against me or to further interfere with my business. Conversations with her turned into 'How are you? What's up?' and she blamed me for being cold and alienated, but suddenly I was able to breathe a little.

Ruth describes two common processes which earned their own term in the jargon. The first is the act of 'going no contact'. It is a tragic solution and perhaps in the most severe cases it might be the child's only way of saving himself. Dr. Ramani

Durvasula, an American psychologist whose field of research is narcissism and narcissistic abuse, likened the damage caused by the behavior and words of the narcissist to the secondhand smoking of the mental health field (Durvasula, 2021). Sometimes, the child has to distance himself in order to cease passively inhaling the smoke emanating from the parent's mental disorder, which renders him ill. The second process Ruth describes is the option less extreme than severing ties – an emotional detachment known as 'gray rock'. The term was coined by an anonymous blogger named Skylar in 2012, following a painful romantic relationship with someone she defined as a narcissist (Skylar, 2012). The term has since been used in the context of all kinds of narcissistic relationships. The intention behind 'gray rock' is to become something which does not attract the narcissist's attention, just as a gray rock on the side of the road draws no attention, thus making the narcissist let go of his object, which no longer provides him with narcissistic supply. The process requires not sharing emotionally significant matters, not being activated by the narcissist-parent's blaming, and not engaging in the struggle that he creates by providing justifications and apologies. An emancipation from guilt is required, by understanding that the parent's dynamics are automatic and do not reflect a personal fault. The relationship is preserved, albeit at a high, unavoidable cost. What relationship remains is superficial, devoid of true intimacy, but the child is liberated from the controlling strings. Durvasula (DoctorRamani, 2021) proposed a parallel concept to that of the gray rock, 'Firewall', an imagery from the digital realm. She introduced this concept, which was suggested to her by an anonymous source, on her popular YouTube channel. It means to prevent the narcissist from gaining an entry which might wreak havoc in the internal world and cause devastation just like a computer virus does.

I believe that the concepts presented express processes that can be understood psychoanalytically and summarized thus: In order to heal, the child is required to halt the processes of projective identification. In this sense, the establishment of a 'firewall' between him and the parent is an extremely appropriate analogy.

In order to fill the void left by throwing up parts of the internalized parental object, the patient will need to internalize a good object in its place. Opposing the resistance is a powerful force which draws the patient to therapy – validation. A validation of his experiences, his essence, his rights, his existence. All of these, the therapist is required to provide him with.

Fairbairn (1943) wrote: "The bad objects can only be safely released…if the analyst has become established as a sufficiently good object for the patient" (p. 70). This constitutes a process that often triggers a serious regression to dependence and is excruciating for the patient and demanding for the therapist. Winnicott (1960/1965) wrote about this, stating that "At the point of transition, when the analyst begins to get into contact with the patient's True Self, there must be a period of extreme dependence" (p. 151). Even with the introjection of the therapist as a good object, the process cannot unfold without the patient experiencing the voids and the depths of agony on his journey toward healing. Additionally, I believe that an introjection of the therapist solely as a good object will not free the patient from a split in which there exists another, brimming with goodness which he, the defective, is in need of. The therapist has to allow himself to also be the bad object. This complex introjection of an object with both positive and negative parts is important so that the patient can bear his own negative parts and unify positive and negative self-representations. This is a treatment of opposites and polarities, a treatment that requires a theoretical 'confusion of tongues' and an almost paradoxical combination of coming in contact with aggression and dark urges (in the parent, in the patient, in the transference, and in the countertransference) along with validation, tenderness, and containment. How can the therapist be a good object and also, to the extent necessary, a bad object? In Kohutian terms – I believe that in therapy, small, gradual failures should (and would naturally) occur, adapted as much as possible to the patient's capacity to bear them, enabling him to gradually develop modulating and soothing psychic structures, and to be less in need of a selfobject. Healing will occur with the therapist's introjection in a manner that would ultimately allow the patient to fulfill parental functions for himself. In the jargon, this is termed 'parenting oneself'. The concept is paradoxical, but the implication is to arrive at a state where the patient has introjected functions capable of calming, of holding faith that there is good in him and in the world, of allowing for mistakes, of loving himself and forgiving himself for his flaws and weaknesses, and of releasing himself from guilt in order to grow out of the swamp and flourish. When meaningful healing occurs, in some cases compassion and renewed love can also be found toward the real parent.

As for our role as therapists to these children – I find it appropriate to quote Racamier (2014):

> The full power of the perverse severance of links becomes manifest when… in the psyche of an individual who has since childhood suffered the silent, secret torments of the perversity of those around him… we, the menders and patchers of psychic life, seek to re-attach the broken links and repair the fabric of scattered, disjoined truths, gauging in the process the immensity of the task… For there are two bedrocks on which the psyche is built. Freud was familiar with them both. He often invoked one of them – namely, that of biology. His concern for the other – the bedrock of truth – was unrelenting.
>
> (pp. 131–132)

Notes

1 In Greek mythology, Styx is the river dividing the world of the living from the underworld.
2 Winnicott's last paper, which was published posthumously and is estimated to have been written in 1963.

Bibliography

Britton, R. (2003). *Sex, Death, and the Superego: Updating Psychoanalytic Experience and Developments in Neuroscience* (2nd Edition). Routledge, 2021.

Durvasula, R. S. (2021). *"Don't You Know Who I Am?": How to Stay Sane in an Era of Narcissism, Entitlement, and Incivility*. Post Hill Press.

Durvasula, R. S. [DrRamani]. (2021, July 14). *How to "Firewall" the Narcissist*. [video]. YouTube. https://www.youtube.com/watch?v=49HGOGy8lzw&t=336s

Eigen, M. (1999). *Toxic Nourishment*. Routledge, 2018.

Fairbairn, W. R. D. (1943). The Repression and the Return of Bad Objects (with Special Reference to the 'War Neuroses'). In: *Psycho-Analytic Studies of the Personality* (pp. 59–81). Routledge & Kegan Paul, 1994.

Freud, S. (1917). Mourning and Melancholia. In: J. Strachey (Ed.), *The Standard Edition of the Complete Psychological Works of Sigmund Freud* (vol. 14, 237–258), Hogarth Press, and the institute of Psycho-Analysis, 1957

Hugo, V. (1862). Les Miserables, Première partie. La Bibliothèque électronique du Québec. https://beq.ebooksgratuits.com/vents/Hugo-miserables-1.pdf

Hugo, V. (1862). Les Miserables, Quatrième partie. La Bibliothèque électronique du Québec. https://beq.ebooksgratuits.com/vents/Hugo-miserables-4.pdf

Kolker, S. (2009). Preface to D.W. Winnicott's 'Fear of Breakdown'. In: E. Berman (Ed.), *True Self, False Self: Essays, 1935–1963* (pp. 199–200). Am Oved Publishers, 2016 (In Hebrew).

Linehan, M. M. (1993). *DBT Skills Training Manual* (2nd Edition). The Guilford Press, 2015.

Lynch, T. R., Trost, N. S., Salsman, N., & Linehan, M. M. (2007). Dialectical Behavior Therapy for Borderline Personality Disorder. *Annual Review of Clinical Psychology, 3*: 181–205.

Miller, A. (1979). *The Drama of the Gifted Child, the Search for the True Self*. Translated from the German by Ruth Ward. Basic Books, 1981.

Modell, A. H. (1965). On Having the Right to a Life: An Aspect of the Superego's Development. *The International Journal of Psychoanalysis, 46*(3): 323–331.

Ogden, T. H. (1989). *The Primitive Edge of Experience*. Jason Aronson, 1989.

Ovid, P. N. (8 AD). *Metamorphoses* (Translators: Sir Samuel Garth, John Dryden, Alexander Pope, Joseph Addison, William Congreve). Passerino, 2017.

Racamier, P. C. (2014). On Narcissistic Perversion. *The International Journal of Psychoanalysis, 95*(1): 119–132.

Skylar. (2012). The Gray Rock Method of Dealing with Psychopaths. *Love fraud.com*. https://lovefraud.com/the-gray-rock-method-of-dealing-with-psychopaths/

Steiner, J. (1993). *Psychic Retreats: Pathological Organizations in Psychotic, Neurotic and Borderline Patients*. Routledge.

The Bible (2017). 21st Century King James Version. Cambridge University Press. (Original work published 1769)

Winnicott, D. W. (1965). Ego Distortion in Terms of True and False Self (1960). In: M. Khan (Ed.), *The Maturational Processes and the Facilitating Environment: Studies in the Theory of Emotional Development* (vol. 64, pp. 140–152). Karnac Books.

Winnicott, D. W. (1974). Fear of Breakdown. *International Review of Psychoanalysis, 1*: 103–107.

Chapter 8

Feeling Like a Vermin and Dying Like a Dog

The Kafkaesque World and the Life of Kafka in Light of His Relationship with His Father

Franz Kafka's book, *The Metamorphosis*, begins thus: "When Gregor Samsa awoke from troubled dreams one morning, he found himself transformed in his bed into a monstrous vermin" (Kafka, 1915).

The title, 'Metamorphosis', is shared with Ovid's masterpiece (Ovid, 8 AD) and I find it to be not coincidental. I believe that the metamorphoses in Ovid's stories (which include 'Echo and Narcissus') and the metamorphosis undergone by Kafka's protagonist epitomize the experience of a fragmented self in a world in which the individual is defenseless against all-powerful Gods or all-powerful regimes (an all-powerful parent). The experience of K., the protagonist of Kafka's story 'The Trial', belongs to the same world, which is interwoven throughout all of Kafka's writings.

Kohut (1984) wrote: "The psyche of modern man—the psyche described by Kafka and Proust and Joyce—is enfeebled, multifragmented (vertically split), and disharmonious" (p. 60). Kohut also wrote that

> Some of the most painful feelings to which man is exposed, unforgettably described by Kafka in The Metamorphosis and observable during the analyses of many people with severe narcissistic personality disorders, relate to the sense of not being human. The awareness of such a central distortion in the personality stems, I believe, from the absence of *human* humans in the environment of the small child.
>
> (ibid, p. 200)

Kafka's relationship with his father, Hermann, was complex and painful, and he grew up in the shadow of his paralyzing fear of him. Max Brod's refusal[1] to destroy Kafka's writings after his death left us masterpieces as well as a window into Kafka's psych. That window is left completely unveiled in 'Letter to Father' – a letter Kafka wrote to his father that spanned 48 pages[2] (Kafka, 1919). Thanks to the letter, it is possible to reconstruct the narcissistic object relations patterns of Kafka's father, which shaped the personality and creation of the son. The letter was written in 1919, when Kafka was 36 years old, and had never reached its addressee. Kafka entrusted it to his mother, who refused to deliver it to the father and returned it to

DOI: 10.4324/9781032625393-8

him. It seems that unlike her son, the mother was free from the repetition compulsion urge and did not delude herself that an attentive ear could be found. The son, however, was trapped in the dissonance between the understanding that the attempt was futile and the inability to forgo it.

> Dearest Father, You asked me recently why I claim to fear you. As usual, I had no answer for you, partly because of the fear I do have of you, and partly because explaining this fear requires too many details that I cannot speak coherently…the fear and its repercussions hinder me in writing to you, and the vastness of the matter goes far beyond my memory and understanding.
>
> (Kafka, 1919)

Thus Kafka's letter to his father begins. Kafka describes his inability to articulate or even grasp the problem as a whole, even though his fear of his father indicates that he feels it with every fiber of his being.

> If you summarize your judgment of me, it appears that you do not accuse me of something outright indecent or malicious (except perhaps for my recent intention to marry), but rather coldness, alienation, ingratitude. And you present it to me as if it were my fault… while you are not the slightest bit to blame, except perhaps for being too good to me.
>
> (Kafka, 1919)

Kafka goes on to describe a relationship in which his father directs 'unceasing accusations' at him, while behaving with righteousness, possessive authority, aggression, and tyranny. He wrote of the father's inability to accept differing opinions or desires, his incapacity to recognize the possibility of ever erring, his judgmental and empathy-lacking attitude toward others. Kafka experienced his father's set of characteristics as if they were aimed at obliterating the other in general and himself in particular, and he felt guilty and responsible for the way things are. This is reflected in his works.

> It's entirely possible that even if I had grown up entirely free from your influence, I might not have turned out to be a person to your liking. I probably would have become a weak, anxious, hesitant, restless person…as a father you were too strong for me… a true Kafka in terms of strength, health, appetite, voice, eloquence, self-satisfaction, superiority over the world… of course with all the accompanying flaws and weaknesses that your temperament and sometimes your quick temper lead you into…perhaps you were more cheerful before your children, especially me, disappointed you and made you feel burdened at home…If one were to calculate in advance how I… and you… would relate to each other, one might have assumed that you would simply crush me, leaving nothing of me behind. That didn't happen… but perhaps something worse did…

You affected me as you had to, though you should stop thinking it was some specific malice on my part that I succumbed to this effect…You are only able to treat a child as you yourself are molded, with strength, noise, and irascibility, and… it seemed to you even more suitable because you wanted to raise me to be a strong, brave boy.

(Kafka, 1919)

Kafka describes a defining incident from his early childhood, when he was whimpering for water at night. In response, his father picked him up and locked him in the inner balcony of the house, dressed only in his pajamas.

I want to use this to characterize your methods of upbringing and their effect on me. I was probably obedient afterward, but I suffered an inner harm from it. My nature would not allow me to reconcile the… senseless pleading for water and the extraordinarily frightening act of being carried outside. Even years later, I suffered from the tormenting idea that the huge man, my father, the ultimate authority, could come almost without reason and carry me from my bed to the balcony at night, making me feel like such a nothing to him…this feeling of insignificance that often dominates me… comes largely from your influence…. you only truly encourage me when it affects you personally, when it concerns your self-esteem that I hurt (like with my intention to marry)… This corresponded to your intellectual supremacy as well. You had… an absolute confidence in your opinions…. In your armchair, you ruled the world. Your opinion was right, any other was crazy… abnormal. And your self-assurance was so immense that you didn't have to be consistent to be right… You took on the enigmatic quality that all tyrants possess, whose authority is based on their person, not on their thought… I was under your heavy pressure in all my thinking… All these thoughts… were burdened from the start with your **disapproving judgment**…I had only to be happy about something, uplifted by it, come home and mention it, and the response would be an ironic sigh, a shake of the head… you always and fundamentally had to provide the child with such disappointments due to your antagonistic nature… these disappointments of the child weren't disappointments of ordinary life, but, as it revolved around your persona, the measure of all things, it struck at the core. Courage, determination, confidence, joy in this or that didn't last when you opposed it, or even when your opposition could just be assumed; and it could indeed be assumed for almost everything I did. This applied to thoughts as well as to people. It was enough that I had a little interest in a person – which didn't happen very often due to my nature – for you to launch into insult, defamation, and degradation… **you compared… to vermin… you had the saying about dogs and fleas ready to use**… Your complete insensitivity to the pain and shame your words and judgments could inflict upon me was always incomprehensible to me.

(Kafka, 1919, bold not in the origin)

'The Vermin' reincarnated into Kafka's 'The Metamorphosis' (1915). The father's 'disapproving judgment' and his degradation of others into 'Dogs' found its way to the story 'The Trial' (Kafka, 1925), both of which will be further discussed. Kafka excelled in depicting the tremendous power that a parent's word holds over his child and the way the father's capricious and inconsistent demands created a split in his psych and an experience of dissonance and confusion:

> As a child, everything you shouted at me was akin to divine commandment; I never forgot it, it remained the most important means for judging the world… you… did not adhere to the rules you imposed on me. This divided the world into three parts for me: one where I, the slave, lived, under laws that were invented only for me and to which I could never fully adhere, for reasons I did not know; then a second world… where you lived, engaged in ruling, issuing commands, and getting angry when they were not obeyed; and finally a third world, where other people lived happily and free from commands and obedience. I was constantly disgraced whether I obeyed your orders… or I was defiant.
>
> (Kafka, 1919)

Kafka noted that the fact that his father, as such, was his entire world, led to the inevitability of him taking everything upon himself (and into himself), and he described the feelings of guilt triggered by his father's judgment of him and by the way the father treated him, a way of 'complete condemnation'. Kafka keenly recognized the reason for his father's aggressive reactions and failure to listen to others – the father experienced dissent as an attack against him. He understood that this was a reaction to something within the father's inner world, that the anger's subject matter is just a pretext to explode, that the father acts this way out of his own helplessness.

Kafka described how this oppression made him introverted and closed off, damaging his social skills and leading to the erosion of his mental strength and resources:

> The impossibility of calm communication had another rather natural consequence: I lost the ability to speak… you forbade me from speaking early on… 'no word of dissent!'…In your presence… I acquired a halting, stuttering manner of speech… and eventually, I fell silent… I couldn't think or speak in your presence… I am the outcome of your upbringing and my obedience…Your extremely effective… rhetorical methods of educating me were: insults, threats, irony, wicked laughter, and – strangely – self-pity… If I started doing something that displeased you and you threatened me with failure, the reverence for your opinion was so immense that the failure… seemed inevitable. I lost trust in my own actions. I became uncertain, full of doubt… a sullen, inattentive, disobedient child, always considering an escape, usually internal.
>
> (Kafka, 1919)

What you had to fight for, we received from your hand, but the struggle for life outside... which naturally is also not spared us, we have to fight only belatedly, as adults with the strength of children.

(Kafka, 1919)

Kafka described the reason for succumbing to the father, the trap in which children of a narcissistic parent are caught, who in order to develop and become independent, are required to relinquish their home:

If I wanted to flee from you, I had to flee from the family as well, even from Mother... Elli [Kafka's sister] is the only example of almost complete success in breaking away from your orbit. In her childhood, I would have least expected it from her. She was such a clumsy, weary, fearful, morose, guilt-ridden, overly submissive... and miserly child. I could hardly look at her... she reminded me so much of myself... I was vanquished early on; what remained was escape, bitterness, sorrow, inner struggle... Ottla [another of Kafka's sisters] has no contact with her father... and for having more confidence, self-assurance, health, and carefree attitude in comparison to me, in your eyes, she is more wicked and treacherous than I am...[Ottla and I] get together... to thoroughly discuss... that terrible trial that hovers over us and you... in which you always assert yourself to be the judge.

(Kafka, 1919)

Kafka notes more than once how different his father seemed when presenting himself outside the family circle. He also mentions how his experiences with his father influenced his writing (as in the motif of the trial itself, which was also mentioned in the previous quote):

The further you were from the business and family, the friendlier, more yielding, more polite, more considerate, more involved you became... just as, for example, an autocrat, once outside the borders of his country, has no reason to remain tyrannical... When I was in your presence I had lost self-confidence and exchanged it for boundless guilt. (In remembrance of that boundlessness, I once aptly wrote about someone: "He fears shame will outlive him.")[3]... You had criticism against everyone I associated with, openly or secretly... the distrust you tried to instill in me towards most people... turned into distrust of myself.

(Kafka, 1919)

Kafka's struggle to break free from the influence of his father was depicted in his writings. This depiction resonates with the character of Gregor Samsa, the protagonist of 'The Metamorphosis', who wakes up one morning to discover he has turned into a vermin. In fact, one may interpret that Samsa-Kafka awakens to a 'reality' that corresponds to his innermost perception of himself, and now he is practically

a vermin. The relationship between Gregor Samsa and his father led to his hor-
rifying and slow death. As he runs away, Samsa is injured by apples hurled at him
by the father he is trying to escape. The wound festers and eventually leads to his
death. The wounds inflicted by the pattern of narcissistic abuse remain festering in
the child's psych, and any attempt to detach from the parent involves an injurious
avulsion. Kafka expresses this in his writings as well as in his letter:

> You were more accurate in your aversion toward my writing and all that was
> associated with it... Here, I had indeed moved away from you to some extent
> independently, even though it resembled a worm that, being trodden on its rear
> part, tears itself loose and drags its front part to the side... My writing revolved
> around you; there, I only lamented what I could not lament in your bosom. It
> was a deliberately prolonged farewell to you.
>
> (Kafka, 1919)

Kafka noticed that his father did not know his 'true being'. The image of the father
occupied his psychic space in a way that left no room for academy or other genuine
interests, and he withdrew into his inner world:

> Ever since I can remember, I have been burdened deeply with concerns of as-
> serting my spiritual existence, that I became indifferent to anything else...my...
> childishly helpless... self-satisfied indifference—a self-sufficient, but coldly
> daydreaming child... was my only defense against having a nervous breakdown
> from anxiety and guilt.
>
> (Kafka, 1919)

> I was always convinced—your disapproving countenance served as hard proof—
> that the more I succeeded, the worse my downfall would ultimately be... Given
> these circumstances, what did education matter to me? Who could ignite a spark
> of interest in me? I was interested in education—and not just education, but eve-
> rything surrounding me at this crucial age—much like an embezzling bank clerk
> who is still employed and is terrified of being discovered, is concerned with the
> small ongoing bank business that he must still conduct.
>
> (Kafka, 1919)

Additional influences that Kafka describes include the loss of the ability to perceive what reality is and to trust his own judgment, along with the appearance of
hypochondriacal symptoms:

> What was all that? Not an actual illness. But since I was uncertain about every-
> thing and needed constant validation of my existence, since I was never truly,
> absolutely, solely in possession of anything that only I unequivocally determine,
> being a disinherited son, I became uncertain even of my own body.
>
> (Kafka, 1919)

It can be said that the narcissistic injury Kafka experienced led to a withdrawal from relations with the external world and to a relationship with his own body, which became an object for him. When Freud described in 'On Narcissism' individuals who choose as a narcissistic object of love someone that represents their own self, he included the hypochondriac which "withdraws both interest and libido... from the objects of the external world and concentrates both of them upon the organ that is engaging his attention" (Freud, 1914, p. 83).

Finally, Kafka addresses his greatest present difficulty, which led him to write the letter – the challenge of forming and sustaining a romantic relationship, a difficulty he also ties to the overwhelming influence of his father (the letter was written due to his father's opposition to his engagement, which was eventually canceled). Here, oedipal themes also seep in, and as they rest on an injury that occurred in an earlier developmental stage, they remain all the more conflictual:

> In reality, the attempts at marriage were the most tremendous and hopeful rescue attempt, and accordingly tremendous was their failure... In these attempts, on the one hand, all the positive forces that I had at my disposal were assembled, and on the other hand, all the negative forces that I described as an outcome of your upbringing also gathered here with almost furious intensity: weakness, lack of self-confidence, feelings of guilt, and they formed a genuine barrier between me and marriage... the idea of marriage itself appeared indecent to me, making it impossible for me to apply what I had heard about marriage in general to my parents... The underlying idea behind both marriage attempts was entirely correct: to establish a household, to become independent... except in practice it turns out like the children's game where one holds and even squeezes the other's hand while exclaiming "Oh, go away, go away, why don't you go?"... you've always, unknowingly, held me back or rather held me down by the strength of your personality... Marriage is certainly the guarantee of the most intense self-liberation and independence. I would have a family, the outmost achievement... you have achieved. I would be your equal... so much cannot be achieved. It's like if someone was imprisoned, and not only intended to escape, which might be attainable, but also simultaneously intended to restructure the prison... Yet, were he to escape, he cannot restructure, and were he to restructure, he cannot escape.
>
> (Kafka, 1919)

In perceiving separation from his father as akin to escaping a prison, Kafka once more demonstrated and emphasized the impossible conflict placed upon the child of a narcissistic parent – if he were to escape he would have to give up the hope of repairing, the repetition compulsion that expresses his authentic need for parental nurture. If he were to escape, he would leave a part of himself behind; if he remained, he would be imprisoned and unable to discover himself.

Kafka passed away of tuberculosis in 1924. He was but 40. He linked his illness to his mental state as reflected in a letter he wrote to Felice Bauer, with whom his engagement had been canceled twice:

These two sides fighting within me, or more accurately, from whose battle I consist... are the Good and the Bad. They sometimes switch these masks... Secretly, I don't really consider this illness as tuberculosis, or at least not initially as tuberculosis; rather, it's my general bankruptcy. I believed I could go on further, but I cannot. The blood doesn't come from the lungs; instead, it comes from a decisive stab of one of the combatants

(Zürau, .September 30 or October 1, 1917)

'Letter to Father' sheds a different light on Kafka's works, which essentially convey the experience of the subjugation of a helpless individual by a tyrannical parent, symbolized by government bureaucrats in some of the stories. In the story 'The Metamorphosis', Gregor Samsa's metamorphosis into a vermin is an embodiment of Kafka's negative self-image and of his perception that he and his needs are loathsome and repulsive. Reading Kafka's work 'The Trial' (1925)[4] in light of 'Letter to Father' also leads to the understanding that it was written in the shadow of childhood experiences of a child who felt there was an authority figure with unlimited power, who is unpredictable and is capable of whimsically punishing him at any given moment, without him even knowing what was his crime. In the judicial system of 'The Trial', there is no 'presumption of innocence', but rather 'presumption of guilt'. This is a system in which the individual does not get a chance to be heard, a system in which he is judged regardless of facts, reason, or justice. In the Kafkaesque world, time dissolves similar to the way children experience time, and the connection between cause and effect is severed, just like the lived experience of the child of a capricious and unpredictable parent. In the conclusion of 'The Trial', the protagonist, Josef K. (it is commonly assumed that K, pronounced as in the German - Ka, represents 'Kafka'), is expected to take the knife from the hands of his executors and plunge it into himself. This conclusion to the story may reflect the masochistic pattern that Kafka developed, which is accompanied by a tendency to criticize and blame himself (an introjection of the bad parental object). Kafka's writing was an outlet for his distress and a hidden rebellion, and thus K. of 'The Trial' actually refuses to stab himself. What happens next perhaps explains why Kafka, like many children in his position, was inclined to internalize the bad object and degrade and humble himself, before the 'authorities' would do so in a more painful manner: "The hands of one of the gentlemen were at K.'s throat, while the other thrust the knife into his heart and twisted it there twice" (Kafka, 1925, paragraph 402). The verdict was executed with sadism, aiming to cause pain and humiliation. "With fading eyes, K. still saw how the gentlemen, close to his face, cheek pressed against cheek, observed the verdict. 'Like a dog!' he said; it was as if the shame should outlive him" (Kafka, 1925, paragraph 402).

I believe that the sense of profound disgrace and the feeling that 'shame should outlive him' are what led Kafka to request the destruction of all of his works. In essence, Kafka sought to annihilate himself, and I believe he did so out of identification with the aggressor, that made him feel that this was what he well deserved. By refusing to comply with his request, Brod, his good friend for 22 years and probably a good object in his life, made him immortal.

Notes

1 Kafka's friend and a writer himself, who published Kafka's writings posthumously rather than burn them as Kafka had requested.
2 45 pages are typewritten and the last 3 are handwritten by Kafka. The original letter, in German, can be viewed under 'Brief an den Vater' in the Max Brod archive in The National Library of Israel's website – www.nli.org.il.
3 These are the concluding words of Kafka's story 'The Trial'.
4 The story was written during the years 1914–1915 and was first published in 1925, after Kafka's passing.

Bibliography

Briefe an Felice Bauer (Letters to Felice Bauer). https://www.odaha.com/sites/default/files/BriefeAnFelice.pdf

Freud, S. (1914). On Narcissism: An Introduction. In: J. Strachey (Ed.), *The Standard Edition of the Complete Psychological Works of Sigmund Freud* (vol. 14, pp. 67–102). The Hogarth Press, 1957.

Kafka, F. (1915). *Die Verwandlung (Metamorphosis)*. https://www.gutenberg.org/cache/epub/22367/pg22367-images.html

Kafka, F. (1919). *Brief an den Vater*. http://www.digbib.org/Franz_Kafka_1883/Brief_an_den_Vater_.pdf

Kafka, F. (1925). Der Prozess *(The Trial)*, VERLAG DIE SCHMIEDE, 1925 (as published in https://www.gutenberg.org/files/7849/7849-h/7849-h.htm)

Kohut, H. (1984). *How Does Analysis Cure?* The University of Chicago Press.

Ovid, P. N. (8 AD). *Metamorphoses* (Translators: Sir Samuel Garth, John Dryden, Alexander Pope, Joseph Addison, William Congreve). Passerino, 2017.

Chapter 9

Only the Happy Bird Can Sing
The Life of Maria Callas in Light of Her Narcissistic Upbringing

Using the life story of Maria Callas, the legendary opera singer, I wish to demonstrate the destructive influence that narcissistic parenthood can have on the child's life trajectory, as well as the patterns of narcissistic abuse within the family and in romantic relationships. Callas grew up with a mother who exhibited abusive behavioral patterns from her birth. In fact, I believe that Callas suffered from what I have termed a 'double injury' due to impaired maternal functioning during infancy. In adulthood, Callas engaged in an abusive romantic relationship with a man who clearly exhibited severe narcissistic pathology, Aristotle Onassis. In this relationship, she experienced exploitation, degradation, and cruelty. I believe that if not for the weakened psychic structure her childhood left her with, she would not have found herself in such a heart wrenching relationship.

Callas's personality encompassed many contradictions, and especially a combination of narcissistic and echoistic traits alike. Both of these aspects had destructive implications on her choices and her ability to cope with life's challenges and sorrows. She is regarded as the greatest opera singer of the 20th century, and in the eyes of many, the greatest there ever was and ever will be. She was dabbed 'La Divina' – the divine one – by a frantic audience. The realms into which she transcended as an artist have led to the enduring fascination with her image, even more than four decades after her death, as she continues to inspire books, plays, and films, and within the opera world, lives on eternally. Over 40 books have been written about her, with their number steadily increasing. The magnitude of her success stands in stark contrast to the emptiness and barrenness she experienced in her private life, where she remained a little girl who perceives life as 'one great struggle for independence against the people who run your life'.

> In a search for the self the person concerned may have produced something valuable in terms of art, but a successful artist may be universally acclaimed and yet have failed to find the self that he or she is looking for… If the artist… is searching for the self, then it can be said that in all probability there is already some failure for that artist in the field of general creative living. The finished creation never heals the underlying lack of sense of self.
>
> (Winnicott, 1971, pp. 54–55)

DOI: 10.4324/9781032625393-9

In regard to actors, there are those… who can only act, and who are completely at a loss when not in a role, and when not being appreciated or applauded (acknowledged as existing).

(Winnicott, 1960/1965, p. 150)

I will weave Callas's story with my own interpretations and hypotheses, yet the exchanges, thoughts, and emotions regarding the characters are in their own words – according to interviews given in the media or books they have written. Much of the information is based on a comprehensive biography of Callas (Huffington, 1981), but above all, I sought to hear directly from her 'objects', and thus arrived at the books *My Daughter Maria Callas* (E. Callas, 1960), *My Wife Maria Callas*[1] (Meneghini, 1981), and *Sisters* (J. Callas, 1989). The fact that they were published by members of her family speaks for itself and about the way she haunted them and they her, even years after their paths diverged forever. A person's life and psych are an endless universe, and I do not purport to comprehensively explore all the factors and influences in Callas's life (such as the trauma of living in Greece during the Nazi occupation or the absence of a father figure, which contributed to her choice of older men as partners). However, I will strive to touch on the key elements, with an emphasis on the impact her mother's personality had on her.

"To sing is an expression of your being, a being which is becoming" – Maria Callas (Huffington, 1981, p. 14)

December 2,[2] 1923 was a cold and snowy day. The storm raged through the streets of New York as Cecilia Sophia Anna Maria Kalogeropoulou[3] made her debut on the world's stage. "Take her away"! (E. Callas, 1960 p. 10) hissed Evangelia Kalogeropoulou, turning her gaze to the storm outside, as she learned that the son she had been expecting was a daughter. For four days, she refused to look at the baby with the great black eyes (E. Callas, 1960; Huffington, 1981). If the nurses tried to talk her into having a change of heart, she did not understand the English they spoke, and her heart remained in Greece anyway, with her Vasili. Only a few months had passed since an epidemic[4] claimed the life of the three-year-old toddler, and Evangelia felt her heart had died with him. Ever since his death, she had prayed for another son to fill the void he left in her heart. Nothing went as she had expected. The happiness Vasili had brought had slightly bridged over the abyss that her marriage to George was marked by, and a daughter she already had, six-year-old Yakinthy.[5] Even the blue clothes she had knitted were too small for the baby-girl, but Evangelia could not foresee the irony in what had so far been a Greek tragedy. After Vasili's death, the distance between her and George steadily grew, and he immersed himself even more in fleeting love affairs. "Do not marry him, Litza", her father warned her, "You will never be happy with him" (E. Callas, 1960, p. 12). If only she had listened to him. A few months after losing Vasili, George informed her that he had sold his successful pharmacy and their home. Against her will they boarded a ship and immigrated to the United States. At the age of 23, pregnant, with a five-and-a-half-year-old daughter and a grieving heart, Evangelia trudged in his footsteps (E. Callas, 1960).

When George Kalogeropoulos brought Yakinthy to the hospital to meet her new-born sister, they found Evangelia staring through the window at the snow, indifferent to the baby beside her. "This is little Cecilia", Yakinthi heard her father say. Without diverting her gaze, Evangelia said, "Sophia. This is your sister Sophia. Say hello to Sophia" (J. Callas, 1989, p. 40). Bewildered, Yakinthi looked up to her father, but he merely shrugged helplessly. Minutes later, George grabbed her wrist and led her outside, angry at Evangelia for refusing his pleas to acknowledge the baby. A few days later, she heard her father announce that 'Maria' would soon be coming home. That was the last time her parents would manage to reach an agreement.

For Evangelia, George was a disappointment. Perhaps she could forgive his infidelities, after all, she knew of many men around who did the same, but she could not forgive him for his lack of ambition, for seeming so common to her, and for the loss of status and economic luxuries that he could no longer provide in the United States. Evangelia regarded herself as deserving much more than that, after all, her father came from an esteemed family and was wealthy. Her family owned orchards, olive groves, and even their own cemetery. She never let George forget this, nor his modest origins from a peasant family. If she were a man, her shoulders would surely have been adorned with ranks, just like her father the colonel, but she was a woman. She dreamed of becoming an actress, but the profession wasn't suitable for a woman from a highborn family like hers, and she resigned herself to getting married and fulfilling the traditional role of a woman. George was so different from her father, Petros the army officer. He was known as 'The Singing Commander'. Some claimed he used to sing even during the Balkan War. His tenor voice was strong and remarkable. Once, he sang an aria at the request of the audience gathered around their balcony. Among the listeners was a famous Italian tenor who had come to perform in town, but hearing Petros, he lost confidence, sneaked back to his hotel, and fled.[6] Petros was always cheerful and full of life, always the center of attention and always commanded respect from everyone he met. George, on the other hand, grew more silent and reserved with each passing day. Only in the presence of other women would his face light up as it used to, and they always gathered around him giggling. At their wedding, Evangelia's heart was heavy. Petros had passed away of a stroke 16 days before her marriage, and she stood at church wearing a plain white dress, mourning. All that was left for her now was a mundane life with a husband who refused the role she assigned him – becoming an important man. Evangelia returned defeated and without a male offspring to their apartment, an apartment she insisted on furnishing extravagantly. The apartment was measly and empty compared to their home in Greece, with its servants and Cook. Even their name became smaller, Callas, as the Americans could not pronounce their true name (E. Callas, 1960).

Evangelia resigned herself to her situation, and following the Greek costume, she nursed the baby, who never cried, until she was one year old. In the silence permeating the apartment, a plan began to form in her mind. The plan formed gradually, first vague and then shining, like a gem she polished in her imagination until it sparkled. If she cannot stand out on her own merit nor through her husband's, her daughters would be the instruments to achieve her goal. She took Yakinthy, now Jackie, to ballet and piano lessons. Jackie was beautiful, good tempered, and popular. Often, her singing would fill the house. Her looks resembled her mother's. Maria's looks resembled her father's. Both girls quickly learned that it was better to stay out of Evangelia's way, knowing there would always be something demanding criticism and requiring 'correction' in their behavior. Sometimes, Evangelia spanked her daughters, and when she suspected they lied, she would put pepper on their lips. It was a trivial matter, a customary Greek punishment for lying. She did not revert to physical disciplining much. The girls were obedient (E. Callas, 1960; J. Callas, 1989).

Little Maria adored Jackie. One day, when she was five years old, Maria ran toward her sister who stood across the street. She was hit by a passing car. In days to come, Jackie would tell how the distance Maria was flung across and the time she remained unconscious kept increasing each time Evangelia recounted the story (J. Callas, 1989). In days to come, Evangelia would blame the accident for Maria's anger at her (E. Callas, 1960).

The cloudy relationship between Evangelia and George cast a tense atmosphere at home, which grew worse with the 1929 stock market crash. George had lost his pharmacy, and they were forced to move to a smaller apartment. He began working as a traveling salesman. If up until now he was emotionally absent from home, now he was physically absent as well (J. Callas, 1989; Huffington, 1981). For Evangelia his absence was a relief. Such contempt she felt toward him! How furious she was with him for causing her this humiliation! Even though they were living from hand to mouth, Evangelia insisted that her daughters receive piano lessons four times a week, ignoring all of George's protests. Not even the fact that the money was needed for rent and groceries could deter her. George faded away, succumbing to her whims. Everything in the house had to be done her way. The soundtrack of the two girls' lives was opera music and the incessant admonishments of their mother's. When George played Greek folk songs on the gramophone, Evangelia would storm in, swiftly replacing the record, lest it corrupt her daughters' refined taste. She would call him a nothing, stupid, a peasant, lazy, belittling him and berating him endlessly in front of their daughters. She never stopped lamenting having married him to them, and he became a stranger and a weak man in their eyes. The Wall Street crash was portrayed as his personal failure, and Evangelia's unexpected dark moods grew worse with each financial blow and each flirtation of his (J. Callas, 1989).

One day, they quarreled in the pharmacy. Jackie and Maria, coming back from school, entered the pharmacy just in time to witness their mother evicted in an ambulance, having overdosed on a medication she had snatched of the shelf. If Evangelia ever felt remorse or shame when she recalled the event, she quickly brushed it off, as if shooing away a mosquito with a flick of her hand. "It is so long ago that it might have happened to someone else, not myself" (E. Callas, 1960, p. 176) she told herself, and in fact, it was George's fault. It would not have happened if she was happy with him. Does anyone appreciate her sacrifice? It is only for the sake of her daughters that she stays with him.

From her daughters, Evangelia demanded absolute obedience and she treated them like a tyrant. She could bend their will at a glance. She would not tolerate being challenged or being presented with desires differing from her own and she was completely blind to their emotional needs. She issued commands relentlessly and controlled every aspect of their behavior and attire. The rules of the house were strict. If Jackie or Maria omitted to make their beds in the morning, their clothes were dumped in the corridor. Evangelia would become furious if they dared to protest, after all her actions were all in their best interest, she did what a good mother should do. How much she invested in her daughters. She nurtured culture and education in them, steering them away from anything that could jeopardize her goal. There was a weekly trip to the library, where she encouraged them to read masterpieces and listen to opera recordings. Evangelia ignited their imaginations with the romantic plotlines and breathed life into the characters. There were frequent visits to the museum. Often, they dined at the nearby Chinese restaurant, which Evangelia's imagination turned into an enchanted, fancy restaurant for her and her daughters. She taught them to dance, and their living room became an elegant ballroom. Evangelia was like a gardener who waters, nurtures, and prunes the plant as desired. There was no room for wild growth, thus there were many restrictions. If Jackie or Maria concealed something, Evangelia sensed it with the keenness of a hawk and extracted the secret from them. Maria and Jackie could barely play with other children; most of them came from families that Evangelia denounces as not good enough, and she forbade her daughters from entering their homes or associating with them. Toys were a waste of time. A strict regime reigned at home, and the girls practiced playing the piano for long hours each day. Evangelia could lecture and scold for days on due to even a minor failure to meet her expectations by one of the girls (J. Callas, 1989).

Both girls became increasingly introverted and withdrawn. For Jackie, whose lively, tomboy's temperament was completely suppressed, it was a continuous torture. One day, at ten years old, she ran down to the river and considered drowning herself in it. They felt relieved only in those few times they were left on their own, when Evangelia's oppressing presence was not home, not physically at least. During such times, Maria would cuddle up to Jackie (ibid).

She loved Jackie, but as years went by, she felt inferior to her sister who was beautiful, wooed, and slender. Evangelia's preference for Jackie was clear as day to Maria, who had developed an uncanny sensitivity to her mother's thoughts, desires, and moods. Maria felt herself to be chubby and plain-looking. Her social skills were meager, and she was a quiet, introverted child, her large, sad eyes hidden behind thick glasses. She loved the library and the records she could borrow there most of all (E. Callas, 1960; J. Callas, 1989). She would listen to opera recordings and imagine magical worlds full of emotion and vitality that were absent from her life, worlds of wonderful love stories and heroism, triumphs and tragedies, princesses and kings, magnificent costumes, and drama (J. Callas, 1989). Those greater-than-life characters, lyric phrases, and witty sentences became a part of her world and of herself. They were food for the soul. She consumed them hungrily and internalized them. With the records, she could be far away from home while still within its walls, suspending reality for as long as she could. When she listened to opera, she felt enveloped in a protective cocoon. Her mind became a source of endless possibilities. She taught herself to retreat into her inner world and could live in it for weeks on end without being bored or having awareness of a sense of loneliness (Adagietto, 2016b). It was a necessary survival mechanism, but like a thin layer of ice over a dark and frozen lake, beneath it lay hidden endless neediness and dependency.

Maria felt her existence was acknowledged only when she sang in ceremonies and competitions at school, where she always achieved success and awards. When she was ten years old, an event occurred that marked a turning point and determined the course of her life. She was singing and accompanying herself on the piano when suddenly Evangelia looked out the open window and saw people gathered on the street to hear her singing. The audience applauded and would not disperse until Maria stopped singing. The gears in Evangelia's mind turned quickly, and the calculation was simple. While Maria dreamed of becoming a dentist, her mother had already decided on a completely different career path for her (E. Callas, 1960). Soon, Maria's life became a series of training, competitions, and performances. In days to come, Maria would say about it, "There must be a law against that kind of thing. A child treated like this grows old before its time. They shouldn't deprive a child of its childhood!" (Huffington, 1981, p. 25). This was not the only way she was deprived of a childhood. In a deeper sense, she was deprived of true maternal love, love for who she really is. Any love she received was conditional, given for her successes. "Only when I was singing did I feel loved", she recounted (Huffington, 1981, p. 26). Her gift was also her curse, a double-edged sword. Always will she think she is loved only for her voice, her money, and her status, and always will she feel that she cannot be loved for who she is. There will always be a split in her. "There are two people in me", she would say in an interview years later (Volf, 2017), "I would like to be Maria, but there is 'the Callas' that I have to live up to". Maria the child felt like an ugly duckling, overweight, clumsy, and rejected. Maria the woman, the admired opera singer, beautiful, elegant, and as noble as a swan, felt the same.

What emptiness she felt Maria tried to fill with food which, perhaps driven by feelings of guilt or by a thought that the weight would benefit her voice, Evangelia provided abundantly. In the absence of close friends or social skills, school was a struggle for her. Against the injury and the sense of inferiority, an internal conviction gradually formed that she was destined for greatness. At the age of 12, she listened with her family to a live broadcast from the Metropolitan Opera. The renowned Lily Pons was Lucia di Lammermoor. At the peak of Lucia's mad scene, Maria suddenly started shouting toward the radio at Pons that she was off-key. When scolded that a child such as herself should show more respect for a star such as Pons, Maria retorted: "I don't care if she is a star, she sings off-key. Just wait and see, one day I'm going to be a star myself, a bigger star than her" (Huffington, 1981, p. 29).

Maria studied avidly from the Metropolitan Opera's radio broadcasts and also from David, Elmina, and Stephanakos, her three canaries. She would study them at length. "That is how it's done", she would mutter, "They know the secret" (J. Callas, 1989). A voice lesson cost ten dollars, a sum they could not afford. Evangelia, who always strove to keep suitors away from Jackie, now attempted to persuade her, at the age of 17, to marry their young and wealthy landlord, in order for him to pay for Maria's lessons, snorting scornfully when Jackie pointed out she did not love him. Jackie refused and Evangelia's wrath of hell fell on her. "I was appalled", wrote Jackie, "The woman would sacrifice anything including her daughter's happiness for whatever was obsessing her at that moment" (ibid, p. 63). Shortly after, Evangelia decided that in order to fulfill her dream for her daughter, they should move to Greece. There, she had hoped, with financial support from her family and their connections, she could get the necessary musical education for Maria. It is unclear why Jackie was sent ahead alone, an 18-year-old girl whose mother still insisted on choosing her clothes. Jackie felt that the act symbolized her mother's anger toward her. At the dock, Evangelia bid Jackie farewell icily, and as if she had not just attempted to marry her off for financial purposes, she warned her to not even look at men throughout the journey. During the voyage, Jackie was offered a Martini. Remembering that her mother had cautioned her against alcohol and ordered her to drink 'only orangeade', but determined to rebel, Jackie requested a Coca-Cola, an audacious act she immediately followed with a quick glance around, expecting to see her mother materializing out of nowhere storming at her (J. Callas, 1989). Evangelia was not there, but she was already deeply rooted within. A few months later, Evangelia and Maria also boarded a ship to Greece, leaving George behind. If he felt sorrow for parting with his daughters, it was diluted in the relief brought about by the sight of Evangelia's figure growing smaller along with the ship. When she told him she was leaving, he fell to his knees in front of her, crossed himself, and said aloud: "At last, my God, you have pitied me!" (ibid, p. 64). Maria would not see her father for the next eight years. Her school days were also coming to an end, and despite the suffering that came with this system, she would always regret the education denied her and feel ignorant.

Maria's singing delighted the passengers aboard the ship that was plowing through the water toward Evangelia's homeland. How proud Maria felt when the ship's captain invited her to sing at a private dinner he held and how excited she was. She sang the aria "Love is a rebellious bird" (Habanera) from Carmen, accompanying herself on the piano. What did 13-year-old Maria understand about the femme fatale protagonist of the opera and her seductive aria? It appears quite a lot. At the end of the aria, Carmen tosses a flower at Don José to enchant him with her charms. Maria sang the aria's final words: "If I love you, beware" (Bizet, Melihac & Halévy, 1875), took a flower from a vase atop the piano, and threw it at the captain (E. Callas, 1960).

How is it that a 13-year-old girl, shy and introverted, whose self-image is poles apart from the voluptuous gypsy woman, identifies so deeply with the character? From where does the dramatic flair emanate, which will characterize her career ahead so much? Maria's ego ideal and grandiosity were projected onto the greater-than-life opera heroines. Outside the stage, she felt small and worthless. To Maria the real world was becoming increasingly threatening. Her internalized bad object was projected and reintrojected repeatedly, and good internalized objects were lacking. Thus, the world of imagination became a refuge for her, and she knew 'how to be' only through identification with imaginary and greater-than-life characters from a world where emotions are distilled and intensified. These characters became her and she became them and only during those moments could she feel whole. They were her good objects, functioned as a selfobject, idealized figures with whom she felt merged. As long as she performed, reality was suspended and imagination became reality. The extraordinary acting talent she possessed arose from her identification with the characters she portrayed and from her super natural sensitivity, which allowed her to perceive the audience's desires and give them back to the audience fulfilled, one dramatic moment after another. Maria felt alive and happy only when she was on stage. Only then was she free to express her creativity and behave authentically. Only when she acted was she herself. On stage, Callas was Maria; off stage, Maria was 'La Callas'.

The captain was enchanted indeed. He kissed the flower and, in return for the performance, gave the 13-year-old Maria a doll. Maria took pride in the doll and was happy with it, even though Evangelia always took pride in the fact that her daughters didn't need insignificant things such as dolls. A seductive gesture and a doll at the same time are a suitable representation of the split in Maria's psych, which contained an introverted girl in need of a mother's love, whose emotional development was stunted, and a deep artist with a natural sense for drama, full of emotion, life, and passion.

Jackie, accompanied by her aunts, came to meet her mother and sister at the train station. Evangelia was dressed in a tailored suit and wore a hat with an enormous feather, a dramatic outfit intended to impress her relatives. Maria looked embarrassed, depressed, and downcast after weeks of confinement alongside Evangelia on the ship. They settled in Athens, back then a small city filled with gardens and perfumed by citrus trees (J. Callas, 1989). Evangelia spoke incessantly about Maria's voice and the great career awaiting her, but her family was not as impressed as she had hoped they would be. She compelled Maria to sing to anyone remotely connected to the local musical scene and forced her to perform in a tavern where guests used to sing opera arias. "Please tell her to stop!" (p. 71), Maria pleaded with Jackie, who was just as helpless. At this stage, there was still a sense of a shared fate and an understanding between the sisters, and Jackie wrote:

Mary stood on the side watching her life being ordered about as if she didn't exist and I suddenly wondered… Was this what she really longed to do or was there some other unspoken ambition locked up behind those wide dark eyes?

(ibid, p. 76)

Eventually, Maria made it into the conservatory and even received a scholarship. She was three years younger than the admission age, but thanks to her height, a minor adjustment of her birthdate in the registration documents resolved the issue (E. Callas, 1960). Her first teacher, Maria Trivella, was to be the first in a series of parental figures who would accompany her throughout her life. Maria would forever need someone to serve as a supportive, believing, and revitalizing figure for her, someone who would mirror her talent and greatness and enable her to believe in herself. From now on, there would be a succession of people who would fulfill this role, and only in the presence of such a figure would Maria be able to work. From now on, only when she worked would she feel she existed.[7]

Jackie's life was also run by Evangelia. She pushed her to date the son of a wealthy shipping magnet, Milton Embirikos. Not long after Evangelia and Maria arrived in Greece, George had stopped sending money and Evangelia had a falling out with her relatives and severed ties with them. They were left without means of livelihood, in an unfurnished apartment, sleeping on the floor. Evangelia urged Jackie to ask Milton for financial support. At first, Jackie refused. She did not love Milton at this point and did not know if she wanted to stay with him. She suggested they returned to the United States, but Evangelia pulled all the strings and did not stop haranguing her and reprimanding her for her 'selfishness', until finally Jackie found herself bursting into tears in front of Milton and became a kept woman (J. Callas, 1989). In the moral norms of those days, that sealed the fate on any prospect of marrying him. This option was actually far-fetched from the beginning, as Embirikos Senior opposed the match and also, in days to come, even after his father's death, Milton detested Evangelia and refused to associate himself with her. Jackie wrote that years later Milton confessed to her that this was the reason he never married her: "her control over me was something too difficult for him to handle... he could see no reason to fall into that trap" (p. 128).

At the age of 16, Maria began studying with Elvira de Hidalgo, a singer who graced the world's greatest opera stages. De Hidalgo's retirement year in Greece was extended into years, perhaps because of Maria, perhaps due to the war that was to come or perhaps because of a romance with a young Greek man. When de Hidalgo first saw Maria, she faced a girl who seemed to wish to disappear into herself. She was overweight, awkward, dressed in baggy drab clothes, and by the looks of them it was clear she took to biting her nails. The idea of that girl wanting to become a singer seemed laughable to her, but when Maria started to sing, de Hidalgo was astonished. The voice was unique, huge, and something in the girl changed the moment she started to sing. There was something mesmerizing about her (Huffington, 1981; Tosi, 2010). De Hidalgo felt as if the girl's eyes were speaking to her. She immediately agreed to take her on as a student. Maria was the first student to arrive at the conservatory in the morning and the last to leave in the evening, listening to the lessons of the other students out of intent to learn from everybody, spending little time at home. De Hidalgo never had to repeat anything twice. Maria would return the next day and perform perfectly what just the day before required improvement (Demonassa, 2010). Maria struggled with the highest range when she started, and some thought she was a mezzo-soprano because of that, but under de Hidalgo's hands, a broad ranged and unique soprano voice was carved out. Maria idolized de Hidalgo, and the more de Hidalgo nurtured her, the more the resentment grew in Maria's heart toward Evangelia's lack of love and blunt preference for her beautiful and buoyant sister. This preference also stood out to those around them as Evangelia used to sew beautiful dresses for Jackie and drab, shapeless dresses for Maria (Palmer, 1978). Jackie, for her part, felt Maria was the favored one and that she herself was invisible, as their mother's entire world revolved around her one goal – to make Maria famous in order to enjoy the glory and wealth. Additionally, despite loving him by then, Jackie felt that she was sold to Milton to finance Maria's studies (J. Callas, 1989), and rancor took root in her heart. She spurned and mocked the appearance of her sister "dumpy Mary", "fat-legged Mary", "spotty Mary" (p. 4).

World War II broke out, and life became harder, but Maria didn't let anything stand in her way. She continued to go, despite the danger, to the conservatory. When it closed, she studied at the home of de Hidalgo. She worked from morning till night, focused on her goal of becoming the greatest singer of all. De Hidalgo was to Maria like a mother who not only raised her into the singer she became but also taught the awkward overweight girl how to dress and how to stand and move on the stage (Huffington, 1981). Why didn't Maria's aspiration for excellence lead her to give more importance to her appearance? Why didn't Evangelia, invested as she was in fulfilling her plan for Maria, make sure her daughter would look like a star, or at least presentable? Perhaps she feared that a more attractive appearance would lead to a romantic entanglement that might derail her plans. Or maybe it was easier for her to bear her envy toward her marvelously talented daughter and her glorious future when she was confined within the body of an overweight sloppy girl dressed in shabby clothes. Evangelia, now in her forties, began to feel the years leaving their mark on her beauty. She used to compare herself to her young daughters and flirt with their suitors. One day, she grabbed a young man, a neighbor's guest, and ushered him into their home, demanding that he ruled who's the fairest among the three of them (Petsalis-Diomidis, 2001). Even if she knew the story of Snow White, Evangelia was surely oblivious to the analogy, and considering that Jackie, too, attempted to conceal her jealousy through flirting with Maria's love interests and by ridiculing her appearance and her very being (J. Callas, 1989), it is no wonder that Maria would later recount how her mother and sister treated her like Cinderella (E. Callas, 1960).

Aged 17, Maria became a member of the Athens Opera, to the dismay of the other female singers. She was reserved and distant, blatantly lacking in social skills and aggressive when she felt threatened – attributes that did not help her endear herself to her fellow company members (E. Callas, 1960; J. Callas, 1989; Huffington, 1981; Petsalis-Diomidis, 2001). She perceived the world as hostile, was always on a defensive mode, and would become aggressive. The world responded accordingly. She did not hesitate to show her sense of superiority over her peers. Over the years, she could reflect on this: "My shyness and insecurity have often made me seem arrogant. It's a form of self-protection of timid people. A person who is really sure of herself doesn't need to act like a dictator" (Dragadze, 1964, p. 69). Her talent and the envy it evoked worsened the hostility toward her. Perhaps because she internalized her mother's projected grandiosity when it came to her professional identity, in everything related to the world of the stage – Cinderella became an Amazon. The war raged around her, in the world and in the opera company, yet she sealed herself off as much as she could. She lived for the sake of singing, and singing saved her life. One day, Italian soldiers burst into the apartment in search of two British soldiers who had been hidden there. The two guests moved to another hideout the previous day, but Maria, knowing that their belongings remained in the apartment and would give her and her mother and sister away, hurried to the piano and began singing an aria from 'Tosca'. The Italian soldiers forgot about their mission right there and then and settled around her. The next day they returned, placing offerings of food on the piano for their new goddess (E. Callas, 1960; Huffington, 1981).

Her voice was a weapon, strength, and an entry ticket into enchanted worlds. In order to challenge the German prohibition on noise, the piano was placed near the balcony. One day she sang Tosca, when suddenly an anonymous voice was carried over responding with the lines of Mario, Tosca's beloved. The duet above Athens' rooftops continued daily. The identity of the mysterious Mario was never revealed, but 'Tosca' became the first professional role of an 18-year-old Maria,[8] when another singer fell ill. She had to fight her way to the stage through the ailing singer's husband, who was sent to physically block her way. Maria jumped him and scratched him in the face, returning home with a black eye and an illustrious triumph as Tosca (E. Callas, 1960; Huffington, 1981).

At the age of 21, as the Second World War ended, Maria was driven out of the opera company due to the hostility of her colleagues and as a result of criticism over Evangelia's involvement with enemy soldiers during the war (J. Callas, 1989). Maria decided to leave Greece. De Hidalgo thought she should stay and continue her studies or go to Italy, but she set sail for America with only 100 dollars in her pocket, not knowing where she would lodge. Completely disconnected by the war, she did not have her father's address or a way to notify him of her arrival, but he spotted her name on a list of passengers in a newspaper and waited for her at the pier. When the ship docked, George approached a young woman who disembarked it and asked her if she knew Maria Kalogeropoulou. Maria, overwhelmed with emotion, fell into her father's arms (E. Callas, 1960; Huffington, 1981).

It did not take long for her to realize that just as it had been difficult to live with her mother, it was equally difficult to live without her. She borrowed money to fund Evangelia's arrival in the United States. What prompted Maria to invite her mother? It is probable Evangelia had written Maria, ordering her to send money so she could join her daughter, and Maria obeyed. One may also guess that Maria, feeling insecure in her mother's love and lacking the temporary validations she received from her mother when singing, felt anxious, empty, and lonely, thus falling back into the familiar pattern of her relationship with her mother. Evangelia lived in her husband's house once more, in separate rooms. Two years in the United

States left Maria's career in a dead-end, however, when she was 23, she secured an audition with the director of the Verona Festival, got the leading role in the opera 'La Gioconda', and set sail for Italy (E. Callas, 1960). The few drab and prudish clothes that Evangelia had packed for Maria could suit the opera 'I Puritani' (The Puritans). Twenty-three-year-old Maria was not given permission to be a woman. A letter of advices accompanied the clothes, in which Evangelia reminded Maria that life is full of disappointments. It ended with the commandment "Honour thy father and thy mother" (Huffington, 1981), a conclusion that may hint at Evangelia's expectation that Maria would provide for her, and in any case, sends Maria on her way with the shadow of her mother falling upon her.

The move to Italy symbolized a transition from the mother to a search for emotional needs fulfillment in other relationships. Upon arriving in Verona, Maria met Giovanni Battista (Titta) Meneghini, a prosperous well-known local industrialist and opera enthusiast. Meneghini was considered to be a 'Romeo', but the contemporary Romeo from Verona was a short, balding bachelor in his fifties who had 12 brick factories and a penchant for young lady singers. As a jest, he was appointed by the festival directors to be Maria's escort in the city. Once he laid eyes on Maria, he decided to take his role extremely seriously (Huffington, 1981). He lavished attention upon the young singer, treated her with admiration, protected her, and contained her without limits. Thus Maria found in one person both a substitute for the mother Evangelia could not be for her and for the father who went out of her life at the age of 13. Soon, Meneghini abandoned his business to become Maria's personal manager. Maria could not be alone. It took two days from her arrival in Italy for her to find in Meneghini a substitute for her mother. It took two years for her to become Maria Meneghini Callas.

Studies at the conservatory included major operatic languages, and only a few months after beginning her studies there, Maria spoke Italian and French (Palmer, 1978). When she arrived in Italy, her mastery of the language quickly grew, and she adopted the Veronese dialect spoken by Meneghini. Her intelligence and linguistic talents allowed her to blend in like a chameleon, but she was like a tree without roots. In America, her birthplace, she was a Greek. When she moved to Greece she was 'the American' who spoke Greek with an accent. As an adult, when she spoke English, it was with a light and indistinct accent that could not be attributed to any specific language. She had her own accent and a grammar that was characteristic of her and idiosyncratic, correct but designed to distance emotions and dissociate them. The deepest sense of not belonging was the one having to do with family. Meneghini's brothers hated her and openly called her a whore (Meneghini, 1981), while her parents and sister were estranged. Her sense of identity was not cohesive, and she clung to her husband like a lifeline. Evangelia, who likely expected Maria to send for her and bring her to Italy, and saw the possibility of Maria building a separate life as a threat to her aspirations and to their relationship, sent reprimanding letters. These letters berated Maria for marrying without seeking her advice, forgetting she belonged to the audience and not to her husband, and for abandoning her family by marrying (Allegri & Allegri, 1997).

Maria's success in Italy was not immediate. Her talent was evident from a young age and she learned fast, but her abilities were honed through hard work and dedication. Music critic Howard Taubman wrote of her voice: "Occasionally it gives the impression of having been formed out of sheer will power rather than natural endowment" (Taubman, 1956, p. 43). Her voice was extraordinary in many ways. It was immense in size and had an exceptionally wide range, but the passages between the higher, middle, and lower registers of her voice were not always smooth, and some said she had 'three different voices'. The timbre of her voice was also unique, thick and dark in the lower notes, acute on the verge of strident in the upper ones. When you hear Callas, there is no mistaking her. The audience was divided between those who adored her and those who disliked her for the imperfections of her voice. Among the latter, a significant amount of fans of Renata Tebaldi, the undisputed queen of the Italian opera world until Callas's rise, used to attend her performances, jeer, boo, and wait like vultures for the smallest of mistakes. They stopped at nothing. Her anxiety grew every time she stepped onto the stage. "Every time I go out there, they are there waiting to get me", she said. She used to grip the arms of the person accompanying her backstage so tightly that it left marks (Palmer, 1978). Once, at the end of her performance of La Traviata, amidst the shower of flowers, a bunch of radishes hit the stage. Maria picked them up as if they were a bouquet of flowers. Interpretations differ on whether she did this knowingly, attempting to diminish the affront with a theatrical gesture, or whether it was her myopia, bordering on blindness onstage without her eyeglasses, causing her to mistake them for flowers. Either way she felt the humiliation and pain (Huffington, 1981; Spence, 2021).

Despite the shortcomings of her voice, few singers reached her level of performance. De Hidalgo taught her the intricacies of the technique well, and she became a virtuoso. Unlike many opera singers, she had more than just musicality. She was a gifted musician, capable of sight-reading an aria, using her voice like a violinist uses a violin. Her unique way to phrase and intonate the words filled them with meaning and emotion. At the beginning of her career in Italy, she sang Wagner's 'Tristan und Isolde'. She got the role by chance, when Meneghini learned that the conductor was struggling to find a suitable singer for the lead role. Maria, who did not know a single note of this opera, claimed to know the role and secured an audition with the conductor, Tullio Serafin. She sight-read the notes (CallasFan, 2015) and Serafin found his Isolde (Meneghini, 1981). This marked the beginning of a fruitful collaboration with one of Italy's leading conductors.[9] Shortly thereafter, Serafin conducted Callas as Brünnhilde in Wagner's 'Die Walküre'. He was set to conduct Bellini's 'I Puritani' featuring another soprano a week later. Maria used to practice in Serafin's hotel suite. One day, she toyed with the score of 'I Puritani', an opera she did not know, and sang an aria of the protagonist, Elvira. Serafin's wife had just put the phone down after speaking to him, hearing him ridden with anxiety because his 'Elvira' fell ill and with only days to the opening night he had not been able to find an alternative. "Tullio is on his way here. Will you do me a favor? When he comes in will you please sing that for him?" She told Maria (Adagietto,

2016a; CallasFan, 2015; Huffington, 1981), and so Maria sang Brünnhilde in the evenings and studied the role of Elvira during the days, within just six days. Brünnhilde is a mythical Nordic warrior, strong and brave. Elvira is a fragile girl whose broken heart renders her insane. The musical style of both operas and the vocal demands of the soprano are as opposed as the two characters and it takes two different singers. Brünnhilde is sung by dramatic sopranos, with a powerful, deep toned voice, while Elvira is a role which requires agile and fast vocal embellishments in the higher range (coloratura). It is the rare singer who is capable of performing both roles, and Maria excelled in both. "Even the most skeptical readily acknowledged the miracle that Callas performed" praised the review in 'Il Gazzettino' newspaper (Galatopoulos, 1998, p. 88; Meneghini, 1981, p. 72). She was a perfectionist and practiced relentlessly until she was pleased with the result, and she was rarely satisfied, always finding flaws in what she did.

She rose to stardom as a Diva, but deep inside her remained an embarrassed little girl. During rehearsals for the opera 'Parsifal', when her character Kundry is supposed to kiss the protagonist, she struggled to do so. Serafin came down from the conductor's podium, approached the singer who portrayed Parsifal, and kissed him. "If I can kiss him surely you can too", he then told Maria (Galatopoulos, 1998 p. 90).

She was the characters she sang. She succeeded in conveying a wide range of emotions through her singing and could interpret the vocally embellishing trills as portraying profound emotional states that could strike at the audience's heart like an arrow. Even without seeing her, one could feel the powerful and clear emotions in the shades of her voice. Callas was a phenomenon that led to a revolution in the world of opera. In a paraphrase, it is said that the world of opera is divided into B.C (Before Callas) and A.C (After Callas). She expanded the emphasis in opera beyond just singing and broadened the repertoire by reviving forgotten operas in unforgettable performances.

Eight hours after her wedding, Maria had set sail to Buenos Aires to participate in several opera productions. She cried like a little girl when she parted from Meneghini, who had to stay in Italy due to his business (Meneghini, 1981; Palmer, 1978). In Buenos Aires, she felt ill and often had fever in the evenings when the performance approached. She wrote: (May 13, 1949) "I damn the day I left and I am furious because you allowed me to leave. I can't live without you: It's time you understood that!" (Allegri & Allegri, 1997, p. 68). Ten days later (May 23, 1949) she described in her letter bizarre symptoms. Each and every day, she would feel fine in the mornings but come the afternoon her temperature would rise, her head would ache and her skin would break all over her body. Though not necessarily tying the symptoms to stage fright, Maria understood to some extent that those were psychosomatic symptoms. She wrote to Meneghini: "Dear, in order to be well I have to be near you, because you are everything to me" (Meneghini, 1981, pp. 93–94, my translation – H.Y.), stating no one can replace him or give her the comfort and sense of well-being that he gives.

A year later, Maria traveled to perform in Mexico City.[10] Once again, Meneghini could not join her. Perhaps due to the difficulties she experienced the last time in his absence, or maybe because of the scolding letters from Evangelia, Maria stopped on her way in New York and invited her mother to come along. She set off for battle and, like a boxer, she needed someone 'in her corner'. Evangelia, who arrived in Mexico after Maria, was received like a royal and thoroughly enjoyed her role as 'Queen Mother'. Her room at the hotel was adorned with fresh flowers daily, courtesy of the management, and she was invited to receptions at the embassy and dinners with the city's dignitaries. The experience was a realization of Evangelia's dream, but it was clouded by a sensation that her daughter had changed. Maria seemed distant, like 'a stranger' and lamented that Evangelia treated her like a child (E. Callas, 1960; Huffington, 1981). The three years that had passed since mother and daughter had last seen each other, and the changes in Maria's life did not prevent Evangelia from expecting that things would be as they once were. From her perspective, there was no margin between them, and in days to come she would see fit to publish in a book how at the end of the performances she would wash Maria's underwear, black from the make-up that turned her into the Ethiopian princess 'Aida'. Evangelia had put this in writing as a testament to her devotion. Was it devotion or ownership? Perhaps it was a covert struggle with Meneghini over the right to be the person closest to Maria, the one most intimate? Whatever the reason, she did not hesitate to violate her daughter's privacy for her own cause and publish it. Before they parted, 26-year-old Maria bought her mother a fur coat and handed her a large sum of money (E. Callas, 1960). The thought that she would never see her daughter again did not cross Evangelia's mind. What caused Maria to sever ties? Perhaps after three years of being separated by an ocean from her mother's control, Maria was fed up with Evangelia's ways. It is possible that the way Evangelia enjoyed Maria's success made Maria feel objectified and used, or it could have been Evangelia's increasing demands for financial support and gifts that led to the rift. Dazzled by her daughter's success, Evangelia felt entitled to share in its fruits. Yet despite her wealth, Maria could never escape her fear of poverty, an outcome of the deprivation in her childhood and youth. It seems that the breaking point for Maria was when her mother made it clear that she intended to move to Italy to live in Maria and Battista's home and be provided for by them. And perhaps what was most unbearable was Evangelia's reaction when Maria dared to refuse. Meneghini wrote that the thought of returning to the discord and dissentions that living with her mother entailed disrupted Maria's sleep, haunting her throughout her time in Mexico and bringing her to the brink of a nervous breakdown. "Battista, she wants to come and live with me", she wrote to him on May 19, 1949 from Mexico. "God forgive me, Battista, but… I have no intention of compromising my happiness, my right to be alone [with you]… How can I tell her that I care about her, but that my love for my husband is different"? (Allegri & Allegri, 1997, pp. 77–78). In that letter, Maria describes how her letters to her mother have been unanswered, making her worried about her. She writes Meneghini that she had arranged a flight ticket for her mother to come to Mexico but believes she would not come because she is angry at Maria's indirect refusal to let her live with them. The anxiety that overtook Maria over having to refuse her mother's will and her constant preoccupation with it are palpable throughout the letter. In effect, Maria is preoccupied with her mother in each and every letter she wrote to Meneghini from Mexico. Meneghini poignantly analyzes the extent of the influence her mother had had on her. He writes that Maria could not get the thought of her mother off her mind, fighting an internal conflict between the wish to 'help' (or rather please) her mother, and her fear of being a victim of her mother's will once more. Meneghini concludes:

> The sadness, the difficulties, the depressions, the irritability, the insomnia that Maria attributed in the letters to the weather, the disorganization, the malice of her colleagues, to being away from me, were all caused in reality by those familial problems that Maria never managed to resolve.
>
> (Meneghini, 1981, pp. 128–129, my translation – H.Y)

Maria's letters to him show just how right Meneghini was:

> May 25, 1950... My dear adored one...tonight I haven't slept a wink...I live in a state of abnormal apathy, with my physical endurance weakened by this damn weather and the altitude that takes away all the strength... My mother doesn't write... I don't see her arriving... I don't know how to live without you... our oness cannot be broken or divided, separation makes one suffer the most.
>
> (ibid, p. 129, my translation – H.Y)

Was it the height that sapped all her strength, or the thunderous silence of her mother, conveying that she was guilty and wicked, shattering her selfhood, and making her need Meneghini even more?

> May 29, 1950... My dear Battista...My mother doesn't write me. What has happened? I hope she isn't unwell. Must I always have worries?...I would die without you, who represent love, fidelity, elegance, finesse, in short all things ideal to me!
>
> (Volf, 2019, pp. 189–191, my translation – H.Y)

> June 1, 1950...My mother sent me a letter, saying I am egotistical, that I think only of myself and let her die in dire striats. I am so fed up I almost decided to sever ties with her...There is no rehearsal hall... I could kill everyone.
>
> (Meneghini, 1981, p. 131, my translation – H.Y)

> June 5, 1950...Today I am in bed, as well as yesterday, with one of my famous colds. This weather is drying out my throat, so they postponed Tosca...will Tosca bring me misfortune?... I don't know what to say to my mother! I mean,

imagine her disappointment when she finds out I'm not going to New York [on the way back to Italy]... I dare not tell her that I won't go.

(Volf, 2019, p. 196, my translation – H.Y)

June 6, 1950... Today, during the dress rehearsal of *Tosca*, I thought I was going to faint. Moreover, the fatal blow is the fact that I can't sleep! I get to 6:30 in the morning and later, without having slept a wink... I have to confess something: I greatly desire to have a baby of our own. I think it will do me good, also for the voice and my cursed skin. What do you think? Do you still not want to?... I send you my greetings...with all my heart that loves you...and declares you're its idol.

(ibid, p. 197, my translation – H.Y)

June 8, 1950...It's 8:30 in the morning and I haven't fallen asleep yet. I believe I'll go mad here in Mexico.

(Meneghini, 1981, p. 133, my translation – H.Y)

June 12, 1950. My dear adored one...I have had so much to study with Il Trovatore[11] and I can't learn anything here in Mexico, it turns one into an idiot... My mother arrived... and we're together... I am very nervous and I torment her.

(Volf, 2019, p. 199, my translation – H.Y)

After Evangelia returned to New York and Maria to Italy, a succession of letters began to cross the Atlantic Ocean, about Maria's obligation to her mother after everything she had done for her, about her financial difficulties, and about her expectations to receive money from Maria. (In one of the letters, she wrote to Maria that she had brought her into this world to provide for her.) (Huffington, 1981; Meneghini, 1981). These letters were seasoned with poisonous reproaches toward Battista, who had never met his mother-in-law, for not supporting her despite being a 'millionaire'. The more Evangelia felt she was losing her grip on her daughter, the more scolding and venomous the demanding and ill-tempered letters became, and Maria drifted further away until she finally ceased to respond. It appears that against her fear of her mother stood the support she found in Meneghini who, recognizing the destructive influence Evangelia had on Maria, wrote to her:

I have felt for some time that the letters Maria has received from home have been upsetting her and making her angry. To prevent this from happening any more, with consequences that could be disastrous, I have decided to write to you myself... To my great displeasure, I saw that the letter [translated from Greek for him] was malicious, vindictive, and offensive, and those things cannot be written by a good mother. You are full of vindictiveness which my wife does not deserve, and I return your insults to you. I also have to think of my wife's health and her dignity, seeing that she can't expect that from you... Think carefully, Signora, about every sentence you write... I have obligations to the family that

I have made with her and to any children we may have. And I will not allow our life to be spoiled by anybody. And I shall send your letters back with the same effrontery as you show in writing them. You are a woman who has lived her life, and I do not think Maria will forget her responsibilities and her family … Be very careful not to behave in a vulgar way, and do not utter any threats. You would do better to consider your station… and not to say whatever comes into your head.

(Petsalis-Diomidis, 2001, pp. 540–541)

Evangelia, by then back in Greece, wrote to George, demanding he forward her any letter the 'swine' might send him (Petsalis-Diomidis, 2001, p. 541). She added that Maria was dead to her, expressed the humiliation Maria made her feel by allowing 'that Italian' to insult her, and she instructed George to demand of Maria the money Maria's stay with him had cost him and to never again say that he has a daughter. It is possible that she did not succeed in manipulating George, but she did succeed in manipulating Jackie, who wrote to her sister that as a Greek "Our whole ethos is to stand by our families no matter what" (J. Callas, 1989, p. 156). Later on, Evangelia was prone to depression every time she imagined Maria's opening nights and the glory that accompanied them, which she missed. When a fortune teller predicted that her daughter will part with the man in her life, she reacted with elation, believing that this would bring Maria back to her. Maria's well-being was not a consideration, and the thought that it might be her second daughter, dependent on Milton for her livelihood, probably did not occur to her. Jackie was now the 'less important' daughter, and Evangelia was entirely absorbed in what she could not have and was completely oblivious to the daughter at her side, which she obliged to come have her meals with her daily and call her every day (J. Callas, 1981). Jackie, wired to do everything to reduce the unbearable anxiety she felt every time there was a possibility that she would not please her mother, obeyed, finding refuge in the solitude and quietness of her apartment between meals. "There was never any way to satisfy her and the only thing was to accept passively whatever she chose to say" she wrote (ibid, p. 176).

I always wondered as I stepped out of the lift and went to open her door just what sort of mood she would be in. Even a good mood was only a question of milder nagging – why had I not taken more care over my appearance, was I sure about the dress I was wearing?… A bad mood meant more cruel, searching questions, a persistent wearing down of the object before her, now always me. No one else would have borne it.

(ibid, pp. 211–212)

The more it registered with Evangelia that she had no one left but Jackie, the harder she strived to thwart any attempt by Jackie to become more independent. She tightened her grip on her, becoming increasingly preoccupied with her need for Jackie to be available for her. In days to come, when Jackie was 52, she refused to introduce her to a man who showed interest in marrying her.[12] Evangelia told her neighbor that Jackie would never marry. "As long as I live, I want my daughter near me" (ibid, p. 214). She made it clear to Jackie that her role in life was to take care of her, that it is the duty of children toward their parents, yet Evangelia herself did not treat her own mother accordingly and forbade Jackie from having any contact with George, with whom Jackie conducted a relationship in secret (J. Callas, 1981).

A decade after Maria and her mother last met in Mexico City, Evangelia published a book titled *My Daughter, Maria Callas* (E. Callas, 1960). The book contains the range of complex emotions experienced by Evangelia, including pride and love, but also devaluation, envy, greed, and above all, as the title of the book betrays, a desire to appropriate the daughter. The book can be divided into two parts. The first part examines the years in which Evangelia actively and influentially participated in Maria's life. In this section, her descriptions of her daughter, while not overflowing with warmth and affection, express appreciation and are mostly balanced. The second part begins with the severance of the relationship between mother and daughter. To Evangelia, this is a ruthless, incomprehensible act by a daughter toward a dedicated mother who had sacrificed her life for her. Her writing undergoes a change in this stage, clearly aiming to 'settle scores' and portray Evangelia as the innocent victim of her daughter. She washes her hands in innocence, disowning responsibility, and does not offer the smallest of insights into the roots of her daughter's hostility toward her. She slams Maria with severe insults. 'Apparently', She writes, "losing one's humanity is part of the price an artist must pay for greatness" (ibid, p. 158). She questions Maria's recollection of her childhood as an unhappy one of a 'friendless ugly duckling', writing that these are "tales she may have told herself as a child and which she still believes" (ibid, p. 163). Of Maria's exceptional acting talent she wrote: "There is no doubt that Maria's histrionics have played an important part in her success" (ibid, p. 147), continuing sarcastically: "She inherited her talent for make-believe from her father, who has been acting all his life" (ibid, p. 148). Of that very same acting talent music critic Teodoro Celli wrote:

> Perhaps, listening to all there is of sadness and terrible nostalgia, of aggression and depression in Callas' voice, we should be able to conclude not only that it is admirably apt for realizing drama in music, but also that it contains a drama within itself, that it is an indication of an unquiet, troubled, spiritual state expressing and purifying itself in sound.
>
> (E. Callas, 1960, pp. 149–150)

It seems that Evangelia was completely oblivious to the profound meaning that Celli's sensitivity perceived – The pain one hears in Callas's voice on stage emanates from the depths of her soul, and such pain does not come out of nowhere.

Evangelia calculated and detailed in the book the sums that Maria had earned in each period of her career, complained about Meneghini the 'Millionaire' for never giving her anything, and presented to the reader a complete inventory count of the: "25 fur coats, 150 pairs of shoes, 200 dresses and 300 hats" (ibid, p. 181) she learned from the newspaper that Maria owned. She complained about Maria's stinginess while mentioning the sums of money Maria had given her and the fur coat, her latest gift, which had cost 500 dollars, "as fine a present as any daughter could make to her mother" (ibid, p. 134). She did not fail to compare Maria to her great rival, opera singer Renata Tebaldi, who (ibid, p. 159) 'was devoted to her mother' (and never got married). The answer that Evangelia gave to herself to the question of why Maria chose to be a "motherless prima donna" is "all genius is tinged with madness" (ibid, p. 174) but she concluded that this answer is not sufficient. Evangelia genuinely could not understand why and how her good-natured baby, who never cried and was always a good and easy child, became an alienated stranger. Finally, Evangelia came to the conclusion that Maria's road accident at the age of five is the reason for her alienation from her mother and sister because Maria "subconsciously associates Jackie and me with this accident" (ibid, p. 175). Guilt also lies with Maria's father, who "did not lead a very peaceful home life" (ibid), while she sacrificed herself and remained married for the sake of her daughters. Finally, she summed it up:

> To say that anyone lacks common sense and a sense of humor-which means a sense of proportion-is, I suppose, considered by many an insult. When I say this of Maria, I do not mean it as an insult but as knowledge offered in all humility and sympathy. If she had common sense, she would never proclaim to the whole world that she does not love me.
>
> (ibid, p. 180)

Evangelia did not hesitate to speak on any platform given to her, relishing the sense of importance and revenge, presenting herself as a victim, and causing Maria reputational damage. At a certain point, Evangelia tried to sell dolls she had made in the likeness of opera heroines that Maria portrayed, like some compulsive magical voodoo ceremony meant to maintain her hold on her daughter.

Does the estrangement from her mother also mark the beginning of Maria's distancing from her husband? There is no doubt she increasingly felt that he saw her as a goose laying golden eggs, and there is no doubt that when they separated, after 12 years together, she persuaded herself that this was all he ever saw in her. Yet all evidence points to the fact that the relationship began with warm mutual feelings, even if it was lacking when it came to passion (Huffington, 1981; Palmer, 1978; Spence, 2021).

Like her mother, Battista wrote a book sharing their relationship with the world (Meneghini, 1981). He included letters that shed light on the process that unfolded between them. Maria, the young and promising singer who had just left her mother behind, needed someone else to take her place as scaffolds for her psych. Battista served in this role for many years, parallel to conductors and directors whom she adored and off whose appreciation of her she fed. These had significant roles at different periods in her life. With some of them, she behaved like a lovesick girl (Huffington, 1981; Palmer, 1978). When she traveled alone, without Meneghini for the first time since they met, she wrote to him:

> My dear Battista…my joy and purpose in life is to receive letters from you and compliments from the maestro [Serafin]… Rome is a beautiful big city… although nothing is beautiful if you are not there…How I would like to have you close right now. I want to hear you say: you speak [Italian] so well! Then I would like you to look at me in that special way of yours and hear that name that you call me.
>
> (Meneghini, 1981, pp. 49–50, my translation – H.Y)

She needed him both as a mirroring selfobject and as an idealized selfobject to merge with. She was insecure and manifested an anxious attachment pattern (Bowlby, 1988). During that same journey, which lasted six days, she wrote him ten letters and anxiously awaited his letters in return. In those letters she tells him how unwell she is without him, how she has no appetite, how lonely she is. She repeatedly begs him not to leave her alone and to write her and she conveys her anxiety at being separated from him, writing of her fear that he would be displeased to see her when she returns (Meneghini, 1981). In subsequent times they will be parted, she would write to Meneghini and share with him the need for perfection and the loneliness born out of fear of people, both tormented her soul and haunted her. She expected to be attacked, criticized, or exploited, and preferred to shut herself, a defense she called misanthropy. Her struggles left her even more dependent on the handful of people with whom she did form relations. She portrayed in her letters the struggle for perfection that paralleled in her private life and her singing:

> You see, dear, I am such a pessimist and everything afflicts and disturbs me. I am convinced that I do everything badly. Then I begin to get nervous and discouraged. At times, I reach the point of begging to die to be freed of the torments and anxieties that always afflict me.
>
> You see, I would like to give so much more in everything I do. In art as in my love for you. In singing I would like my voice always to do what I want. Yet it seems I ask too much. My voice is ungrateful and doesn't come out as I want… I would even say that it is rebellious and will not be commanded or, rather, dominated. It always wants to escape and makes me suffer. If I carry on like this, you will have a nervous breakdown on your hands.
>
> (Allegri & Allegri, 1979, p. 58)

It is the same with my love for you. I suffer because I cannot give you more… I suffer because of your distance, because I can't share everything about you… Without you I am alone. I don't have nor do I want friendships. You know what a 'misanthrope' I am. And I am rightly so. I live only for you and for my mother: and I am torn between you both!

(Meneghini, 1981, p. 62, my translation – H.Y)

Eleven years later, when she informed him that she was leaving him, her words expressed the other side of a symbiotic relationship and how much like her mother he was to her: "You are like my jailer. You never leave me alone. You control me in everything. You're like a hateful guardian and you have kept me in chains all these years. I'm fed up" (Meneghini, 1981, p. 291, my translation – H.Y).

What has transpired between them? Perhaps Battista in the eyes of 'La Callas' was not the same Battista a 23-year-old Maria had met as an unknown singer, without a penny, all alone in a foreign land. Meneghini was a well-known and respected man in Verona, and it was easy for her to be impressed by him. He was kind and generous to her and assisted her with his connections. She sought, and for a time found in him, "a shelter and screen to protect me from the outside world" (Volf, 2017). La Callas, having conquered La Scala, the pinnacle of every opera singer's aspirations, and having won the hearts of the sophisticated Milanese, found herself a woman of the world, speaking four languages fluently, courted by the world's most important dignitaries. Alongside her stood a man who seemed to her unrefined, lacking in intellectual depth, who spoke only Italian and haggled with opera house managers over her fees like a horse trader, harming her career by doing so. In his book, Meneghini wrote: "As a singer, Maria was a product to me. Instead of selling bricks... I began to sell a voice" (Meneghini, 1981, p. 272, my translation – H.Y). Maria had changed, and their marriage was nearing its end. The transformation Maria underwent was both internal and external. She began to hear criticisms from her colleagues about her weight, and in a review of her performance in 'Aida' at La Scala, it was written that it was impossible to distinguish between the legs of Aida and those of the elephants on stage (Huffington, 1981). The offended Maria decided to strive for perfection in her appearance to par her singing. She invested such efforts in portraying young, consumptive, tormented women, while her sizable physical attributes ruined the spell. She shed about 80 lbs. at a dazzling pace, keeping in her mind's eye the skinny, elegant figure of Audrey Hepburn. Maria became a beautiful woman, tall and slim. Her eyes were large, and their expression was deep and fascinating. She started to wear the latest fashion and always looked like she stepped out of a magazine. She was the embodiment of elegance. Despite the transformation from an ugly duckling into a real swan, she continued to feel deep insecurity about her appearance. She increasingly surrounded herself with fashion designers, hair stylists, and high-society figures.

To what extent did Maria's narcissism play a role in her separation from Battista, 12 years after they first met? It seems that the more she advanced in her art and her status, the more Battista failed to meet her perfectionistic standards. The critical, demanding, and un-empathic image of her mother was evidently internalized in Maria. She was stubborn and unforgiving, primarily toward herself, but also toward those around her. "I am personally incapable of enjoying what I have done well because I see so magnified the things I could have done better", she said (Huffington, 1981, p. 41). It seems that 'Titta' was never a separate person in her eyes. According to his description, she demanded his presence by her side when she woke up in the morning and reacted with a tantrum if he was not there (Meneghini, 1981). The great Diva treated him like a two-year-old child behaves with his mother. At the beginning of their relationship, when she was 24, Maria wrote to him:

> I want the best of the best. I want my man to be the best of all. I want my art to be the most perfect. I want, in short, to have the best of everything. Even my clothes: I want them to be the best possible to be had. I know that all this is not possible and it torments me greatly. Why? Help me Battista, don't think I'm exaggerating. It's the way I am.
>
> (Allegri & Allegri, 1979, p. 59)

She also wrote to Meneghini how much she needs him to love her, how deeply it hurts her if he is the least displeased with her, desperately beseeching him to love and understand her.

To Maria, the world was monochromatic and her skin was extremely thin. Twelve years from the day they first met, Battista was no longer 'the best man'. Unfortunately, her perspective on who was 'the best man', even at the age of 36, was that of one easily dazzled and devoid of the ability to contain contradictions and complexities, much like that of a child or, at most, an adolescent.

Aristotle Socrates Onassis did not like opera. To him it resembled a bunch of Italian chefs shouting risotto recipes at each other in a language he did not understand. But Onassis loved to rub shoulders with celebrities, and Maria was one of the greatest celebrities of her time. They met at a glamorous party, where they were introduced to each other as "the two most famous living Greeks in the world". She was dressed in a magnificent designer outfit and was adorned with borrowed diamonds worth millions. Onassis, a shipping magnet and savvy businessman, immediately assessed the magnitude of the prize before him. He examined his meticulously combed-back hair, his sharp facial features tightening in determination, and quickly seated himself next to Maria, his wife following in his footsteps. Shortly after, Maria and Meneghini received an invitation to sail aboard the Christina, his luxurious yacht (Huffington, 1981).

Maria's acquaintance with Onassis found her at a crossroads in her professional and personal life. Since she had noticeably lost weight, there had been a change in her voice. She had always struggled with her voice, but it seemed to deteriorate rapidly. It lost strength, became unpredictable, and she struggled to control it. Sometimes she was at her best, and at other times, she received hurtful reviews. When she sang a high note, the sound was unstable with an increasingly uncontrolled wobble. She had to cancel performances more frequently, provoking the audience's anger who considered this a haughty Diva's behavior. Her heart broke when someone put a dead dog in her car and her home's gate was smeared with excrement, the audience's reaction to the cancelation of her 'Norma' performance at the end of the first act, with the President of Italy at the audience. Poor Maria went onstage ill and did her best, but could not go on (Huffington, 1981; Meneghini, 1981). The Italian audience saw the interruption of the performance as an insult to the President and the Republic, and their ruthless reaction felt to Maria like a public execution. She wished to reduce her busy performance schedule but faced resistance from Meneghini, who pushed her to continue for economic reasons (Spence, 2021; Stancioff, 1987).

The reason for the deterioration of her voice is not entirely clear. Possible factors include her rapid weight loss, the price she paid for the reckless use of her voice, which she never spared, singing demanding and dramatic roles at a very young age before her voice matured into them. She must have increasingly used compensatory muscles and mechanisms, leading to further weakening of her vocal cords and an erosion of the technique she had worked so hard to master. She spent time around heavy smokers, and at some point, she occasionally smoked herself, and there are claims that she suffered from an autoimmune disease[13] that affected her throat tissues (Fussi & Paolillo, 2017). There is no doubt that psychological factors were also a significant part of Callas's vocal decline, and it seems that she was aware of this herself. "Like anyone else I have to be praised and boosted up all the time because I am a born pessimist. Remember always that only a happy bird sings while an unhappy one creeps into its nest and dies", she said (Dragadze, 1964, p. 69).

With her confidence further undermined with each betrayal of the voice, the necessity of going on stage became a torment. Fever became a recurring phenomenon on opening nights. As expectations grew, and her audience increasingly included presidents and princes, it became increasingly difficult to sing. Her fright increased, and memories of a jeering, cruel, unforgiving audience overwhelmed her. The venom she faced made her feel detached from the audience (and also move her residence to Paris eventually). The satisfaction she once derived from the roaring, admiring crowd was now tainted by these experiences. Maria, who in her private life had always been reserved and kept to herself, detached in a world of her own, began seeking refuge in her professional life as well. It is reasonable to assume that the more her voice betrayed her the more she felt that Meneghini, who showed no understanding of her difficulties, regarded her as a milking cow. He was no longer a supportive and empowering presence in her inner world, which made it even more challenging to go on stage. Her longing for a child remained unfulfilled as well, perhaps because Meneghini did not want her lucrative career to be affected, or perhaps, as he claimed, because she could not conceive (Meneghini, 1981). Despite public declarations about the depth of her love, intended to deny her marital situation primarily to herself, shortly before she accepted Onassis's invitation and boarded the Christina for the first time she requested that her income from her upcoming professional commitment will not be transferred to her joint account with Meneghini (Huffington, 1981).

The Christina was precisely the refuge Maria needed, and Onassis was the ideal host. In fact, the man resembled his beloved yacht: a showboat, extravagant and lecherous, with a zest for life and designed to grab attention. Next to him, the aging Meneghini appeared even gloomier, stingier, and more tedious. They sailed together for three weeks in the company of Churchill and his entourage, basking in the sun that gilded the ocean, sipping champagne, enjoying the swimming pool, and savoring the delicacies emerging from the ship's galley.

Onassis was captivated by Maria. They found a common language, both literally and metaphorically. The 17-year gap between them was no obstacle, not for Maria, whose need for a big, powerful man to protect her was as strong as ever, and certainly not for Onassis, who was known for his conquests and skills as a lover. The fact that she was almost a head taller than him was also not an issue. Their bond was strong and immediate. Both of them were of Greek origin, both began their lives in difficulty and poverty, both endured the hardships of war. Both achieved greatness in their respective fields. Both harbored a hidden, insecure, and plebeian side, wrapped in glamor and wealth. He saw in her a fighter like himself, a winner, and a worthy adornment symbolizing his status and power. She loved to listen to his stories and provide the admiration he so greatly needed. With him, the girl who had felt loved only for her voice finally felt like a woman, loved for who she was. With his larger-than-life gestures and the passion he was known for, Maria experienced for the first time the emotions and desires that had previously only been realized on stage. Despite her moralistic principles, Maria found herself falling into his arms like a ripened fruit (Huffington, 1981; Palmer, 1978; Spence, 2021).

The Christina anchored in Istanbul, where the Greek Church Patriarch received Onassis and his guests. He called Onassis the 'new Ulysses' (Odysseus). Onassis and Maria knelt side by side before him to receive his blessing. For Maria, the experience was like a divine blessing that united them, and she appeared to be distraught (Huffington, 1981; Stancioff, 1987). She was not the only one who saw it this way. "But she is already married", murmured Meneghini, who looked on from the side on what for him was a curse (Huffington, 1981, p. 203).

His struggle against the new Ulysses was flaccid. He saw Maria dancing all the time, always with Onassis, vibrant and full of life, and he suppressed the meaning. One night, she did not return to their room. At dawn, he went looking for her and encountered Onassis, smug and smiling on the deck. Suspicion pierced his heart, but he remained silent. When Maria returned to the room, she exploded and demanded that he stopped being her shadow. She criticized his appearance, attire, and uncouth behavior. He did not ask anything. He heard about the affair from Tina Onassis and kept silent, hoping in vain that Maria would come around. When they returned to Italy, she demanded that they each go to a different house (Meneghini, 1981).

Onassis did not anticipate the following developments. Tina, his wife who had turned a blind eye to his constant affairs, demanded a divorce. Although his ability to adorn the world's most famous singer like a jewel was a significant factor in his relationship with her, it seemed he loved Maria. However, he had no intention of separating from his wife and tried to appease her as best as he could. Tina was resolute in her decision, and Maria became the 'first lady' of the Christina. For the first time in her life, she felt liberated from the constant worries of commitments and performances. Life alongside her Ari was all that she desired. "You cannot serve two masters", she told her good friend, director Franco Zeffirelli (Huffington, 1981, p. 212). She listened to Onassis's mythology stories and stories about his business ventures like a child listening to her father telling fairytales. Her time by his side transformed her significantly. The Diva who was nicknamed 'The Tigress' became a kitten. Perhaps because she felt more loved and fulfilled, she had softened and became more forgiving. She bent herself to his will and started to take an interest in his areas of interest. She adopted his friends and his lifestyle, deprived of a separate life of her own, living for him and in his world. She bore in silence the humiliating status of a lover and the headlines in the newspapers, including the words of her mother who all of the sudden praised the attributes of her son-in-law (Huffington, 1981). "Maria will never be happy… Women like Maria can never know real love… I was Maria's first victim, now it's Meneghini. Onassis will be the third" she was quoted as saying (ibid, p. 209).

At this stage of their relationship, Maria had never been happier. Ari, too, was more serene than ever, his famous outbursts of anger subsiding. They sailed and partied in the company of princes, heads of state, and Hollywood starlets. Maria's performances dwindled and waned. The lack of training, late-night revelries, smoking, and weeks in the sun and in the sea breeze deteriorated her voice further. The vocal cords are muscles, and opera singing requires their constant training, along with other muscles in the body that support voice production and breath control. The vocal abilities of an opera singer are much like those of an athlete – if he stops training, he will lose them. Maria, who used to train for hours every day, now went for weeks without singing at all.

The rarer her performances became, the more in demand they were, and the seats filled with celebrities, which only heightened her anxiety. In the end, she had to resort to pills and tranquilizer-injections in order to take the stage (Huffington, 1981).[14]

Maria sought a new meaning in self-fulfillment as a woman. Her entire life had been devoted to art, relegating her other dream of starting a family to the background. She was deeply connected to the cultural values she came from, and despite her lifestyle, she believed in traditional gender roles (Huffington, 1981). In her eyes, a marriage proposal was just a matter of time, but Onassis saw it differently. No one could pinpoint the exact moment when their romantic idyll was tarnished for the first time. Perhaps his divorce stirred resentment toward Maria within him, and his anger at himself was turned toward her. Maybe he felt dependent on her, now that he had lost his wife. The more he loved Maria, the smaller and weaker he felt in comparison, and the need to maintain a power balance through control and humiliation grew, blinding his already limited ability to see the other, much like the Cyclop in the Odyssey. Despite the monstrous cruelty that emanated from him, she continued to see a Ulysses in him and responded with absolute submission. Gradually, he began to speak to her with jabs disguised as affection, and over time, he made less and less effort to hide his mockery. A cloud of fear of losing him loomed and grew in her heart, overshadowing her happiness. She cut her hair short as he wished, lengthened her nails, and stopped playing the piano. He used to call her dress maker with instructions. Since he liked her in black, she bought one black dress after another. He told her she looked ugly in her glasses, and Maria wandered around blindly, holding her glasses in her hand, occasionally peering through them, then hurriedly removing them. His two children hated her, blaming her for the separation from their mother. She walked wordlessly in the street behind the three of them, silently enduring the curses and insults that his children hurled at her while he remained quiet. He relished mocking her and demeaning her in front of others (Huffington, 1981; Stancioff, 1987). The more she yielded to him, the more he felt an inexplicable urge to be crueler, and he did so with the same proficiency he used to pursue and satisfy women. He knew Maria's weaknesses well. "What are you? Nothing. You just have a whistle in your throat that no longer works", he said in front of their friends (Huffington, 1981, p. 212). He reveled in his cruelty and her humiliation in front of others. Once he made her lend a dress of hers to a guest, then said: "Maria!... Look how beautifully her bust fills out that dress of yours!" (Stancioff, 1987, p. 156). Her performances revolved around his sailing schedule and decreased in frequency. He did not like her to sing. "If a person is in love, he does not want to see you on stage. That is comprehensible" (Adagietto, 2016b), she told herself. The person in love increasingly set sail without her, not even telling her where. He was ostentatiously absent from some of her most important and successful opening nights. There was no reason for it, except for the green-eyed monster that possessed him when her success turned too threatening for him, but after her failures, he could offer comfort. When her voice cracked on a high C during a performance of 'Norma' at the Paris Opera, the audience booed and shouted insults at her. She stopped, signaled the conductor to start over, and successfully sang through the 'C'. Behind the scenes, he expressed his pride in her and supported her (Huffington, 1981). When she showed a fighting spirit, he could feel solidarity and closeness.

She surrendered herself to his game of dominance and gave herself to him. She assumed it was an expression of great love between a man and a woman. In a television interview, unaware of the full implications of her words, she said, "we loved each other, maybe too much. And strong men... they usually want to completely domineer a woman, dominate them, and I want to be dominated of my own accord" (MariaCallasMuseum, 2011). Her few friends found the way he treated her difficult to bear, and some of them distanced themselves. When she could no longer bear it, she would erupt, leaving the room in rage, and he would pursue her again. She used to blame herself. When she underwent sinus surgery, he was not by her side. Her fortieth birthday arrived. The glamor of Aristotle's world was fading, a world to which she had never truly belonged. She longed for love and connection with another soul, something Onassis provided less and less of (Huffington, 1981; Palmer, 1978).

In 1965, she sang Norma again, the role she loved the most and had performed more times than any other. On the premiere night, filled with tranquilizers, she felt she could barely stand on stage, let alone sing, but she was too afraid to cancel once more. Just before stepping onto the Paris Opera stage, she crossed herself, as she always did before a performance, desperately searching for something to hold on to and regain an illusion of control. She managed the performance well, but on the evening of the last performance, nothing helped. She went on stage a nervous wreck, against her doctor's advice. When the curtain fell on the third scene, Maria lost consciousness. The audience did not watch the rest of the opera that evening. She apologized feebly to the audience gathered outside the opera house as she was being carried out on a stretcher. A decade earlier, she had said in an interview: "When my enemies stop hissing, I shall know I'm slipping" (Huffington, 1981, p. 272). The audience was mostly silent, pitying, and she knew.

There were four London performances of Tosca left to which she had committed. Her nerves have failed her. She was ill, her blood pressure was low, and her doctor forbade her to fly. The people who had slept for a week on the street waiting for tickets watched her understudy. She yielded to the pleas and made it to the final performance, attended by the queen and all the dignitaries, but not by true opera lovers, who had to settle for another Tosca. Oblivious to the irony that, like in her private life, she chose the people of empty image over those who could have given her true love, she stepped onto the stage to a chillingly cold reception. The date was June 5, 1965. Maria was 42. The opera concluded with enthusiastic and prolonged applause and cruel reviews in the newspapers (Huffington, 2002/1981). The Evening Standard wrote: "Yesterday only the ashes were seen, the fire was extinguished" (Spence, 2021, p. 307). That was the last opera she ever performed.

That summer, her relationship with Onassis deteriorated, and he became increasingly abusive. She stood guard, anticipating his moods, which were only becoming worse due to business difficulties he had encountered. She was riding his emotional rollercoaster with him. Many times after he had hurt her, he showered her with flowers and jewelry. She could not understand how he could treat her so well and so bad and could not imagine a life without him. "He really does love me", she told herself, "you can't lie in bed" (Huffington, 1981, p. 343). "He is hurt because Prince Rainier has turned his back on their friendship and is relegating his business out of Monaco", she tried to comprehend. He was like two different people, and she was caught in the contradiction between the two personalities, unable to reconcile the gap in her psych that was accustomed to seeing the world in black and white. She blamed herself and was caught in the same pattern again and again, hoping this time things would change. Now, without opera, she felt even more wretched and empty and dependent on him.

A glimmer of hope came to her in the form of an offer to star in the film 'Tosca', alongside Tito Gobbi, the famous baritone, one of her few colleagues who had become a friend and whose acting talent equaled her own. The marvelous tenor, Franco Corelli, was also part of the cast. Her friend the brilliant director, Franco Zeffirelli, was to direct. Had the project come to fruition, it might have opened a new path for Maria's career, free from the anxiety of a live performance, but Onassis sabotaged the negotiations that would have made her greater-than-life performance eternal. The second act of 'Tosca', with Callas and Gobbi, directed by Zeffirelli, staged in The Covent Garden in 1964, was filmed. It only makes one mourn what Onassis denied the world.[15] Her relationship with Onassis had changed her as a woman, and her 'Tosca' was now painted with far more diverse shades, drawn with a finer brush compared to her previous interpretations. Zeffirelli said that in Scarpia, the character portrayed by Gobbi, he saw Onassis. Scarpia is a powerful chief of police, and his relations and very being are based on his power. He is determined to conquer Tosca, the admired and beautiful opera singer, at any cost, deriving apparent sadistic pleasure from tormenting her. "For love of her Mario, she will yield to my pleasure" he sings, then adds: "The taste of a violent conquest is stronger than that of sweet consent" (Puccini & Illica, 1900). Had Onassis loved opera, he could surely have found himself in Scarpia's words: "I desire something, I pursue that which I desire, satisfy myself, then throw it away, seeking new prey. God created diverse beauties and diverse wines; I want to taste as many of these divine creations as I can". For Scarpia, just like Onassis, the Diva whom the world worshipped was a particularly large and satisfying prey.

"I didn't like the idea of Scarpia portrayed as a one color villain", told Zeffirelli (Palmer, 1978).

> There must be shades… in this character of this man who is extremely ruthless but also extremely charming. That is what attracted, in a dangerous way, Tosca… Scarpia…he had a deep wound to heal and he never healed, the fact that he could not be loved… little by little I was conveying to her the idea that Scarpia was a bit like Onassis. I suddenly found myself a little short from saying: "he's a kind of Aristo". I didn't say it but she read my mind and she understood where her Scarpia was.
>
> (Cole, 2003; Palmer, 1978)

The tension between Gobbi and Callas onstage is palpable, like fumes of explosive material waiting to ignite. Zeffirelli breathed life into Callas's Tosca as an admired and proud diva, who harbors within her an attraction to Scarpia's power. In her life, Maria interpreted Onassis's aggressive domination over her as love, and a part of her took masochistic pleasure in succumbing to him. It is no wonder for a child whose relationship with her mother manifested in aggressive domination.

Onassis presented extensive demands to the producers of the 'Tosca' film and it seemed that he was not interested in the film being made. When Maria tried to intervene during the negotiations, he exploded: "Shut up! Don't interfere, you know nothing about these things. You are nothing but a nightclub singer!" (Huffington, 1981, p. 274). Without a word, Maria stood up and left the room. Shortly after, she announced that she would not participate in the project (Huffington, 1981; Palmer, 1978).

In 1966, Maria renounced her American citizenship. She did so following legal harassment from the wounded Meneghini and due to a Greek law that suggested that under Greek citizenship as a sole citizenship, her marriages to Meneghini were null and void. She had hoped that Onassis would finally marry her, but he responded to questions from the press on the matter with a smug, sardonic reply that humiliated her: "We are very close, good friends. This new event changes nothing... It is wonderful for her to be a Signorina[16] again" (Huffington, 1981, p. 277).

That year, a 43-year-old Maria found herself pregnant. There was nothing she desired now more than a child; she had longed for it since she was a girl, but Onassis threatened to leave her if she did not terminate the pregnancy. Against her moral beliefs, Maria gave up the one thing that could have given meaning and purpose to her empty life, for the sake of a relationship that would soon come to an end (Huffington, 1981; Stancioff, 1987).[17]

Poor woman! All alone, abandoned
In this populous desert called Paris.
What can I hope for? What must I do?
Enjoy myself and in the vortex of pleasures perish

From "La Traviata" (Verdi & Piave, 1853),
first act. (My translation – H.Y)

She purchased an apartment in Paris; Onassis sailed more and more without her. When she knew he would arrive, she made sure to go to bed early so as to meet him 'fresh'. She knew all along that he kept on having affairs, but the next affair was different. His next target was set as the glamorous widow of the American President Kennedy. Here was a famous woman of a high social status that did not pose a threat for him by succeeding on her own. In his eyes, she was a greater prize than Maria, and his mind calculated the business he could conduct in America as her husband. When he took Jackie Kennedy for a cruise aboard the Christina, Maria could no longer turn a blind eye. He instructed her to wait for him in Paris, saying he intended to host someone in August and she will be in the way. She knew who he was talking about and tried to resist. When she realized it was futile, she said, "I'm leaving you". He responded with a characteristic dismissal: "I'll see you in September after the cruise". "No, you don't understand. I'm leaving you. You're never going to see me again – ever!" (Huffington, 1981, p. 288). While Onassis and Jackie sailed together, Maria accompanied them in her mind's eye, tormented. From now on, she would not sleep without relying on sleeping pills.

"I lived for art, I lived for love", sang Tosca (Puccini & Illica, 1900). Maria had nothing left to live for. For the first time, she was alone, without a supportive figure to merge with, lonely with a disintegrating psych. The thought of returning alone to her apartment in Paris terrified her, so she flew to the United States. There, wounded and bitter, she poured her heart out to acquaintances. "After nine years, not a child, not a family, not a friend!... you have a girl... If today she says she'll love forever, and then tomorrow she treats you…very badly…you'll be a nervous wreck" (Huffington, 1981, p. 291), she told her friend and admirer, music critic John Ardoin, breaking up for an instant and crying in his arms, then quickly collecting herself. Her sentences disjointed and without context, recalling painful memories from her entire life one after the other in endless circles.[18] Her words were filled with sadness, bitterness, anger, and despair. She experienced the breakdown she had tried to escape all her life – a deep, primal loneliness mixed with present day loneliness.

> I also wonder will I ever really be happy, or will I really pass my life always struggling to survive?… They [people] care for one day, one month, one year. And then what?… What does one do? Sit in the four walls? I've been facing four walls all my life!
>
> (Silver Singing Method, 2009)

Those who witnessed her pain found it difficult to bear the spectacle.

About two months after she last disembarked the Christina, she heard on television that Onassis and Jackie were to be married the following day. He did not bother to tell her (Huffington, 1981).

She tried to move on and starred a movie that failed. The film was a non-operatic version of the Greek tragedy 'Medea', which was one of her greatest operatic roles. Now, more than ever, she identified with Medea. The director of the film, Pasolini, poignantly described the likeness of the two: "Here is a woman, in one sense the most modern of women, but there lives in her an ancient woman – strange, mysterious, magical, with terrible inner conflicts" (Huffington, 1981, p. 296). Medea, who also appears in Ovid's 'Metamorphoses', is a priestess of the goddess Hecate and therefore possesses magical powers. She loses herself and her powers in her love for Jason. Pasolini described the role to Maria:

> Suddenly she finds in love which humanizes her a substitute for her lost religious sense. In the sensual experience she finds the lost rapport, the sacred identification with reality. So the world, the future, her well-being, the meaning of things, all take shape again suddenly for her. It is with gratitude, like one who feels reborn, that she lets Jason possess her.
>
> (ibid, p. 297)

In her biography of Callas, Huffington suggests that the filming of 'Medea' enabled her to exorcise some of the bitterness she harbored after her separation from Onassis. Callas undoubtedly dealt at the same time with far more ancient bad objects, that her experience with Onassis had stirred up and whom she would never exorcise from her psych. "That's like cancer, I'll never get rid of her and the consequences", she wrote to her godfather, after another humiliating interview with her mother was published (Huffington, 1981, p. 250).

In her final years on the opera stage, Callas limited herself to only three roles: Tosca, Medea, and Norma. The plot of Norma is very similar to that of Medea – a high priestess who had sacrificed everything for a man who lost interest in her and betrayed her with another woman. There are several recordings of Callas's Norma. One can hear the difference in the range of emotions and their complexity in the latest recording from 1960, conducted by Serafin, which contains different intensities of tenderness and of jealousy and pain, her experiences with Onassis. When Norma discovers that her beloved has betrayed her, she says to the other woman:

> Oh, you are the victim
> Of such a cruel and fatal deception!
> Rather than meeting him
> Death would have harmed you less!
> A fountain of eternal tears
> He has opened for you too
> Just as he deluded my heart
> The wicked will betray yours
>
> From the opera 'Norma' (Bellini
> & Romani, 1831), first act. [My
> translation – H.Y.]

Maria could not free herself from the role of the victim. A victim of her mother, of a world she experienced as jealous and cruel, and a victim of Onassis's betrayal. Her thinking was greatly magical, steeped in superstition, and she defined herself as fatalistic. "Destiny is destiny and there's no way out" (Volf, 2017), she said. Her childhood experiences prevented her from developing a sense of agency and an understanding that she can make choices, giving her some control over her life.

All alone with her maid, Bruna, and her butler, Ferruccio, who were like family to her, pleading with them to forego their weekly day off, Callas was a wreck. "God, give me what you want, I have no choice, good or bad, but give me the strength also to be able to overcome it", she used to pray (Volf, 2017).

Onassis's honeymoon was short. Within a few weeks, he was already beneath Maria's window, forcing her to let him in by threatening to start a commotion on the street (Huffington, 1981, Palmer, 1978). Jackie was a brook on which he gazed like Narcissus. She was too much like him, a mirror that did not return love. Had he continued to gaze at her he would be surrounded by death, and aside from that, the mirror was spending a budget totaling hundreds of thousands of dollars a month on clothes and various whims, and demanded more. Onassis realized his mistake fast, albeit too late. Maria, like Echo, withered away waiting in the apartment on Rue George Mandel in Paris. When he came back into her life, it was as if she came back to life as well. She hosted a dinner party, inviting friends to ease the excitation that gripped her upon his arrival, wanting to update him on everything that had happened to her while they were apart. Her expression and tone were those of a flustered girl (Huffington, 1981). The goddess, the tigress, the fierce diva were absent; instead, there was a little naive girl dreaming of loving and being loved.

Jackie was not as naive. She undoubtedly anticipated that he would graze in foreign pastures. Her first husband was a womanizer and a president, her second husband was a womanizer and a millionaire. Onassis did not anticipate that the fragile president's widow would turn out to be a worthy rival for him. In February 1970, the headlines roared. Letters that Jackie had sent to an old friend were published in the newspapers, revealing too great a closeness. Onassis served his meticulous revenge gradually. He flew to Paris. Newspapers around the world were filled with photos of Onassis and Maria dining in the glamorous restaurant 'Maxim's'. Jackie was able to bear infidelity in silence, but she could not bear the public humiliation. The next day, she was already in Paris. She ensured that a photograph of her and Onassis dining at the very same table in Maxim's would make the newspaper's front pages. Maria served as a prop for two master artists in a game whose rules she did not know. When she saw the morning newspaper with the picture of Onassis and Jackie dining at Maxim's, she understood. That night, Maria could not sleep. How could he? Why had he used her so? She took one sleeping pill after another, seeking solace for her tormented soul. In the morning, she was hospitalized, barely conscious.

The game continued. Maria lived from one visit of her Ari to another, forgiving him time and again, while he and Jackie escalated the stakes in their abusive game. When Jackie demanded more money, Onassis made sure that items about her unfettered shopping trips were published. The game would have ended in a resounding victory for Onassis, had he not spent the rest of his days attempting to escape his marriage without Jackie laying her hands on his money. In November 1972, nude photos of Jackie, sunbathing on Onassis's private island of Scorpios, were published in the pornographic magazine 'Hustler'. "Call your lawyers! Sue them, Ari!", she demanded, distraught, unaware that he was the one who tipped the photographers where and when they could obtain the final ingredient for his meticulously concocted revenge (Huffington, 1981).

Onassis felt that he was struck with the famous Kennedy curse.[19] Ever since Jackie came into his life, troubles never ceased. First, his daughter Christina married against his wishes. He quickly cut her off from the inheritance, and within six month the pressure he exerted on her led to her divorce. Then, his ex-wife married his business and emotional nemesis. Further on his business dealings also faced difficulties. He felt the whole world was against him. Maria was there to support him, taking comfort in knowing that she was his best friend and the person closest to him. Eventually, he suffered the blow from which he would never recover. In January 1973, his beloved son Alexander, in whom he saw himself reflected and whom he treated like a tyrant, died in a plane crash. Overwhelmed by guilt, he was consumed by thoughts that his enemies had killed his son to hurt him. He became a paranoid and broken man. Even the wonders he once knew how to work in his business dealings were gone. Too late he realized that he had cast aside the realest thing he had had. Now, only a shadow of the man he once was, he held on to Maria, and she was there for him, but their relationship appeared to be primarily friendly, and the world became an emptier place than ever (Huffington, 1981).

Maria sank deeper into despair and withdrew further into seclusion in her Paris apartment. "The less you give, the less you're hurt. Even if you meet something that's good you don't want it because you are so afraid. So even that is spoiled" (Huffington, 1981, p. 307, Silver Singing Method, 2009) she said in her unique way of speaking, but using the third person did not really distance the pain. The experiences that were ingrained in her early life grew ever more persecutory. She kept her distance from people, fearing they would use her for her name and fame, afraid of getting hurt. She spent her days sleeping until noon, watching westerns and cartoons, trying to delay the tormenting going to sleep. When she could not sleep, she would spend the night listening to her own old records. What few projects she engaged in have failed. First, there was the film 'Medea', then she attempted to direct an opera. Master classes she gave at Juilliard generated broad interest, but it did not bring her any relief (Huffington, 1981; Palmer, 1978). Even though what the students received from her was priceless, teaching was not for her, she did not find comfort or fulfillment in imparting her knowledge to the younger generation. For her, the master class was an opportunity to feel her way around and sing without being exposed to criticism.

She worked on her voice, trying to restore its lost brilliance. In a perfect timing, her colleague from days gone by, tenor Giuseppe Di Stefano, approached her and suggested they go on a joint concert tour. He needed money for his sick daughter who had cancer; she needed a reason to get up in the morning (Huffington, 1981). "Dear Pippo, every day, fortunately, is one day less" (Palmer, 1978), she told him when they met. Once again, Maria had someone by her side to bolster her shaky professional confidence, someone who soon became a lover. Maria was inextricably bound to Ari, and Di Stefano was bound in matrimony, but they both needed each other. Di Stefano persuaded and pressured her, and she agreed to perform again, eight years since she last set foot on stage. The result was sorrowful. "Like a monochrome reproduction of an oil painting", was the London Times' review of their first performance (Huffington, 1981, p. 326). Both of them were far from their days as the greatest singers of the 20th century. Maria's acting talent was still moving, and at times one could hear in her voice an echo of its greatness, but it was evident that she was struggling with the broken Stradivarius in her throat and was cautious with it. Despite everything, just as she expected, an hour-long program was stretched to two hours due to the applause. The grateful audience wanted to see La Callas, and what was lacking of her they completed with their mind's eye. She was painfully aware of it, but she gulped the love of the audience down like someone lost in the desert longing for water. The music critics and journalists did not spare her, subjecting her to harsh reviews and cruel questions. The pressure mounted, and the fact that Di Stefano's wife joined him added tension. On the eve of a performance in New York, she took one sleeping pill after another. In the morning, a psychiatrist was called to her room. The audience received a notice of the cancelation of that evening's performance due to 'acute upper respiratory tract inflammation' (Huffington, 1981). The concert tour deteriorated, as did her relationship with Di Stefano, who would recall that when Maria was in love she was "possessive, invasive, and jealous" (Allergri & Allegri, 1997, p. 157). On November 11, 1974, Callas gave the last performance in her life, in Sapporo, Japan.

The hope of singing again faded, and Onassis's life was fading away as well. He was afflicted with myasthenia gravis, his muscles weakening as a tangible reflection of his declining spirit. When hospitalized for surgery in Paris, the cashmere blanket Maria once bought him was among the few things he took with him. He knew that the end was near but tried to ignore it. The last time she saw him, he said to her, "I loved you. Not always well, but as much and the best I could. I tried" (Volf, 2017). He never regained consciousness after the surgery. He lay so close to Maria's home, yet Jackie prevented her from seeing him. Led to think that his condition might last for weeks and unable to bear the pain, Maria fled to Palm Beach, pacing restlessly in the hallways of the rented house. Within a few days, she received word of his death. When his coffin was laid to rest in Scorpios Island in Greece, she lamented agonizingly in the United States (Huffington, 1981).

The year was 1975 and Maria's life ended with his. She returned home, driving away her friends and lovers with empty phone conversations in which she had no real interest or content to contribute, and in last-minute cancelations of the meetings she had scheduled with them. She suffered from severe insomnia and was addicted to strong sleeping pills that were prohibited in France. She sent money to Jackie, who, in return, purchased them for her in Greece. As she needed increasingly higher doses, there were others who obtained pills for her as well (J. Callas, 1989). To recover from their effects, during the daytime hours, she used stimulating pills. She used to call friends in the middle of the night (Huffington, 1981; Palmer, 1978). Jackie described that their conversations were comprised of disorganized ramblings about her loneliness, the loss of everything she had lived for, about Onassis, whose grave in Scorpios she visited, kneeling and praying (J. Callas, 1989). To her long-time friend and colleague, Tito Gobbi, she used to ring and say: "I don't have anything to say, I just need to hear your voice" (Huffington. 1981, p. 257).

Her desperation was palpable, and only a few did not seek to run as far away as possible from the abyss engulfing her. The photographers who continued to chase her during her dwindling outings captured a woman whose depression was etched in every feature of her face, and whose sadness cried out from her tormented eyes from a distance. Anyone who looked into her eyes could see that the soul behind them was in a distant and dark world. She no longer found a reason to live. Once, she heard from Jackie about an acquaintance who had passed away and said to her: "I want to die too. Since I lost my voice, I want to die" (J. Callas, 1989, p. 220).

Meneghini (1981) recounted that in the summer of 1977, Maria had handwritten a note, which was later found in the prayer book by her bedside. Despite not being in contact with her for years, he claimed that at the top of the note, she had written: 'To T.', as she used to address her notes to him ('To Titta'). The contents of the note were the opening lines of an Aria from the opera 'La Gioconda':

In these terrible moments
You alone remain for me

And my heart tempts me
The last voice of my destiny
The last cross of my life's-road

From the opera 'La Gioconda'
(Ponchielli & Boito, 1876), fourth
act [my translation – H.Y.]

Maria omitted the first word that opens the aria, the one Gioconda cries out desperately and vehemently: 'suicidio' – suicide.

In the book by Allegri & Allegri (1997, p. 162), there is a photograph of the note, written in her characteristic handwriting. It cannot be determined if the note is authentic and if Meneghini's claims are true, but it can be speculated that it is an act she indeed considered doing.

September 16, 1977 started like any regular Friday. Maria Callas woke up around noon as usual, after yet another night filled with sleeping pills. She went to the bathroom. Shortly after, Bruna's scream shattered the silence that engulfed the apartment. She found Maria sprawled on the floor. She regained consciousness, unable to explain what had happened. Bruna and Ferruccio carried her to her bed and had her drink coffee. Suddenly, she was no longer with them again. They rushed around panicked and called for a doctor (Huffington, 1981, Meneghini, 1981).

That evening, Evangelia was alone in her apartment. The television was broadcasting the six-o'clock news in the background. Suddenly, her eyes caught the captions on the screen: "Maria Callas dies at the age of 53 of a heart attack"[20]

Notes

1 Maria Callas Mia Moglie.
2 There is uncertainty regarding the exact date of Callas's birth, which may reflect the reluctance her mother had toward her arrival into the world. The birth documents record December 2, 1923, and Callas celebrated her birthday on this date (in some documents, December 3, 1923 is recorded). However, her mother claims she was born on December 4, 1923.
3 Greek surnames are given suffixes according to gender, therefore the name Kalogeropoulos and Kalogeropoulou will be used alternatingly.
4 Different sources claim the death of the infant was caused by either typhus or meningitis.
5 Also transcribed as Jakinthy.
6 Jackie Callas describes Evangelia's overactive imagination and tendency to tell tall tales and hints this story might be the byproduct of these attributes.
7 "I don't agree with Descartes: 'I think therefore I am'. My motto is 'I work therefore I am'" – Callas in an interview to 'The Observer' (Allegri & Allegri, 1997, p. 76).
8 Tosca was also the last opera she ever sang onstage.
9 Serafin had conducted Callas's Italian debut in 'Gioconda' at the Verona festival, but it was not until their second engagement together that he fully grasped her abilities and their collaboration began.

10 Bootlegs of these performances from 1950 are among the few that showcase her voice at its peak and in all its glory, despite their quality.
11 An opera by Verdi callas first performed in Mexico City.
12 It was customary in Greece back then that marriages were arranged.
13 Dermatomyositis.
14 Drugs that, being muscle relaxants, have probably further aggravated the condition of her voice.
15 The entire second act with subtitles can be found on YouTube (La Divina Callas, 2020).
16 Miss/Maiden.
17 Stancioff writes she was told of the abortion by Maria. Huffington wrote that she based this information on interviews with acquaintances who knew Maria at the time of the abortion and on information she received from Stancioff. There are other stories that, after exploring I assessed to be not credible, including a claim Callas had the baby who passed away shortly after delivery.
18 Amongst the people she poured her heart out in front of was her old friend and music critic John Ardoin, whom she encouraged to record her stormy emotional monolog.
19 A series of accidents and premature deaths that occurred in the Kennedy family.
20 Due to Meneghini's claim and the fact that her body was cremated hastily and without a request from a family member, the circumstances of her death remained shrouded in mystery. No one can know for sure, but I believe that suicidal thoughts were no stranger to her, but that she had probably passed away as a result of the cocktail of medications she had taken. The body was cremated at the initiative of a pianist who had fussed her way close to Maria, possibly to prevent the discovery of traces of the illegal drugs she had been sending her.

Bibliography

Adagietto. (2016a, June 30). *Maria Callas Discusses her Art* (*Interview with Lord Harewood for BBC2, April, 1968*) [Video]. YouTube. https://www.youtube.com/watch?v=-8y8HjPcMBg

Adagietto. (2016b, September 16). *Maria Callas Interview with Mike Wallace (1973)* [Video]. YouTube. https://www.youtube.com/watch?v=VDoyFth1OnU

Allegri, R., & Allegri, R. (1997). *Callas by Callas: The Secret Writings of La Maria.* English Translation: Peter Eustace, Universe, 1998.

Bellini, V., & Romani, F. (1831). *Norma: An Opera in Two Acts* [Musical score].

Bizet, G., Meilhac, H., & Halévy, L. (1875). *Carmen: An Opera in Four Acts* [Musical score].

Bowlby, J. (1988). *A Secure Base Clinical Applications of Attachment Theory.* Basic Books.

Callas, E., with Blochman, L. G. (1960). *My Daughter Maria Callas.* Fleet Publishing Corporation.

Callas, J. (1989). *Sisters.* Pan Macmillan, 1990.

CallasFan. (2015, June 15). *Callas: In Her Own Words Part 1 of 4 (By John Ardoin)* [Video]. YouTube. https://www.youtube.com/watch?v=OS2GN8vnPJg

Cole, S. (2003). *Maria Callas- Living & Dying for Art and Love* [Documentary]. BBC.

Demonassa. (2010, June 11). *The Callas Conversations Volume Two (2) (Elvira de Hidalgo Interview for Peirre Desgroupes, L'invitee du Dimanche April-20-1969)* [Video]. YouTube. https://www.youtube.com/watch?v=8MWmCcioY2k

Dragadze, P. (1964, October 30). Return of Maria Callas: Close-up of the World's Most Tempestuous Opera Star. *'Life' Magazine, 57*(18): 61–69.

Fussi, F., & Paolillo, P. N. (2017, May 10). *Analisi Spettrografiche dell'evoluzione e Involuzione Vocale di Maria Callas alla Luce di una Ipotesi Fisiopatologica*. Franco Fussi. www.francofussi.com/analisi-spettrografiche-dellevoluzione-e-involuzione-vocale-di-maria-callas-alla-luce-di-una-ipotesi-fisiopatologica/

Galatopoulos, S. (1998). *Maria Callas: Sacred Monster*. Simon & Schuster.

Huffington (Stassinopoulos), A. (1981). *Maria Callas: The Woman behind the Legend*. Cooper Square Press, 2002.

Konstantinos Paliatsaras. (2012, October 31). *Maria Callas – Dallas Interview 1968. (Inteview for John Ardoin 13.9.1968)* [Video]. YouTube. https://www.youtube.com/watch?v=SrNlDtiVOs4

La Divina Callas. (2020, January 25). *Maria Callas and Tito Gobbi at Covent Garden, 9.02.1964-Tosca, prod Franco Zeffirelli, atto II* [video]. YouTube. https://www.youtube.com/watch?v=xnFlg1z1hPc

MariaCallasMuseum (2011, October 9). *Maria Callas: Today Interview with Barbara Walters (New York, April 15, 1974)*. [Video]. YouTube. https://www.youtube.com/watch?v=TjBAqTAYSdk

Meneghini, G. B. (1981). *Maria Callas Mia Moglie (My Wife Maria Callas)*. Rusconi Libri.

Palmer, T. (1978). *Callas: A Documentary* [Documentary]. Alliance.

Petsalis-Diomidis, N. (2001). *The Unknown Callas: The Greek Years*. Amadeus Press.

Ponchielli, A., & Boito, A. (1876). *La Gioconda: An Opera in Four Acts* [Musical score].

Puccini, G., & Illica, L. (1900). *Tosca: An Opera in Three Acts* [Musical score].

Silver Singing Method. (2009, May 12). *Maria Callas Talks*. [Video]. YouTube. https://www.youtube.com/watch?v=lii1EkG4wMk

Spence, L. (2021). *Cast a Diva: The Hidden Life of Maria Callas*. The History Press.

Stancioff, N. (1987). *Maria Callas Remembered*. Da Capo Press, 2000.

Taubman, H. (1956, October 30). Opera: Maria Callas Sings in 'Norma' at 'Met'; Soprano Makes Debut as Season Begins. *The New York Times*.

Tosi, B. (editor) (2010). *The Young Maria Callas*. Guernica.

Verdi, G., & Piave, F. M. (1853). *La Traviata: An Opera in Three Acts* [Musical score].

Volf, T. (2017). *Maria by Callas* [Documentary]. Sony Pictures.

Volf, T. (2019). *Maria Callas: Cartas y memorias*. Ediciones Akal, 2022.

Winnicott, D. W. (1960). Ego Distortion in Terms of True and False Self (1965). *International Psycho-Analysis Library, 64*: 140–152. Karnac Books.

Winnicott, D. W. (1971). *Playing and Reality*. Tavistock Publications.

Chapter 10

Checks and Balances

Understanding and Forgiving

Throughout this book, I strived to maintain a complex and sometimes contradictory perspective, discussing the validation that abuse has occurred without turning the offender, the parent, into a monster (although there are cases where the behavior is monstrous). It is a challenging task, and I am sure I have failed at it more than once, both in my writing and in my clinical work. When we sit with suffering patients, we must bear with them the psychic pain they bring. We have to validate the reality and feelings of the patient, who often underwent a repetitive traumatic denial of his experience, as a legitimate one, and at the same time, we have to avoid losing our therapeutic stance and identifying with his sense of utter helplessness, as we risk being trapped in the patient's abyss with him. In the transference, the patient's pain and rage may manifest as intense bitterness and aggressiveness, and the therapist, may struggle to remain 'experience near' the way the patient needs, and may even be tempted to 'speak for' the abusive parent or take on a stance of complementary identification (Racker, 1957), feeling hostile toward the patient's 'grievances'. In such cases, the patient would feel abandoned. The patient is walking the tightrope drawn between a blinding identification with the aggressor and a blinding rage. It is difficult not to try to calm the patient along with our own anxious apprehension, in light of the sensation that the defenses are about to crumble, dropping the patient into the abyss, but if we do this, we abandon him to face that abyss alone. It is challenging to remain close to the patient on such a tightrope. With narcissistic abuse the truth heals, but we must also remember that we do not possess it and that the path to it is winding and endless. Here, we have a never-ending paradox. The injurer is injured, the injured injures. The echoist is also a narcissist. The phenomenon of 'narcissistic abuse' dwells in the twilight zone of 'was or wasn't'. It was. Yet it is also a subjective experience. We must illuminate the darkness while remembering that the parent, in most cases, was also loving and nurturing to the best of his abilities, all the while remembering that we must not mistake him for a healthy parent. The patient needs to step out of the blindness and acknowledge the truth in order to heal, but recognition of the truth breaks down the defenses and opens within him a fountain of pain. Like Narcissus, if he knows himself, he dies; like Echo, if he doesn't know himself, he cannot live. In other words, recognizing the truth brings the patient in touch with emptiness and psychic death, but only then

DOI: 10.4324/9781032625393-10

can the seed of the true self germinate. If he sees, he is not as helpless, but he feels rage toward the parent; if he understands and forgives, the perception of reality becomes murky once again. If he consumes the toxic nourishment (Eigen, 1999), it causes him harm; if he refrains from it, he starves. The patient has to die in order to live, and, as in Victor Hugo's quote (1862) that was already mentioned, he must save himself through what is destroying him.

In my view, the American-born terminology of the jargon that has evolved illuminates dark corners and helps anchor the patient's perception of reality and give it a name. However, it carries a degree of de-humanization of the hurtful parent, and it entails a danger that the patient might assume the role of the victim as an identity in a way that prevents growth. In contrast, the psychoanalytic terminology leaves something lacking or too obscure. I presented Alice Miller's criticism that without validating the patient's true childhood experiences, we prolong his stay with us in his darkness (Miller, 1979), but it appears that we cannot shortcut and pull the defenses out from under the patient's feet prematurely. "The slowness of the analytic process is a manifestation of a defence the analyst must respect" (Winnicott, 1971, p. 72). Therapy is not 'psycho-education', but are there not cases where a relationship is so abusive that the therapist must take a stand? The paradoxes inherent to the phenomenon also accompany its treatment. The bad object cannot be expelled until the therapist is introjected as a good object, but he must not be 'too good' an object. The patient also needs to experience the therapist as a 'bad' object, adequately frustrating at times, to facilitate growth. It is a prolonged process, a developmental therapy, Sisyphean; painful yet healing for the patient and requiring at times infinite patience from the therapist. Progress may be slow, in small steps, but even a small motion can divert a planet from its orbit.

Elizur and Alon (2016) wrote about

> the phenomenon of prolonged hostility towards elderly parents by their adult children, who make claims against the parenting they received by them and the damages it had caused... The serious implications of this reckoning on the lives of the elderly and on the family structure... and the role of popular psychology in demonizing the parents.

I believe that in the case of narcissistic abuse, the risk of a harsh reaction from the child toward the parent is great. There is no avoiding going through negative and harsh emotions. There are many cases where emotional distancing and even severance of ties are necessary. However, there are also cases where such severance of ties reflects being stuck in a bitter and unprocessed stage which leaves both the patient and the parent hurting. I am not certain there is a solution to this paradox. The patient has to lose the parent as an object of love before being able to see him realistically, and only then, perhaps, he can really love him. Not always it is possible. I have no solution, but one word keeps coming up in my head, and it seems to me all the therapist can do is to hold on to it for the patient and the parent alike – compassion.

Bibliography

Eigen, M. (1999). *Toxic Nourishment*. Routledge, 2018.

Elitzur, E., & Alon, N. (2016). *"Score-settling" with Ageing Parents*. Hebrew Psychology (in Hebrew). https://www.hebpsy.net/articles.asp?id=3382

Hugo, V. (1862). *Les Miserables.* https://www.gutenberg.org/cache/epub/17489/pg17489-images.html

Miller, A. (1779). *The Drama of the Gifted Child, the Search for the True Self.* Translated from the German by Ruth Ward. Basic Books, 1981.

Racker, H. (1957). The Meaning and Uses of Countertransference. *Psychoanalytic Quarterly, 26*(3): 303–357.

Winnicott, D. W. (1971). *Playing and Reality*. Routledge, 1991.

Index

For Product Safety Concerns and Information please contact our EU
representative GPSR@taylorandfrancis.com
Taylor & Francis Verlag GmbH, Kaufingerstraße 24, 80331 München, Germany